SOMETHING MORE PASTORAL

Catholic Standard *photo by Paul Fetters. Used with permission.*

SOMETHING MORE PASTORAL

*The Mission of Bishop, Archbishop,
and Cardinal Donald Wuerl*

By Ann Rodgers and Mike Aquilina

The Lambing Press
Pittsburgh
MMXV

At the Cathedral of St. Matthew the Apostle in Washington. Catholic Standard *photo by Jaclyn Lippelmann. Used with permission.*

A note on the type: The type is based on punches and matrices given to Oxford University by John Fell. The Fell Types are digitally reproduced by Igino Marini, www.iginomarini.com.

FOREWORD

By Bishop David A. Zubik

Cardinal Donald Wuerl is a leader of gutsy courage and untiring service to Jesus and His Church. I know this firsthand. I worked closely with him for every bit of sixteen years. You won't be surprised to know that of all the ways I can describe the man who is the Cardinal Archbishop of Washington, the one that is most on spot is "teacher." For decades, he has been known as "The Education Bishop." He has been "teacher" to me and many, many others. He is a natural.

When I first started serving as Bishop Wuerl's Priest Secretary in the Diocese of Pittsburgh back in February of 1988, the first thing he told me on his first day as Pittsburgh's Bishop was that he hoped to put the Diocese of Pittsburgh "on the map." He hoped to do this on many levels:

- with the faithful of the diocese;

- with all of the parishes of the diocese;

- with the civic leaders in Southwestern Pennsylvania;

- with the Church in the United States;

- with its loyalty to the Holy Father.

In his mind and heart, putting the Diocese of Pittsburgh "on the map" was to place the spotlight on the Church as the Body of Christ and not on himself.

There are many ways in which Cardinal Wuerl's ministry continues to be a gift to the Church far beyond his former See of Pittsburgh or his current charge as Shepherd of the Church of Washington. Faced with the difficult task of choosing the major contributions which Cardinal Wuerl has made to the Church, permit me to list my five.

1. Becoming an ardent champion of, and voice for, those within the Church and beyond who need the opportunity for a better life, any who are in need of the healing touch of Jesus in and through the Church.

2. Promoting and practicing the zero-tolerance of child sexual abuse, long before it became mandated or even a widespread practice in the Church, let alone the wider society.

3. Having an acute vision of where the Church needs to grow and developing a highly consultative process to address demographic and cultural shifts that continue to impact the landscape of a local Church.

4. Being a respected voice of and for the Church not only among her members but in all the professional "worlds" of American society.

5. Devoting long, arduous hours to service of the Church in the United States through his proactive service in the United States Conference of Catholic Bishops and to the Holy See by his participation in nearly every major Synod of Bishops in Rome, where he has had a steady and increasing hand in shaping the message and priorities of the Church Universal.

I trust that you will see the rationale for my "top five" notables in the leadership of Donald Cardinal Wuerl. And maybe, after reading this book, an in-depth reflection of one of the most credible leaders today in the Catholic Church, you will come up with your own "top five."

But, whatever the case, I can guarantee you that once you have read *Something More Pastoral*, you will either come to know Cardinal Wuerl or you will come to know him better with both admiration and gratitude.

It takes courage to be a leader in the Church these days. *Something More Pastoral* not only presents a glimpse of a leader in the Church who knows courage and lives it. It's the story also of a true teacher from whom we can all learn to be true leaders in a day when God's people need our courage too!

Join with me in taking our hats off to Donald Cardinal Wuerl: a gutsy leader and a tireless servant of Jesus and His Church.

Acknowledgments.

We owe far too many thanks to list everyone by name. Well over a hundred people gave generously of their time so that this story might be complete. Whenever you see a name cited or quoted, know that the authors are profoundly grateful for that source and for every source.

Bishop David A. Zubik supported us with encouraging words and by making himself available for background on numerous issues. He placed the resources of the Diocese of Pittsburgh at our disposal, and we drew much from the diocesan archives and from the files and back issues of the *Pittsburgh Catholic* newspaper.

Mark Zimmerman, editor of the Washington, D.C., *Catholic Standard*, was heroically generous in helping us, as were the newspaper's photographers, whose works appear throughout this book.

We owe thanks to John Robinson Block, David Shribman, and Angelika Kane for giving us access to the library of the *Pittsburgh Post-Gazette*. We're grateful to Jane Belford for extraordinary hospitality in arranging and facilitating interviews in Washington, D.C.

We are deeply indebted to the diocesan and archdiocesan staff in Pittsburgh and Washington, and to clergy and lay leaders in both sees, for sharing their time and recollections. The same is true of ecumenical, interfaith, and civic leaders, as well as journalists and other independent observers, who were eager to share their recollections of Cardinal Wuerl. Bishops and staff from the U.S. Conference of Catholic Bishops, as well as some clergy from outside the United States, were likewise extremely accommodating with interviews. We hope that we have conveyed their descriptions and assessment accurately and in in the spirit with which they spoke.

Finally, we must acknowledge the tremendous generosity of our subject, Cardinal Donald Wuerl, who gave us access to needed sources and made himself available as often as we needed him.

A note on sources: We have used notes only for published sources. All other quoted material comes from personal interviews. To cite and date each conversation would have made the book cumbersome and cluttered the text with superscripts.

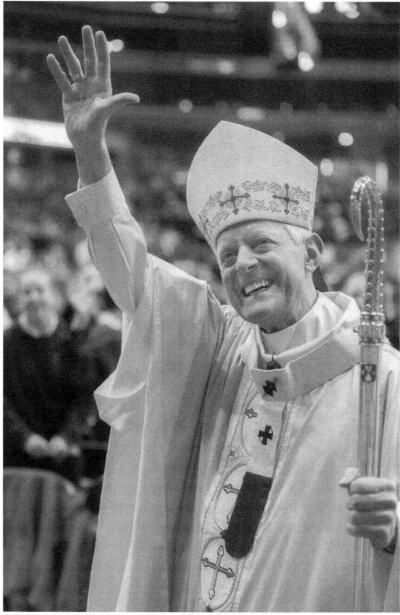

Cardinal Wuerl waves to the crowds of young people gathered inside the Verizon Center in downtown Washington on January 22 for the 2015 Youth Rally and Mass for Life.

Courtesy of the Diocesan Archives of the Diocese of Pittsburgh.

INTRODUCTION

One day late in 1979 Father Donald Wuerl was summoned into the presence of the Holy Father.

It was not an unusual event. He and the Pope knew each other. Father Wuerl had been, for years, an official with the Vatican Congregation for the Clergy. Pope John Paul II, during his years as Cardinal-Archbishop of Krakow, had been a member of the Congregation. Father Wuerl had spent time in Poland as a guest of Cardinal Wojtyla. When the Polish cardinal became pope, he still treated Father Wuerl as an old friend.

At Clergy, Father Wuerl served as assistant to Cardinal John Wright, prefect of the Congregation. When Cardinal Wright died in 1979, Father Wuerl no longer wished to remain in Rome.

"I understand you don't want to stay here any longer," the Pope said to him.

Father Wuerl replied that he would like to go back to Pittsburgh and "do something more pastoral."

"Oh, and what I'm doing isn't pastoral?" the Pope asked with a smile.

• • • • • • •

"Something more pastoral" is what Father Wuerl proceeded to do: as an auxiliary bishop in Seattle, a bishop in Pittsburgh, and an archbishop in Washington, D.C. As this book goes to press, he has served in the Catholic episcopacy for almost thirty years. A bishop does more than occupy an office and bear a title. According to the most

ancient Christian tradition, he is a shepherd entrusted with a particular flock. He cares for a congregation of believers who belong to Jesus the Good Shepherd. *Pastor* is simply the Latin word for shepherd, and Christians have always applied it to their clergy, especially
those who are bishops.

No matter what Father Wuerl was thinking during his 1979 ex-
change with Pope John Paul, he went on to do the most pastoral sort
of work. Indeed, he has come, in a sense, to exemplify the word for
his colleagues. In more than a hundred interviews conducted for this
book, it was the word most often used to describe the man.

Now, Cardinal Wuerl has become one of Pope Francis' most
trusted pastoral advisors, not only in formal positions such as his
seat on the Congregation for Bishops but in private consultations
that aren't part of Pope Francis' posted schedule.

This book is an account of Donald Wuerl's pastoral years, his years
as bishop. It is not a biography—that will be left to more qualified
historians years in the future. It seeks only to examine the various aspects of a bishop's ministry through the lens of how he fulfilled that
mission.

This book is not about management style or about how to move
up the ecclesiastical ladder. It is about the hard work, wisdom,
courage, and sacrificial love that it takes for a Good Shepherd to
guide his flock and to protect lambs from wolves.

The authors of this book have each known Cardinal Wuerl for
more than a quarter century.

Ann Rodgers was a religion reporter who covered him throughout
his eighteen years in Pittsburgh, originally for the *Pittsburgh Press*
and later the *Pittsburgh Post-Gazette*. Then-Bishop Wuerl was always accessible, passing along what amounted to an unaccredited
graduate education in Catholic doctrine and ecclesiology.

Mike Aquilina was editor of the Pittsburgh Catholic for three
years of Bishop Wuerl's tenure (1993-1996). He later co-authored
three books with Cardinal Wuerl: *The Mass, The Church*, and *The
Feasts*.

We sought to supplement our own records and memories with
those of others who have worked with him. Among them was Bishop

Paul Bradley of Kalamazoo, who was a priest and auxiliary bishop during then-Bishop Wuerl's tenure in Pittsburgh. He succinctly summed up something we had perceived but never articulated. "I think he can be imitated, but I don't think he can ever be replicated," Bishop Bradley said. "He just doesn't fit in a box."

• • • • • • •

We decided to write this book because we closely observed most of the years of Cardinal Wuerl's ministry as a bishop and believe he is a role model for a Good Shepherd. Both of us have learned a great deal from witnessing his love for the Church and his single-minded dedication to building the Kingdom of God. He worked heroically to communicate Catholic doctrine—"the teaching of Christ"—at a time of widespread confusion. He invested in education when others were abandoning the field. He consistently spoke of his mission as a *trust*, not something that belonged to him, but rather as something entrusted to him—something that required his faith and forbade his meddling.

He showed tremendous moral courage throughout his ministry, most significantly for taking a stand—against some powerful forces in Rome—on behalf of children and all parishioners who were at risk from sexual predators among the clergy.

We, like the cardinal, are Pittsburghers, and in Pittsburgh he remains "Bishop Wuerl."

Just a little while ago, he told us this story: Recently he was in a Pittsburgh restaurant, where he was spotted by an older woman dining with her grown son.

"There's Donald our bishop," the cardinal heard the woman say,

"He's a cardinal now, mother," the man responded.

"For 20 years we prayed for Donald our bishop. That's who he is," she retorted.

"That's Pittsburgh," the cardinal said.

And it is. But it's Catholic, too. It's the doctrine of the Church from the time of the Apostles.

"Cardinal" is an honorific title, an ornament that, but "bishop" is a matter of personal identity. The title signifies that its bearer holds the fullness of the sacrament of holy orders. He has been changed by his ordination, equipped by God to do the work of a shepherd—equipped by God to do something most pastoral.

Young Donald Wuerl, Mount Washington, Pittsburgh. Courtesy of the Diocesan Archives of the Diocese of Pittsburgh.

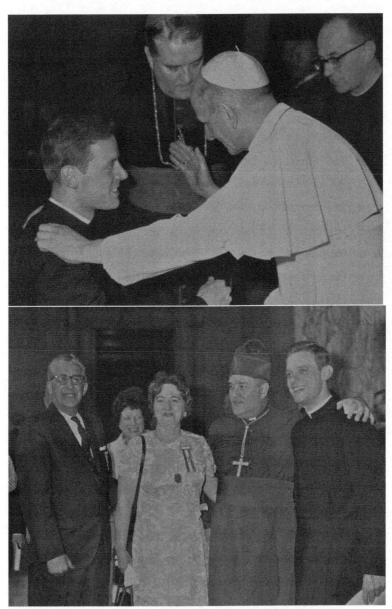

Courtesy of the Diocesan Archives of the Diocese of Pittsburgh.

CHAPTER 1:
BECOMING FATHER WUERL

Donald Wuerl was born in Pittsburgh on November 12, 1940, a frigid day when the smoky industrial city narrowly escaped a storm that had sunk five ships on the Great Lakes. The newspapers were filled with news of distant wars in Europe and Asia—news that struck home that day as three workers died at a munitions plant out-side Pittsburgh, one of a dozen to suffer explosions in coordinated acts of apparent sabotage.

Donald was the second son of railroad worker Francis Wuerl and his wife Mary Ann. The couple had him baptized at St. Wendelin Parish, near their home in the quiet hilltop neighborhood of Carrick. Their third child and only daughter, Carol, was born just over a year later, days after the Japanese military bombed Pearl Harbor.

Francis Wuerl enlisted in the Navy. He would return home safely, but his young wife died of cancer in August 1944, leaving him with three young children.

In April 1946, he married 21-year-old Kathryn Cavanaugh, the only mother Donald Wuerl would remember. He returned the same wholehearted love to her that she offered him and his siblings.

The family moved a short distance to the neighborhood of Mount Washington, perched on a steep hill overlooking Downtown Pitts-burgh and the confluence of the Monongahela, Allegheny, and Ohio rivers. Today its Grandview Avenue is lined with luxury homes, but

in postwar Pittsburgh it was a blue-collar enclave. Cable cars carried
thousands of workers daily up and down the steep incline to the mills
and railway on the banks of the Monongahela River. The panoramic
view was often obscured by dense smoke from the steel mills below.
The Wuerl children used to go sledding on the steep streets, coming
back home covered in soot from the coal cinders that neighbors
threw on icy roads for traction.

The youngest Wuerl, Dennis, was born there and baptized at St.
Mary of the Mount Parish, where all of the children went to school.

· · · · · · ·

The era of the baby boom also saw a faith boom. Men who had
found God in the foxholes of World War II took their young families
to church. Virtually every parish built a school, and classrooms were
overcrowded. Thousands of men became priests in a vocations surge
so large that bishops sometimes lacked places to assign them all. So
many young women wanted to be sisters that religious communities
turned away qualified applicants.

"We had two basic reference points, our home and the parish,"
Cardinal Wuerl recalled. "It wasn't just the church, but the school.
The gym served as a social center for the neighborhood." The family
attended parish festivals that celebrated their German and Irish
roots, as well as those of their Italian neighbors. Above all at St.
Mary's, there was Mass.

Early each Sunday morning, Kathryn Wuerl had the children up
and dressed for church before their father returned from his night
shift at the railroad yard. Then they all went to early Mass. "It was
important to him that we would all be at Mass together," Cardinal
Wuerl recalled. "Then we would all go home and he would go to bed.
His quiet conviction made an impact on me. His faith was just un-
shakeable and assumed. We never debated it; he didn't discuss it; it
was just there."

The family prayed the rosary together after supper, went to the Stations of the Cross on Fridays and wouldn't have dreamed of breaking the fast before Communion.

Cardinal Wuerl said: "My parents were not only practicing Catholics, but it was clear that the faith was the frame of reference for their lives. All of us kids went to Saturday-afternoon Confession. My mother would remind us that it was time for us to go to church, but it was more than just going to church. The Catholic faith permeated the house in that we knew there was a right and a wrong, and that we were supposed to do what is right because that is what God asks of us."

• • • • • • •

Francis Wuerl, Donald Wuerl's father, worked nights weighing freight cars for the Pennsylvania Railroad, and sometimes took the children to watch the loading and unloading of massive freight trains. His job required hard work, precision and organizational skills, all traits that Francis Wuerl passed to his middle son.

When Francis Wuerl died in 1994, neighbors remembered him as a man who constantly looked out for others, shoveling the walks of widows, repairing the bicycles of other people's children, visiting the sick and bringing food, even when he had become elderly himself. His children recall times when a bank teller gave him too much money and he returned it. Throughout his life he attended daily Mass.

Wayne Wuerl remembers a father who was always available if his children needed him, but who believed that they needed to make their own choices. Wayne and Dennis became businessmen, Carol an engineer.

Their father "taught us to think for ourselves, to make our own decisions based on the values he had instilled in us, the values of integrity and honesty," Wayne Wuerl said. "Once you made a decision or said to a person that you would or you would not do something, then he expected you to be a person of your word. That was his hall-mark.

"He would discuss very freely and openly the career choices or decisions that you were considering, and not try to dissuade you or push you into what you said you wanted to do. Rather, he talked through the issue with you to make sure you had thought it through thoroughly."[1] Throughout his ministry, Cardinal Wuerl strove to model his dedication to the Church on the way his father took care of the family. Francis Wuerl had "a profound sense of responsibility, of duty. He put his wife and children at the very top of the list for those for whom he had a responsibility of loving care. He put himself at the bottom of the list," he said.

But what he most admired in his father was the virtue that he admits to having the greatest difficulty with: Patience. "He never came to lose his temper with us or get angry. It was more like he was communicating to us how disappointed he was when we did something wrong," Cardinal Wuerl said.

• • • • • • •

Wayne Wuerl recalled that his younger brother was born with a desire to do things right, and would have set exacting standards for himself whether he had become a priest or a plumber. He didn't have patience with hobbies that required relaxed waiting, such as fishing, he told the *Pittsburgh Post-Gazette* in 1996.

"Don was always studious, inquisitive. He was always eager to turn the next page, to see what lay beyond it."[2] The Wuerl children learned a work ethic early. The two oldest boys delivered newspapers, and in high school Donald served sodas and ice cream at a neighborhood drug store. He attended the Friday-night school dances at St. Mary's with his brothers, both of whom would marry. But he felt called to a different path. From childhood he had "played Mass," drafting his older brother to be the altar boy.

In high school he came under the influence of Father Joseph Bryan, an assistant at St. Mary's. Just three years out of seminary, the young priest arrived at St. Mary of the Mount when Donald Wuerl was 12. He became a mentor to a circle of teenage boys there, encouraging them to go deeper into the life of faith.

"It wasn't just that he was friendly and asked if we wanted to go visit the seminary. He was genuinely interested in whether we were learning to pray," the cardinal recalled. He would ask whether they took time for prayer and urged them to challenge themselves to attend daily Mass. Much of this spiritual direction took place in Confession. But he knew Father Bryan was having the same discussion with his peers because they were asking each other, "Where can you get that book?"

"That book" was *Introduction to the Devout Life*, by St. Francis de Sales, which Father Bryan urged them to read and to put into practice. Donald rode the ten-cent trolley from Mount Washington to Downtown and tried to order it from the book section at Gimbel's Department Store. After he was denied credit, his mother ordered it for him. He keeps that same, worn copy on the prie-dieu in his apartment today.

"A couple of us went into the priesthood. Most went on to be married. His point was that you needed to be close to God in any case," Cardinal Wuerl said.

• • • • • • •

As a high-school senior, Donald Wuerl went to the diocesan vocations office to inquire about seminary. Bishop John Dearden, then in his final year as shepherd of the Diocese of Pittsburgh, had started a summer program for prospective seminarians to learn Latin. Donald Wuerl was among nearly fifty young men enrolled in that summer of 1958. Their instructor was a young priest, Father Adam Maida, who, like Bishop Dearden, would go on to become the Cardinal-Archbishop of Detroit.

At the time Pittsburgh had no diocesan seminary, so in September 1958, he was dispatched to St. Gregory College Seminary in Cincinnati, part of a larger seminary known both as the Athenaeum of Ohio and Mount St. Mary of the West.

In the summers he returned home, earning money for the school year by laboring on an Allegheny County road maintenance crew.

"You know those road posts you see all over the county?" he once asked a reporter, referring to an old system of street signs. "Well, I painted about half of them."[3] For two years he excelled at his studies. In the spring of 1960, the vocations director in Pittsburgh urged him to apply for a Basselin scholarship to attend the Theological College at the Catholic University of America. These prestigious scholarships were funded through an endowment that lumber magnate Theodore B. Basselin established in 1914 to train priests who would be exceptionally skilled in philosophy and preaching. . In addition to their philosophical studies, Basselin scholars were required to have a second major in English literature. The program still provides a full scholarship, including room, board and tuition, to seminarians who have already shown great promise in their studies.

"It was one of the great blessings of my life to have received that scholarship," Cardinal Wuerl said. The Diocese of Pittsburgh normally didn't send students to the Catholic University of America due to the expense. But his studies there opened important doors.

His three years in Washington were a time of optimism and excitement. America had elected its first Catholic president. Preparations for the Second Vatican Council were underway in Rome.

"The whole world seemed so young then," he told People Magazine in 1979. "John XXIII was pope. Americans had just elected John F. Kennedy. Everything seemed so fresh and new."

His dreams centered on becoming an assistant in a parish. The pastor had been a distant figure in his childhood.

"I envisioned the priesthood to be all the things that Father Bryan did. He said Mass, he visited the sick, heard Confessions, helped people with their problems. The assistant priests—we call them parochial vicars now—were always there to reflect the goodness of God in our lives."

But the path of his priesthood was about to branch away from that vision.

A few months after he had entered the seminary in Ohio, Bishop Dearden was transferred to the Archdiocese of Detroit. Apart from his confirmation, Donald Wuerl had never met Bishop Dearden, since bishops of that era considered it unnecessary to get to know their seminarians. In January 1959 Pope John XXIII sent the brilliant young Bishop John Wright of Worcester, Mass., to lead the Diocese of Pittsburgh.

Bishop Wright was already a renowned speaker. When he came to Washington, D.C., to give an address at the Catholic University of America, Donald Wuerl, the only Pittsburgh seminarian on campus, was assigned to meet the bishop's train at Union Station.

There was no small talk during their ride to the university. The intellectually omnivorous Wright "grilled me on what I was writing for my thesis, and what sources I was using," Cardinal Wuerl recalled.

His responses about his work on natural law in the writings of Thomas Jefferson apparently impressed his new bishop, who soon after invited him to spend the summer organizing his personal library. After further observing his intelligence and work ethic that summer, Bishop Wright decided to send him to his own alma mater, the Pontifical North American College in Rome.

Donald Wuerl arrived in Rome in September 1963. For the first time in his life he was not within a day's travel of home by car or rail.

"I learned that you do have to begin to rely just on the Lord," he said. "Your prayer life has to be the source of your energy."

Known as "the NAC," the college is a residence where American seminarians develop their spiritual life while attending classes at the international Pontifical Gregorian University. The lectures were in Latin. Now they are in Italian, but today's students credit Donald Wuerl in part with devising a study system in which the best linguists were assigned to take notes for a specific class, distributing them to the other students to study. (He allows only that he may have "perfected" an informal system of long standing.) Today the cardinal, a longtime board member, still stays at the NAC every time he visits Rome.

· · · · · · ·

When the young Donald Wuerl arrived in Rome, the Second Vatican Council was in full swing. Pope John XXIII had died a few months before, and Pope Paul VI now presided at the Council, where Bishop Wright was one of the most influential participants.

Initially Bishop Wright brought staff from Pittsburgh to assist him. But the bishop was increasingly impressed with the diligence and organizational skills of the young seminarian from Mount Washington, and came to rely on him. Though he was occasionally allowed inside the Council meetings to deliver papers to Bishop Wright, he learned about it mostly from Bishop Wright's conversation.

Bishop Wright was instrumental in bringing about the Council's endorsement of religious freedom over theocracy as the best way to spread the gospel. He also had a critical role in the decisions to honor Orthodox and Protestant believers as fellow Christians and to denounce anti-Semitism. Bishop Wright stood for a church that would proclaim the Christian gospel in love, not try to impose it by fiat or force. He stood for a Church that defended human rights, the right to religious freedom first among them. He stood for a Church that would engage any argument that its critics offered with love and logic, but also a Church that would not water down its beliefs to satisfy popular trends.

Even as he reformed the Church's engagement with the wider world, he modeled a new way of engaging seminarians. While most bishops continued to ordain new priests sight unseen, whenever Bishop Wright came to Rome he took the Pittsburgh seminarians out to lunch.

"All of us got to know him. We were the envy of many of our classmates," said Cardinal Wuerl.

Seminarians at the NAC are ordained priests before completing their final year of studies. Donald Wuerl was ordained a priest on December 17, 1966 in St. Peter's Basilica by Bishop Francis Reh, the rector of the NAC. He returned home in June 1967 and was assigned to St. Rosalia Parish in Greenfield.

* * * * * * *

Greenfield was a blue-collar Catholic neighborhood, where people walked to church and to work in the steel mill.

"You could walk around and talk to people, carrying on your ministry from porch to porch," Cardinal Wuerl recalled. "They were good, hard-working people who loved their families and loved the Lord. And their defining characteristic was that they loved the Steelers," Pittsburgh's legendary National Football League team.

He was assigned the 4:15 Sunday Mass, but the pastor explained that the assigned time didn't mean 4:15. "It meant 15 minutes after the Steelers game ended," Cardinal Wuerl recalled.

"It worked," he said. "Everybody in that parish knew that 15 minutes after the game ended there would be Mass. That was where I learned pastoral flexibility."

He was the junior assistant priest. In addition to the pastor and a senior assistant priest the rectory had a priest-in-residence who was working on a doctorate at Duquesne University. "It was another era," he said, noting that today St. Rosalia has just one priest.

Father Wuerl also had duties outside the parish. Bishop Wright had drafted him as a part-time secretary. The two were of markedly different temperaments. Bishop Wright was a free spirit who didn't abide by schedules and thought nothing of calling his aides in the middle of the night. Father Wuerl was a paragon of organizational skill who never complained about being on constant call.

The late Bishop Anthony Bosco, a chancery official in Pittsburgh during those years, once described how young Father Wuerl imposed order on Bishop Wright's happy chaos.

"Bishop Wright was breezy, loose and free. If he scheduled an appointment for three o'clock, it really meant sometime that afternoon," he told the *Pittsburgh Press* in 1989. "I felt that then-Father Wuerl was a magnificent counterbalance to that in his attempts to keep some order in the office, on the desk, and assure you that the three o'clock appointment might at least occur that same day. That was due to Father Wuerl's organizational abilities, his precision and the fact that he's somewhat of a neatnik."[4]

"We worked very well together," Cardinal Wuerl said of Bishop Wright. "Whether he would make a point of it or not, he appreciated the fact that there was someone there trying to make all of these things move along. At the same time, I always appreciated that his effectiveness lay precisely in the fact that he was always there for everybody. I would explain to the people waiting for an appointment when we were 45 minutes behind schedule that one of the joys of meeting him is that you know you are not going to be rushed."

As different as Father Wuerl was from his mentor, he absorbed valuable lessons about how to be a bishop. While Bishop Wright was a man of many interests, "he had only one love in life, and that was the Church."

Bishop Wright's conviction that the Church must be engaged with the wider society led to the creation of new diocesan offices to address societal issues, especially racism. He was a champion of ecumenical cooperation, and led the way in creating Christian Associates of Southwestern Pennsylvania, which brings together the Catholic, Orthodox, and many Protestant traditions.

Bishop Wright helped him to understand in his heart what he had known intellectually: that the Church isn't just an institution dedicated to Jesus, but is the body of Christ on Earth. The bishop's most important lesson was that "you can't love Christ apart from his Church," Cardinal Wuerl said.

"If you are a priest, if you are a bishop, the Church has to be your life. You have got to love the Church just as if you were married and you would love your spouse or your children. You have to love the Church with that same love, and it has to be there every day, all the time." Once when speaking to priests in Washington, in response to a question, Cardinal Wuerl spoke of the Church of Pittsburgh as his "mother" and the Church of Washington as his "spouse."

• • • • • • •

While serving as Cardinal Wright's secretary, Father Wuerl met a young auxiliary bishop from Atlanta who would also have an important impact on his ministry. In 1968, Bishop Joseph Bernardin, who had been made a bishop while still in his thirties, was general secretary of the National Conference of Catholic Bishops. When he came to Pittsburgh to confer with Bishop Wright, Father Wuerl picked him up at the airport. They quickly formed a friendship that lasted until Cardinal Bernardin's untimely death in 1996.

In 1967 Father Wuerl became chaplain to the University Catholic Club, an organization for college graduates in an era when most Pittsburghers never went to college because the steel mills provided high wages without a degree. Some of its members became important leaders in the community and the Church. In 1968 he began teaching theology part-time at Duquesne University. All the while he continued as an assistant at St. Rosalia.

But his life was about to change in a radical and unexpected way. Not yet thirty, Father Wuerl was about to go from hometown priest to Vatican insider.

Father Wuerl's ordination as a priest. Courtesy of the Diocesan Archives of the Diocese of Pittsburgh.

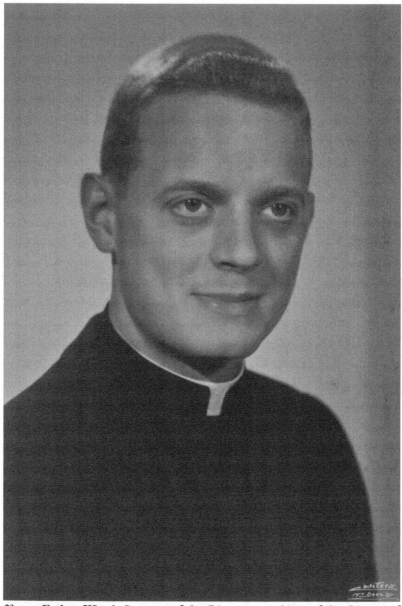

Young Father Wuerl. Courtesy of the Diocesan Archives of the Diocese of Pittsburgh.

Courtesy of the Diocesan Archives of the Diocese of Pittsburgh.

CHAPTER 2:
INSIDE THE VATICAN

The political philosopher Christopher Wolfe tells of a visit he made to Rome when he was a teenager. His uncle had been Cardinal Wright's attorney in Pittsburgh, and when young Christopher traveled to Rome on vacation he went with orders to visit his uncle's highly placed client.

Christopher had lunch with Cardinal Wright—and with Father Donald Wuerl, who as the Cardinal's secretary was usually by his side.

Father Wuerl was content to stay in the background, saying nothing as Cardinal Wright allowed his teenage guest to dominate the conversation. When Cardinal Wright asked what he thought of the Vatican, young Chris dismissed it as "a culture of lackeys."

Father Wuerl spoke up for the first time. "Hey!" he said with a smirk. "Go easy on the lackeys."[5]

Father Wuerl knew what he was talking about. He spent years doing the everyday office work of the Vatican—an experience from which he learned that it is often the unappreciated, nameless "lackeys" who get things done.

In April of 1969, Pope Paul VI made Bishop Wright a cardinal and appointed him prefect of the Congregation for Clergy, the first American in the top post of a Vatican office.

It was a position that would require careful organization, and Cardinal Wright knew exactly the man for the task of organizing. He appointed Father Wuerl his full-time secretary and asked him to continue that role in Rome.

This was a challenging time to be in global Church leadership. While the Catholic Church in Africa was on the verge of tremendous growth, the Church in Eastern Europe was suppressed by communist governments; in western Europe it was eroded by secularism; and in North America it was mired in confusion.

The implementation of Vatican II had proved a mixed blessing. Many Catholics rejoiced at having Mass in their own language and appreciated the attention to social issues. But others—who had expected changes that didn't come—were bitterly disappointed. A different group grieved the loss of the Latin Mass, and legitimately felt betrayed when some priests stopped promoting traditional devotions such as the rosary. As sisters shed their religious habits and ways of life, some sisters felt that their community had abandoned them. A variety of well-intentioned efforts to teach the faith in ways that were more relevant and experiential ran off the theological rails and failed to convey central doctrines to a new generation.

In the 1970s all of this led to waves of resignations from the priesthood, flight from the convent, and a generation of young priests and laity who were confused about what the Church taught, what it meant to be a priest, and how to be a good Catholic.

As prefect of the Congregation for Clergy, which oversaw issues pertaining to priesthood and the teaching of Catholic doctrine to the laity, Cardinal Wright was in the eye of that storm. Part of his mission was to observe the ongoing education of priests worldwide, to see what was and wasn't effective in their education. Father Wuerl accompanied him on those travels. Before he turned thirty, he began to see first-hand how the Church lived out its mission in many different cultures and contexts.

Founded in 1564, the Congregation for Clergy was housed in a modern building that a journalist once described as "spacious, airy, and somewhat antiseptic." The staff of thirty-five priests, plus a handful of lay office workers, oversaw the education and supervision of more than 400,000 diocesan priests. One of the cardinal's more depressing tasks was to respond to a surging number of requests from men who wanted to resign from active priesthood. He met with them personally whenever possible—visiting the Americans on summer travels home—and approved about 80 percent of the requests.[6]

One of Cardinal Wright's gifts was to bring joy to his work, no matter how painful the subject at hand. "Even if it was a serious discussion, he always found a way to interject something light enough to get a chuckle," Cardinal Wuerl said.

But Cardinal Wright was increasingly denounced by liberal Catholics who had once regarded him as their champion. They viewed him as a turncoat because he didn't support their interpretation of the Second Vatican Council. The idea took root in some influential Catholic circles that the Council had turned the Church into a democracy, along the lines of many Protestant denominations. These Catholics were suspicious of, even antagonistic toward, Rome.

Often in homilies or speeches, Cardinal Wright would name some idea that had taken root in the Church of the 1970s, whether it was a married priesthood, permission to use contraceptives for family planning, or the notion that Jesus was merely a good man and not the divine Son of God. "I never heard that at the Council," he would say.[7]

An editorial in the August 4, 1972 edition of the *National Catholic Reporter*, an independent liberal Catholic newspaper, described him as "a man whose beliefs are dangerous in the long run" because his "actions and words demonstrate a harmful bias in favor of the institutional church and against the freedom, growth and development of the individual Christian."[8]

But Cardinal Wright believed in being open with the journalists, even when they were unkind to him, a lesson he passed along to his protégé. Before entering seminary Wright had earned a master's degree in journalism and had paid his tuition at Boston College by working as a reporter for the *Boston Post*. He understood the importance of keeping a good relationship with the media, hosting reporters at his apartment in Rome.

• • • • • • •

In Italy Father Wuerl witnessed the danger of tethering the Church to any political faction. While most Italian women practiced their faith no matter what, he was shocked to discover that the men regarded Mass as something only for members of the Christian Democratic Party. The party—which the Church had encouraged as an antidote to communism after World War II and which advocated important elements in the Church's social teaching—had unintentionally politicized the sacraments and weakened the impact of the gospel. It was a lesson that Father Wuerl took to heart.

He admired the way that Pope Paul strove to hold the Church together in a time of polarized reactions to both the Second Vatican Council and to wider cultural changes, including the sexual revolution. Some decisions, such as his reaffirmation of the ban on artificial contraception, incited anger and rejection in the wider Church, including the charge that he was non-consultative. But Pope Paul's careful, quiet, pastoral approach made a lasting impact on Father Wuerl's ministry. It helped him to cultivate a gift for identifying gray areas in matters of Church life, where people of different visions can come together and find pastoral solutions to difficult problems.

"When you think of Paul VI, whom history is going to point out to be an extraordinarily significant pope, the whole idea of holding the family together means that it's not all just black and white," Cardinal Wuerl would say later.

Remembering how grateful he had been to have lunch with his bishop in his seminary years, Father Wuerl regularly invited the Pittsburgh seminarians to his apartment. It still wasn't easy for him to live so far from home. His mother was battling cancer, and she died in July 1972, at the age of forty-seven.

His work continued. As Cardinal Wright's executive secretary he was a member of the Curia, the Vatican bureaucracy. He saw the good and the bad up close, concluding that most of those who worked in the Vatican sincerely sought to serve both Christ and the Vicar of Christ, though they sometimes had different visions of what that meant. He was most troubled by a pattern common to bureaucracies, in which officials would ignore a problem because it was outside their area of responsibility.

"You can spend a great deal of your life's energy going from office to office" in search of assistance, he said. It made him long for a Church in which officials might say "we don't do that here, but let me find you someone who can help you get that done."

His years of service in Rome would later lead other bishops to seek his advice on how to get things done there.

He saw many new offices created to implement the ideas and decisions of Vatican II. There were pontifical councils to promote Christian unity, justice and peace, the family, the sciences.

"That all seemed like a very positive thing," he said. "You saw all of them multiplying. But it struck me then that this was the institution of the Holy See trying to find a way to keep alive all that energy of the Council. Now I think we realize, I certainly do in the archdiocese, that the creation of a new office is not the response to the issue. Teaching the issue becomes the response to the issue."

But he has long challenged the stereotype of Vatican officials as fundamentally authoritarian rather than collegial.

"That's just a false dichotomy," he said in 1988. "I see Rome today seeking consultation—all kinds of input from a variety of sources before decisions are made—not just giving orders. That's a caricature and like all caricatures, it doesn't tell the whole truth."[9]

• • • • • • •

As Father Wuerl had done in Pittsburgh, in Rome he multitasked. He earned his doctorate in theology at the Pontifical University of St. Thomas, where he also taught one day a week. His dissertation on the nature of priesthood criticized the efforts of some popular theologians to reduce the sacramental nature of priestly ordination to the power to be CEO in a parish. He also began writing books and articles, ranging from stories for the the Vatican newspaper *L'Osservatore Romano* and the popular American Catholic weekly *Our Sunday Visitor,* to books on critical aspects of Church life.

His first book, published in 1971, was *The Forty Martyrs,* about a group of Reformation-era saints whom Pope Paul had recently canonized. He followed with *The Church: The Hope of the World* in

1972, *Fathers of the Church* in 1975, and *The Catholic Priesthood To-day* in 1976.

But his major work, destined to be a worldwide Catholic bestseller for decades, was his collaboration with two brothers, Thomas Lawler and Father Ronald Lawler, O.F.M., Cap., on the adult catechism *The Teaching of Christ,* a project about which we will hear much later on.

•••••••

In Rome, Father Wuerl established as much of a routine as possi-ble, given Cardinal Wright's unpredictable schedule and tendency to improvise. He began the day at dawn by running four miles on Rome's cobblestone streets. His early morning rituals also included praying the Liturgy of the Hours, celebrating Mass for two nuns on Cardinal Wright's household staff, and meditating for some time. Only then would he launch "another unpredictable nine to 10 hours of work as Wright's aide and troubleshooter," according a brief pro-file in People Magazine. He ended his days around midnight, listen-ing to music that ranged from Beethoven to the Beatles, and reading both theology and historical novels.[10]

Sometimes hard work is rewarded. Sometimes it is scorned as am-bition. The Vatican, like any bureaucracy, can foster petty jealousies. Some of his contemporaries in Rome recalled peers who resented this young Yankee who not only represented a powerful cardinal, but was making a name in his own right. But many others developed a deep appreciation for his single-minded focus on building the King-dom of God.

"He was a very nice, gentle guy," the late Father F. X. Murphy said in an unpublished interview in 1995. The Redemptorist scholar —popularly known as Xavier Rynne, the pseudonym he used to chronicle Vatican II for *The New Yorker*—was teaching in Rome during the first two years that Cardinal Wright and Father Wuerl served there.

He remembered some Vatican staffers making dismissive com-ments about Father Wuerl, but recalled him as intelligent and efficient. He said the young man kept a low profile. He was known for graciously entertaining the cardinal's friends when they came to Rome.

The priest-sociologist and popular writer Father Andrew Greeley, now deceased, was among their visitors late in the decade, when Cardinal Wright was showing signs of neurological disease. "The cardinal was not a well man,'" Father Greeley said in 1996. "As fond as I was of him, he would have driven me crazy in a couple more hours. Don was marvelously gentle and patient with him, he took care of him and directed him. It was a tour de force."[11] In 1978 Cardinal Wright was diagnosed with a progressive neuromuscular disease, polymyositis, that causes weakness and painful muscular inflammation. When Pope Paul VI died that August, the cardinal was hospitalized in Boston. Father Wuerl was the homilist for the pope's Memorial Mass in Pittsburgh.

"Pope Paul dedicated his reign to the struggle for peace among nations, justice among peoples and that brotherly love that is the privileged heritage of the Judeo-Christian tradition," he told the faithful.[12]

Because of Cardinal Wright's illness, he and Father Wuerl were not in Rome for the conclave that elected Albino Luciani as Pope John Paul I. Thirty-three days later, news of the new pope's death shocked the world. The Cardinal was still gravely ill, but he rallied to travel with his aide to the Church's second conclave that year.

• • • • • • •

Cardinal Wright arrived for the conclave in a wheelchair, and needed Father Wuerl to assist him. Thus Father Wuerl—bound by the same promises of secrecy as the cardinals—was the only non-cardinal present during the cardinals' deliberations in that conclave.

One of the other cardinals was an old friend of Cardinal Wright's, the Polish archbishop of Krakow, Karol Wojtyla. Though Cardinal Wright was more than a decade older, both had been among the youngest bishops at Vatican II, where both had been crucial advocates for its endorsement of religious freedom as a God-given right.

Both shared a concern that too many Catholic theologians were in-ferring changes to Church tradition that the Council had never in-tended. They became close friends. Cardinal Wojtyla had visited Pittsburgh shortly before Cardinal Wright moved to Rome, and Car-dinal Wright and Father Wuerl visited Cardinal Wojtyla in Krakow. The Polish cardinal was a member of the Congregation for Clergy, which meant he often visited Cardinal Wright in Rome, where the two would dine with their secretaries, Father Wuerl and then-Father Stanislaw Dziwsz.

On the first night of the conclave Cardinal Wojtyla asked Father Wuerl for help practicing his English. So they walked together in a walled section of the Vatican Gardens, conversing.

About forty-eight hours later Father Wuerl was awestruck to see him vested in the white robes of the successor of the Apostle Peter. No non-Italian had been pope since 1522.

"I felt like I had been ordained all over again," he said. "The joy of ordination came flooding back. There was a sense of starting all over again with the election of this pope."[13] That night Father Wuerl, who was fetching Cardinal Wright's miter, took a shortcut through an off-limits passage in the Apostolic Palace and literally ran into the new pope and his entourage. He very nervously fell to his knees. Throughout his experience, popes were distant figures, exceedingly formal even with those they knew well.

Pope John Paul II stopped, asking, "What are you doing down there, Father Wuerl?" and pulled him to his feet.

"The protocol response," Cardinal Wuerl remembered years later, "would have been for him to keep on going and not even recognize that anyone was there. Instead he created a situation that relieved my anxiety."[14]

It was a harbinger of a renewed papacy, of a pope who trampled protocol and often left Rome to be an evangelist to the world. But Cardinal Wright would see little of it.

· · · · · · ·

Jerry Filteau, then a new reporter for Catholic News Service in Rome, reminisced more than thirty years later about visiting Cardinal Wright's apartment early in the papacy of Pope John Paul II. Father Wuerl "was then quietly running almost all affairs of the Clergy Congregation because of Wright's illness," he wrote.[15] Pope John Paul himself came to the apartment to bless his terminally ill friend.[16] Cardinal Wright died at the age of seventy on August 10, 1979, while hospitalized in Massachusetts. He bequeathed to Father Wuerl the bishop's ring that Pope Paul VI had given to him in commemoration of his role in the Second Vatican Council. It was a statement of faith, of commitment to the Church, and also a vote of confidence that Father Wuerl would one day wear a bishop's ring.

Cardinal Wright also left an intangible inheritance.

When they had first worked together, Father Wuerl had been impatient with the long hours that Bishop Wright poured into perfecting documents for the diocese or for the National Conference of Catholic Bishops. The bishop responded that Church documents are reference points of faith that remain regardless of the personalities or priorities of individual priests, bishops, and popes.

"I realize that structures, documents, and institutions are not the soul of the church. The Holy Spirit is the soul of the church. And I know those things are not the fabric of the Church. God's people are the fabric of the church," Bishop Wuerl would say thirty years later. "But the church can't be amorphous. All the time you spend on a teaching document or all the time you spend on putting some program...together is worth it. Because that is part of the skeleton that holds the body of the Church together."[17]He had seen the cardinal struggle with disappointment in how the Council was received and adversity in how he himself was perceived. His years in Rome were "a particularly difficult time in the life of the Church," Cardinal Wuerl recalled.

"One of the things that I learned from the cardinal is that you have to keep your eye on the big picture; that the Church is in this for the long haul, and that continuity counts as well as freshness. You can't have one without the other. If we are trying to freshen the presentation of the faith, you have to make sure that it is in continuity with what the faith has always said. That was a great lesson to learn. It helps you sort things out. It's not all black and white. There is so much gray, but you have to make your way through seeing what really counts and what is just passing."

After Cardinal Wright's death Father Wuerl asked to be relieved of further assignments at the Vatican so he could return home to Pittsburgh. He hoped to once again become an assistant in a parish—"to do something more pastoral," as he told the Holy Father. In spite of his amusement at the phrasing, Pope John Paul II understood, and Father Wuerl was soon on his way back to Pittsburgh.

• • • • • • •

The Diocese of Pittsburgh he returned to was led by Bishop Vincent Leonard, a beloved Pittsburgh native who had been an auxiliary bishop during Bishop Wright's tenure. The steel industry was showing signs of instability, but wasn't yet in free fall. The skies of Pittsburgh were still smoky, the 321 parish churches filled with nearly a million Catholics. Bishop Leonard did his best to care for the poor and to steer a middle course through controversies of church and society.

When Father Wuerl called on Bishop Leonard at his residence, it was typical of the bishop's informality that he invited his newly returned priest to watch the evening news with him. During a commercial break Bishop Leonard told him that he was to become vice-rector of St. Paul Seminary. The appointment was announced in February 1980, and he was swiftly promoted to rector.[18]

Father Wuerl was never again assigned to parish ministry. His two years at St. Rosalia were his last in a neighborhood church. Asked whether he believed he would have been a better bishop had he had more time and responsibility in a parish, he said he isn't certain.

"Parochial ministry is a form of pastoral ministry, but not the only form of pastoral ministry," he said. "I think I learned good pastoral skills working with Cardinal Wright in Rome and helping in his parish there. Also, you develop pastoral skills as rector of the seminary. So the parish is not the exclusive experience of pastoral ministry, but I loved that time in the parish."

His years at St. Paul Seminary were among his happiest. He enjoyed guiding young men along the path to priesthood. But, as usual, he was multitasking. He also taught part-time at Duquesne University, was state chaplain for the Knights of Columbus, and even co-authored an illustrated children's book, *A Visit to the Vatican for Young People.* Dedicated to his niece and nephews, it covered topics from the architecture of St. Peter's to the work of Vatican Radio, but also served as a mini-catechism on the mission of the Church.[19]

He worked hard to make St. Paul Seminary into a model for the education of priests. He hired the first female faculty member, a sister who supervised the seminarians' field service, in part so the future priests would learn to respect women in Church leadership.

The man who is now coadjutor Archbishop of Newark and apostolic administrator of the Archdiocese of St. Paul-Minneapolis, Bernard Hebda, was a young attorney at a prestigious Pittsburgh firm when persistent thoughts of priesthood led him to have lunch with the seminary rector.

Father Wuerl "started talking about the importance of building the kingdom, and how we each have to take responsibility for that. He was so persuasive, I wanted to sign on the dotted line right then. I remember thinking I would be willing to sign over my life to that man," said Archbishop Hebda, who was ordained five years later.[20]

Pope John Paul II soon tapped Father Wuerl's expertise and experience for part-time service in the wider Church. In 1982 he was named executive secretary of a Vatican-mandated study of all seminaries in the United States. He visited theological schools nationwide. The study produced reforms in seminary education—reforms that later research by experts at John Jay College credited with ending the vast majority of child sexual abuse by priests, even before the problem was identified.[21] At every stage of the ten-year seminary study, Father Wuerl went with the study's apostolic visitor, Bishop John Marshall of Burlington, Vermont, to report to Pope John Paul.

The pope "would always graciously have us come to supper. That is when I began to have an even deeper respect for the pope. He was a great listener. But as he was absorbing what was being said. You could see the body language that told you what you needed to say again, or he would simply say 'What does that mean?'" Cardinal Wuerl re-called. "I found it intriguing, the interaction with him and his hu-mility. He is the pope, the Vicar of Christ and the successor of St. Peter, sitting at the table with the two of us and his secretary, listen-ing to what we were reporting on and asking questions that had to do with what we were talking about. It was a great lesson in collabora-tion."

In 1984 he was named a consultor to the Congregation for Clergy, the office that he had served for a decade in Rome. At the same time the new bishop of Pittsburgh, Anthony Bevilacqua, drew him into diocesan leadership as associate general secretary of the Diocese of Pittsburgh.

The next year Pope John Paul II turned to him again. This time it was for a far more difficult assignment in Seattle—a task that sent shock waves through the Church in the United States.

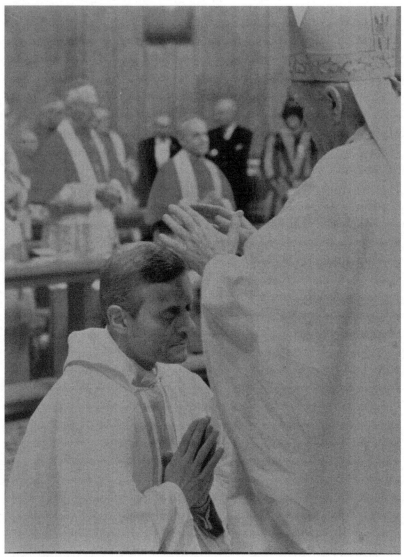

Pope John Paul II ordains Donald Wuerl as auxiliary bishop of Seattle.
Courtesy of the Diocesan Archives of the Diocese of Pittsburgh.

CHAPTER 3:
THE UNWANTED BISHOP

The situation in Seattle was complicated, to say the least. It was so complicated that no one really knew what was going on.

Some Catholics from the Pacific Northwest had complained for years about Archbishop Raymond Hunthausen. Many of the complaints were about matters that did not trouble the Vatican, such as the archbishop's decision to withhold some of his taxes as a protest against militarism. But others had to do with important matters of Church teaching and practice.

In 1983 Pope John Paul II had sent Cardinal James Hickey of Washington, D.C., to investigate matters of doctrinal significance. The investigation identified five areas of concern:

1. The process of granting marriage annulments; liturgical abuses including widespread use of general absolution instead of private Confession.

2. Sterilizations in Catholic hospitals.

3. Permitting priests who had been laicized to have liturgical duties that Rome had forbidden to them.

4. Allowing a dissident ministry for gay Catholics to have Mass in the cathedral.

5. Failure to properly educate priests on critical doctrines including Church unity exercised through a bond with the pope.

These were not new or isolated issues. The same 1972 issue of *The National Catholic Reporter* in which the interview with Cardinal Wright appeared had reported on dioceses allowing divorced Catholics who had remarried without an annulment to receive Communion if they sincerely believed that their first marriage was not a true marriage and that their current one was.²²

Pope John Paul II did not want to remove Archbishop Hunthausen, whom he understood to be a caring, pastoral bishop who had left the administration of the archdiocese to others. So the pope conceived a plan to send in an auxiliary bishop—who would ordinarily have no governing authority—empowered to make decisions in the five problem areas. According to a chronology later released by the pope's representative in Washington, D.C., Archbishop Pio Laghi, Archbishop Hunthausen had agreed to the arrangement as long as he, rather than the pope, was the one to formally delegate authority to his new auxiliary.²³

It was an unusual plan, and it would require an unusual auxiliary bishop—one who would be diplomatic and self-effacing enough to make it work. The Pope decided that his old friend Father Wuerl had just that unusual combination of traits.

So Donald Wuerl was ordained bishop and sent to Seattle to help sort things out. The pope believed this diplomatic solution could be quietly carried out with no public embarrassment to Archbishop Hunthausen. He knew Donald Wuerl's personality: he was confident he had made the right choice.

But the problem facing the new bishop was not his own personality. It was the imaginary personality some people in Seattle had already constructed for him as soon as his appointment was announced.

. . . .

When the appointment was announced on November 30, 1985, the reaction in Pittsburgh, where few people monitored West Coast Church politics, was simply one of pride in a local priest who had become a bishop. But in Seattle, both clergy and media were immediately suspicious, given the previous investigation and the oddity of an auxiliary who wasn't from the archdiocese or even the region.

At a press conference in Seattle, Archbishop Hunthausen was already denying political implications. The archbishop said that his new auxiliary's "background and experience are clear indications of his ability and they match what we needed for this archdiocese." Bishop Wuerl would answer to him, he said, and the appointment of an auxiliary would free him to do more of what he loved: visiting parishes.

The motto that Bishop-elect Wuerl chose for himself was "Thy Kingdom Come.". It reflected his struggle with the contrast between Jesus' vision of a just and peaceful world, and the reality of the pain that humans inflict on one another. God hadn't failed; people had failed to follow God.

Pope John Paul II personally ordained him a bishop in St. Peter's Basilica. There he presented Bishop Wuerl with the miter he had worn during a visit to the Netherlands, where liberal Dutch Catholics had jeered the pontiff.

That was the first signal to Bishop Wuerl's family and friends that trouble lay ahead.[24]

Initially offered a choice of apartments, Bishop Wuerl said he preferred to live in a parish. He was given a room in the rectory of Holy Rosary parish on the city's rough-and-tumble West Side.

Arhbishop Hunthausen "gave me the task of doing a lot of confirmations," Cardinal Wuerl said in 2014. "He said it is the one way you can really get to know the archdiocese. And I did." The Seattle archdiocesan newspaper, The Progress, later described him driving his Honda Civic throughout the archdiocese, meeting parishioners who found him to be "dedicated, articulate and talented."[25]

But for eight months, Archbishop Hunthausen didn't delegate any authority to Bishop Wuerl.[26]

• • • • • • •

Before his appointment was even announced, Archbishop Pio Laghi, the pope's representative in the United States, had given him and Archbishop Hunthausen copies of the same letter. In it Archbishop Laghi had thanked Archbishop Hunthausen for agreeing to welcome a new auxiliary and to grant him authority in five specific areas.

"It was the interpretation of Archbishop Laghi's letter that was the center of the difficulty and not any secret instructions," Bishop Wuerl said in 1987. "Obviously he didn't understand the instructions the same way that I did."

Bishop Wuerl had "accepted the assignment on the understanding I was acceptable to the archbishop and the whole concept of helping him was acceptable."[27]

The impasse was exceedingly awkward for the new auxiliary who, at forty-five, was a decade younger than the average priest and nearly two decades younger than the average bishop. From the start some archdiocesan staff members refused to speak to him.

"I always greeted people, even if they chose not to respond. I always felt that they are responsible for their actions, I am responsible for mine," Cardinal Wuerl said long afterward.

Matters came to a head in March 1986, during a disagreement over how to respond to a proposed city gay-rights ordinance. Bishop Wuerl felt duty-bound to ask if this wasn't an issue on which he should make the final decision.

The chancery staff stopped speaking to him altogether. Archbishop Hunthausen appealed to Rome for clarification, which was three months in coming. It was another two months before he ceded the authority to Bishop Wuerl.[28]

Members of the archdiocesan staff mobilized protests. Although Vatican officials had assumed the transfer of authority would remain quiet to preserve the dignity of the archbishop, the archbishop sent a letter to explain the situation to priests and parishioners.[29]

That letter ignited media attention. So in early September Archbishop Hunthausen and Bishop Wuerl held a press conference.

Father Thomas Reese, a Jesuit political scientist and journalist, happened to be in Seattle researching his book *Archbishop* on the day of the press conference. Although his ecclesiastical instincts led him to sympathize with Archbishop Hunthausen, he empathized with Bishop Wuerl.

"He appeared like someone who was dropped into the middle of this mess and then abandoned and left to the wolves," he said. "He was being attacked and pilloried by everyone in Seattle, and

it really didn't seem that it was his fault. Obviously it was causing
him a lot of pain and suffering. Just looking at his face and his
posture and listening to him during the press conference showed
that."[30]

The press conference was just the beginning.

· · · · · · ·

Suddenly Bishop Wuerl's assignment was on all the national
nightly news broadcasts. Newspapers across the nation sent reporters
to Seattle. The usual story line was that malevolent Vatican forces
had sent Bishop Wuerl as an agent of repression in a crackdown on
benevolent pastoral practices. Many stories also intimated it was a
conservative political move against the archbishop's stands against
war and for human rights.

Archdiocesan chancellor Father Michael Ryan held a meeting for
priests to endorse an appeal to Pope John Paul to restore the archbishop's authority.[31] Stories were circulated to the media claiming
falsely that he had demanded a luxury condominium in downtown
Seattle.[32]

The real problem, Cardinal Wuerl would say years later, wasn't
that he had undermined the archbishop's authority because, in practice, that had long been delegated to members of the chancery staff.
Those staff members were up in arms because he was a threat to their
power, he said.

"There was a sense in which the archbishop provided the umbrella
under which a lot of things were being done. I'm not always sure he
was aware of everything that was going on. They had a sense of protection and they saw my arrival, particularly in the mandate to begin
to address some of these things, as the closing of the umbrella."

Special Masses, prayer services and meetings were held regularly
throughout the archdiocese, calling for his removal. More than
13,000 Seattle Catholics signed a petition calling for full powers to
be restored to Archbishop Hunthausen. In the media coverage both
priests and lay leaders in Seattle spoke of the Vatican not as a center
of unity but as a hostile force and the pope as an alien usurper rather

than a Holy Father. *The National Catholic Reporter* quoted one homily in which a priest preached that Bishop Wuerl represented a "winter of repression emanating from the Vatican."[33]

Father David Jaeger, Seattle's director for seminarians and an organizer of Concerned Catholics, a group formed to oppose Wuerl's assignment, said that "the real issue is a church that is no longer children, no longer under the thumb" of the hierarchy.

"I think it's been a real surprise to Donald that people are not willing to be intimidated," he said.

When Bishop Wuerl met with Concerned Catholics on October 1, 1986, people shouted at him. Some people there charged that he warned them that, if they didn't tone down their opposition, the pope might take stronger action against Archbishop Hunthausen. They then accused him of making a threat, which he denied, saying that they were fomenting division in the Church.[34]

The executive board of the National Federation of Priests' Councils called for full restoration of authority to Archbishop Hunthausen. Two bishops from the region criticized the assignment as a "drastic reprimand" that had the "appearance of unfair treatment."[35]

Even a small group of priests back home in Pittsburgh eventually called on Bishop Wuerl to resign from Seattle, saying they were "scandalized by the injustice" to Hunthausen.[36]

Most of Bishop Wuerl's critics insisted that the real reason for the transfer of power had been Archbishop Hunthausen's anti-nuclear activism.[37] But high-ranking Vatican officials repeatedly and explicitly denied this. A statement that Archbishop Laghi released on October 27, 1986, insisted that "at no time did the Holy See pursue with Archbishop Hunthausen the criticisms it received on controversial issues, e.g. nuclear weapons and the payment of taxes. The concerns were strictly and solely of a doctrinal and pastoral nature." A 1985 letter to Archbishop Hunthausen from Cardinal Joseph Ratzinger, then the head of the Vatican's Congregation for the Doctrine of the Faith and later to become Pope Benedict XVI, had dismissed the archbishop's critics on social-justice issues.

Vatican officials do not wish to "encourage extremist groups who are wholly lacking in a spirit of cooperation and seek to destroy or suppress whatever is not to their liking. It is our intention, rather, to support what you have done to promote the renewal of the Church in Seattle and to point out, at the same time, areas which we consider are in need of correction and improvement," Cardinal Ratzinger wrote.[38]

Archbishop Hunthausen called for civility even as he disputed the Vatican's interpretation of his ministry. He urged everyone to "rise above any contentious spirit and let us do all we can to preserve the bond of unity that is ours as faithful members of the church, committed always to witnessing to the truth in love."[39]

The situation was so tense, public, and potentially volatile that Seattle's police chief assigned an officer to protect Bishop Wuerl on his daily sunrise run from Holy Rosary to a school about a mile distant, where he ran the track.

"I noticed in the morning when I would come out, there was a police car parked there. And as I would run it would drive very slowly behind me," he said. The patrol car stayed at the school while he ran, then followed him back to the parish.

He had never felt physically threatened. One day when he happened to see the police chief he told him that the protection was unnecessary. The police chief, he said, responded, "Bishop, how about if we agree that I won't tell you how to preach if you don't tell me how to police."

· · · · · · ·

The irony is that, by all accounts, Bishop Wuerl never exercised his authority to make changes in Seattle. To do so, he said later, would have been like throwing accelerant on a raging fire. And much of the ministry he saw in Seattle was exemplary, he said.

"There were a few people on one side saying 'Everything is wrong here' and a few people on the other side saying 'We are the way it should be. This is the new church and we are going in a new direction.' But if you concentrate on that large center in between, you would find a lot of good going on in the Archdiocese of Seattle," Cardinal Wuerl said. "I didn't want to go in and just start making judgments about the situation but to begin to become a part of it."

In order for changes to take root, he said, people must be persuaded to buy into them. "My style is to get a lot of people involved and get them to have ownership. You can't do that overnight."[40]

In some cases, he said, problems identified by the apostolic visitation had been resolved before he arrived. To the best of his information, sterilizations no longer took place in the Catholic hospital.

Acting on earlier direction from Rome, the archdiocese had already started its own ministry to gay Catholics. That ministry was "well conducted," Cardinal Wuerl recalled. "It was clear that there were people of same-sex attraction who are a part of the Church and they would come to church and have their Mass."

In fact, "there were a lot of good things going on in that ministry," he said. "I used to ask them why they didn't just go to Mass with everybody else and they would say, 'No, we have our own problems and our own needs.' I never challenged that. What I did say was that you can't insist that the Church change her teaching about the purpose of human sexuality. But none of them said that I had to."

The Rev. Michael Evernden, a Paulist priest who worked with that outreach to gay Catholics, later said that the personal attacks on Bishop Wuerl were unjust.

"He always held the party line, but I felt that he was very pastoral and sensitive to the problems of gay and lesbian Catholics. He exudes kindness and warmth," he told the *Pittsburgh Post-Gazette* two decades later.[41]

But serious problems remained, including situations in which pastors granted permission for divorced people to remarry without going through an annulment process in a Church court. Bishop Wuerl never doubted their sincere desire to help Catholics repair relationships with the Church that had been damaged due to turmoil in their personal lives. The priests may have mistakenly believed that their informal process of approving the remarriage was faithful to Church teaching. But it didn't meet canonical standards. The couples involved would be in for a painful awakening if they were, for instance, asked to be godparents to a child in another diocese and couldn't be approved for it.

"There was a lot of focus on what to do when you have marriages that have broken down. How do you welcome back people who feel alienated from the Church because they had to get a divorce? I think that is what Pope Francis is asking us to do now, face this and try to find some pastoral solution," Cardinal Wuerl said.

"The indissolubility of marriage is a teaching we cannot change, but reception of Communion is another issue. They are two different things. Part of the problem in Seattle was that they were all sort of mixed together."

"With regard to doctrine, there was never any compromise," he said. "Everyone knew from my articles and homilies what the teaching of the Church was.

"But when you get into the whole issue of 'Okay, how do you implement or enforce this?' I always kept in mind the one thing that was written in the papal bull that appointed me. What Pope John Paul II said to me on more than one occasion was 'Your job is to maintain the unity of that church, the unity of the church among its members and its unity with me.

"So many times I would have to make a judgment call: 'Will doing this so exasperate people that the victory is a Pyrrhic one? Or can I do this in steps so that at the end of the day you have been able to win people over and the unity is maintained?'"

His choice was always for unity in an archdiocese teetering on the brink of schism.

His worst grief "came from realizing how the Church there was being torn apart. Also, on a personal level, some petty, vindictive things were done that were unnecessary and beneath what you would expect of 'Church,' something you don't expect from Christians."[42]

Looking back, he recalled: "I don't think I was ever seen as an individual human being, but more as a symbol of the visitation. It was necessary for me to remember that any unpleasantness done to me was aimed at the symbol."

· · · · · · ·

Matters came to a head at perhaps the most contentious meeting in the history of the National Conference of Catholic Bishops. Media interest in the five-hour closed-door session on Seattle completely overshadowed the passage of the bishops' long-awaited pastoral letter on economic justice.[43]

While some bishops reportedly argued for some words of protest about overriding the authority of a diocesan bishop, the official statement said that the Holy See's action in Seattle "deserves our respect and confidence." They expressed concern about abuse directed at Pope John Paul II and the Vatican. And they offered "any assistance judged helpful and appropriate by the parties involved."

Archbishop Hunthausen issued his own statement, asking the bishops for help in resolving the situation. He criticized the way the Vatican had handled the investigation of his archdiocese, and denied that he had violated doctrine or canon law.[44]

Three months later the Vatican named three American prelates—Archbishop John Quinn of San Francisco, Cardinal John O'Connor of New York, and Bishop Wuerl's old friend Cardinal Joseph Bernardin of Chicago—to assess the crisis in Seattle.

Meanwhile, some Seattle priests threatened to suspend all Eucharistic celebrations for three weeks unless the archbishop's full power was restored.[45]

On May 27, 1987, with all parties describing the situation as "unworkable," a compromise was announced between Pope John Paul II and Archbishop Hunthausen. Full authority was restored to the archbishop. Bishop Wuerl was removed from the diocese, amid praise from the commission for his work there. Bishop Thomas Murphy of Great Falls, Mont., with whom Archbishop Hunthausen was friendly, was made coadjutor archbishop, with no immediate authority but the right to eventually succeed Archbishop Hunthausen.[46]

• • • • • • •

Bishop Wuerl's farewell Mass at Holy Rosary in West Seattle was packed.[47] *The Seattle Post-Intelligencer*, which had been scorchingly critical of his assignment, now ran an editorial praising his "dignity and dedication to healing." It said he "never responded to anger in kind" but kept "a low public profile, not issuing edicts or engaging in sharp rhetoric." That "his church had imposed a difficult if not impossible administrative arrangement upon him and the archbishop was not Wuerl's fault," the newspaper said.[48]

"I'm glad it's over. I'm glad it's settled," Bishop Wuerl told Catholic News Service. He played down the hostilities he had endured, saying, "I haven't felt any bitterness. This was not a question of personal animosity but of issues. What we're talking about here, what this is all about from the start, is issues...not personalities."

Regarding the future he said. "I don't have any expectations. I haven't concretized any plans...I think one possibility would be to return to Pittsburgh and take a vacation—which I think I've earned by now."[49]

In Seattle, he said, he was sustained by what he had learned about reliance on God when he was a seminarian in Rome. He had also reminded himself "that I was sent here by the Vicar of Christ. I could say to myself, 'I am here because I was sent.' I used to think back to when I first started to work for Bishop Wright and he said to me, 'You didn't ask for this assignment. It's not going to be an easy assignment but I'm giving you this assignment. So when you look in the mirror you can say, 'What a mess this day has been, but it's *his* fault.' He told me, 'If you ask for an assignment you look in the mirror and say, 'It's my fault.' I did not ask for this assignment but I was sent by the successor of Peter. If it's difficult going, that is not my fault."

A homecoming story in *The Pittsburgh Catholic* noted that his hair had visibly grayed, and he had lost weight from his already slim frame. "I'm physically and psychologically tired," he told reporter Patricia Bartos.

In that interview, he framed the anger and conflict in Seattle in the larger story of the gospel.

"It is part of the life and work of the Church and a natural part of life to have disagreements and misunderstandings, but the Church is bigger than any human misunderstandings. It was that thought that really sustained me through all of this. What is important is not that there are misunderstandings, but the manner in which you resolve them. That should always be with patience, understanding and, above all, love."

His assignment taught him priceless lessons about the importance of finding ways to bring people with different worldviews together, about being slow to pass judgment on those whose beliefs are different than one's own and the art of finding gray areas in which the Church can make room for Catholics whose lives fall short of the Christian ideal.

Seattle showed him that "the world of gray is bigger than the world of black and white. You can't be judgmental if you are trying to bring people together, and patience really is a beautiful virtue," he said.

He resolved that in any future assignment, if difficulties or protests arose, he would meet with the people involved. "That was one of the things I was so grateful that I learned in Seattle. Going and doing all those confirmations that first year made me a person and not an abstraction they read about or heard about in the media."

But he's more reflective in interviews today than the sensitivities of the situation allowed him to be at the time. He left Seattle "with mixed emotions," he said. He sometimes thinks that, if people had been given enough time to calm down, he could have fulfilled his assignment.

And despite everything that happened, Archbishop Hunthausen became a friend, with whom Bishop Wuerl would remain in contact for decades to come.

• • • • • • •

He realized in June 1987 that "the one place, the only place that I could go to would have been back to Pittsburgh and wait and see what the Holy See was going to do with me. I refer to that as my

Food Stamp period. I was unemployed and living off the kindness of the Diocese of Pittsburgh."

He hoped to receive a diocese of his own, "but I assumed it would probably be a smaller one somewhere to get reoriented," he said.

He was grateful to the many Pittsburgh priests who wrote to welcome him home. He moved back into St. Paul Seminary, where he continued to write, to work on projects for the bishops' conference, and to consult on the last stages of the papal seminary study. That July, when he met with Pope John Paul about that study, there was media speculation that he was being given his new assignment. But that would not materialize until six months later.

In early 1988 he was in Dallas for the National Catholic Bioethics Workshop for bishops when Archbishop Laghi stopped him in the hallway and asked to talk during the next coffee break. At that break the nuncio revealed that he had just received word that Pope John Paul II had chosen him as the next bishop of Pittsburgh.

"He said, 'Come with me to my room and we will call Rome right now,'" Cardinal Wuerl recounted. They made the phone call, and the appointment was confirmed. But he was also told that it couldn't be announced until Bishop Bevilacqua, who had been named to succeed Cardinal John Krol of Philadelphia, was formally installed there. Normally that would not have been a problem, but Cardinal Krol had asked to remain in office until the crozier was literally handed to his successor. Therefore Bishop Bevilacqua was still in office in Pittsburgh and couldn't be replaced until he was installed in Philadelphia.

Bishop Wuerl readily agreed. He was elated to be made bishop of his beloved home diocese, where his family lived and where he knew the priests—and the only place in America where people's impressions of him had been shaped by more than the news from Seattle.

On February 11 he was in Philadelphia at a luncheon in honor of newly installed Archbishop Bevilacqua, when Archbishop Laghi turned to Archbishop Daniel Pilarczyk of Cincinnati and asked if he had congratulated Bishop Wuerl yet on his new assignment.

"Archbishop Pilarczyk asked 'What new assignment?' and the nuncio said, 'He's going to be the bishop of Pittsburgh.' Dan said,

'Why didn't you say something?' and I said that I didn't know I was allowed to," Cardinal Wuerl said.

Archbishop Laghi interrupted the congratulations with news that a massive snowstorm was expected to ground air traffic later that day. He directed Bishop Wuerl to rush back to Pittsburgh so he would be there when his appointment was announced the next day at six a.m.

"So I got on the plane and got back in time," he said.

Before that first press conference, he said his first Mass as diocesan bishop for the thirty-one seminarians at St. Paul Seminary. Afterward he hugged them and asked them to "pray real hard for me."

He knew he had an enormous task ahead.

"I tried to hit the ground running," he said.

Courtesy of the Diocesan Archives of the Diocese of Pittsburgh.

CHAPTER 4:
BISHOP OF PITTSBURGH

"Pittsburgh!"

If I close my eyes I can still hear that name resound as if from a distance—from down a corridor or across a room. It was the name by which Blessed John Paul II identified me.

My acquaintance with the Holy Father predated his papacy. I first met him when he was Archbishop of Krakow, Poland, and I was working in the Vatican Congregation for the Clergy. I got to know him because he enjoyed practicing his English with native English-speakers. To the end of his life, he spoke English well, but with an accent, which made my nickname all the more endearing.

Why did he call me "Pittsburgh"? He had several good reasons. He knew it as the city where I'd been born and raised. He had visited the city himself in the 1960s and had great affection for its people. And it was he who named me bishop of my home diocese in 1988.

Thus I was easily identified with "Pittsburgh." To him, my face recalled the Church in my city, the people of that city. To the man entrusted with the keys to the kingdom of heaven, I personified a particular corner of the realm. When he showed affection to me, I knew it was directed beyond me: to my people, to our people, to

God's people back home. On my return, I took great pleasure in relaying his greetings and blessing to "Greater Pittsburgh," the city and the surrounding counties.

Wherever I go in the world, my words, and my deeds are not simply my own. They represent the Church, especially the Church I serve as bishop, and the same principle applies to every bishop. Once I represented the Church of Pittsburgh. Now I represent the Church of Washington.

I am intensely aware of it, especially as I travel and find myself among people who do not know me. To them, at first, I am the priest in the next seat on the plane—just another stranger about whom they will form their first impressions. When they realize I am a bishop, they may project their impressions onto the Church I represent.

—Cardinal Donald Wuerl, *Seek First the Kingdom*.

After the agony of Seattle, Bishop Wuerl now led a diocese filled with people eager to embrace him—both because he was a hometown boy and because of their ingrained respect for the office of bishop. It was, for him, the best assignment he could have dreamed of.

But many bishops would have considered Pittsburgh a penance.

Its parishes and finances had been drained by the collapse of the steel industry, as tens of thousands of younger Catholics left the region. Unemployment was at 25 percent in parts of the diocese. A diocesan deficit was expected to reach $3.8 million that fiscal year. A separate issue was that 48 of its 333 churches owed the diocese a total of $5.6 million for insurance and other costs.[50]

On top of that, there was open anger over his predecessor's decision not to wash the feet of women on Holy Thursday. And, though it was not yet public, the new bishop was aware that three of his priests were on administrative leave, accused of conspiring in the sexual abuse of two altar boys.

All of that faced him at his installation Mass on March 25, 1988, when every pew in St. Paul Cathedral was jammed and an overflow crowd watched on television from the hall next door.

"We have a long walk ahead of us," Bishop Wuerl told them. "It may be tiring, but what makes it beautiful is that we will be making that walk to God's kingdom with the love that we share."

"Thy Kingdom Come" was still his motto, and in his eyes the bishop's role was to organize and guide his people to build that kingdom. He urged those in the cathedral to take up that commission: "We make God visible. We build within our own midst, time and lives that kingdom where there is peace and justice and understanding and faith and love."[51] He saw himself as the steward in Jesus' parables, who tended the people and resources his master had entrusted to him.[52]

· · · · · · ·

One of the first things Bishop Wuerl told Father David Zubik—then his secretary and eventually his successor—was that he intended to put the Diocese of Pittsburgh "back on the map." He resolved to build it into an organization that local leaders respected, trusted, and turned to for assistance in building a better community.

He quickly signaled his intention to bring healing by washing the feet of exactly six women and six men on his first Holy Thursday at St. Paul Cathedral.

The next year he moved the ritual to the Allegheny County Jail, saying that Jesus was a prisoner during the first Holy Week. As he prepared to wash the inmates' feet he told them that paintings show a few people around Jesus' cross, but none with the two thieves alongside him. "I thought I would like to remedy that by spending time with you," he said.[53]

In other years he went to nursing homes and other institutions for marginalized people, where he continued to wash the feet of both men and women.

But the administrative crises needed more than charity: they needed careful handling. The most urgent "was the hemorrhage in the budget. We were spending far more than we had, and we were spending down the reserves," Cardinal Wuerl said.

No bishop is asked to acquire an MBA. Yet a bishop typically over-sees a multi-million dollar central operation, a school system, an in-surance-and-benefits operation, a court system, a news organization, hospitals and health systems, scores of parishes, and a multifaceted social-service network that may include low-income housing, clinics, and immigration and refugee services. He must govern all of them according to two sets of laws: those of the state and those of the Church.

That list "is why the Church, in her wisdom, says the bishop must have a finance council. This is not an option," he would tell rookie bishops years later at the Vatican's annual "school" for new members of the hierarchy.

In approaching the administrative crisis, Bishop Wuerl's bywords were *consultation, collaboration,* and *communication.* Vatican II had called bishops to listen to their priests and value the advice of laity, and his experience on the Vatican seminary study had shown him the value of listening to critics.

At the beginning of that study everyone affected was invited to help design the process. The first draft of the questionnaire was sent to all bishops and religious superiors, with a request for suggestions to improve it. One recipient was very critical—using the word "in-quisition"—but sent suggestions.

When the revised copy was circulated, he wrote to Father Wuerl, thanking him for incorporating all of his suggestions. He became a great supporter of the study.

"What a good lesson for me to learn," Cardinal Wuerl said years later. "Collaboration, consultation, and communication became three norms."

• • • • • • •

To begin dealing with the financial problems, Bishop Wuerl held a meeting to inform all the priests of the financial realities of the diocese. Then he appointed an eleven-member deficit-reductions task force filled with lay financial experts.

All decisions should be made with prayer, but Cardinal Wuerl admits that he has never once heard the Holy Spirit audibly whisper, "Do it this way." He seeks the advice of many experts, but ultimately weighs that against the two greatest commandments: to love both God and his neighbor.

And he always insisted on transparency. The Church should not be hiding things from its own people. "If something that was a problem happened in the diocese, he insisted that there would be a story about in the *Pittsburgh Catholic*," Bishop Zubik said. "Until then, the *Pittsburgh Catholic* basically just printed the good stuff. He used to say over and over, 'You can never communicate too much.'"

Pittsburgh's longtime diocesan spokesman, Father Ronald Lengwin, recalls that one of Bishop Wuerl's constant refrains was "you have to have a team on the field." The football reference meant that the other side will win if you don't show up to engage critics.

Whenever logistically possible, he has been willing to meet with reporters, answer their questions and give his own take on a situation, even one that reflects poorly on the Church.

"If the news media report things that are wrong, you have to be able to respond," Father Lengwin said.

Once reporters have the interview, Cardinal Wuerl said, "if they distort it, manipulate it, that doesn't rest on my conscience. What would rest on my conscience is if I refused to give my side of the story and then faulted them for having it wrong."

The bishop wanted to build bridges to any group that had a difficult relationship with the Church, including those who felt marginalized or hurt by its doctrines or clergy.

That was one reason he placed a high priority on bringing women into leadership positions.

· · · · · · ·

His conviction about the importance of women's voices came partly from his close relationship with his sister, Carol. "When I was ordained, she would critique my homilies. It was a blessing for me, a frame of reference," he said.

Soon after his installation he began to ask why there were no women on various boards and commissions, and was often told that it was difficult to find qualified women. But he would meet them at events—and ask about their friends. "Once you got into the world of networking women, you could find all kinds of people," Cardinal Wuerl said.

Dr. Rosemarie Cibik, a former public-school superintendent, became the first lay superintendent of Catholic schools. Rita Joyce, a canon and civil lawyer, would become the first layperson to serve on the diocesan marriage tribunal. Bishop Wuerl chose a woman, Sister Margaret Hannan, to take his former position as associate general secretary of the Diocese. She would eventually serve as chancellor, the highest canonical post that can be given to someone who isn't ordained.

Bishop Wuerl showed her respect, clearly signaling that he expected others to do likewise, she said.

The chancellor administers the oath of fidelity to newly appointed pastors. One new pastor arrived in her office, clearly unhappy. Later they became friends, and he confessed why he had appeared so irritated.

When Bishop Wuerl handed him the envelope of papers for his appointment, he directed the priest to see Sister Margaret for the oath. He replied that he would rather go to the priest who had been chancellor before Sister Margaret.

The bishop, Sister Margaret recounted, "looked at him and said, 'Then please return my envelope.'"

· · · · · ·

Bishop Wuerl built up especially close relationships with the religious, and those relationships were crucial to his work with Catholic social-service and health-care institutions. Because Jesus commanded his followers to care for the sick and suffering, the Catholic Church must be involved in health care. It is a complex ministry, technically, ethically, and financially.

The Diocese of Pittsburgh requires any ministry to the sick and the poor with "Catholic" in its name to have "some verifiable, structural linkage to the Diocesan Bishop at the level of institutional oversight," though the details of that linkage are to be worked out on a case-by-case basis. Those structures "ensure that what is being done is truly a reflection of the Church, her mission and teaching," Bishop Wuerl told new bishops in Rome.[54] As a ministry, he said, health care "comes under the direction of the bishop, even though all of the technical aspects of the delivery of health care are the responsibility of those engaged directly in the service." In Pittsburgh he inherited extensive medical ministries, but moved to expand them even in the midst of resolving the diocesan budget crisis.

His predecessor had closed a Natural Family Planning clinic that had come under fire from some Catholic groups for working closely with secular family-planning organizations. Bishop Wuerl created a Natural Family Planning advisory committee of health-care professionals and other experts, which developed a medical program of instruction based at Catholic hospitals.

Early in his Pittsburgh ministry he worked with hospitals and community groups to transform a former Catholic personal-care residence into a home for persons with AIDS, a bold move at a time when AIDS was poorly understood and nearly always fatal.[55]

In 2003 he designated $250,000 as a challenge grant to raise funds for the eventual creation of a $2.5 million Catholic Charities Free Health Care Center for the uninsured. Opened by his successor, it served the working poor who made too much money to qualify for government assistance.[56]

But medical institutions face serious financial pressures. Many have closed. There have been worries over whether sale to a secular health-care chain would result in abortions at facilities founded to support life. In the early 1990s the U.S. Conference of Catholic Bishops asked Bishop Wuerl to oversee a subcommittee on Catholic health care to address those issues. That familiarized him with the complex situations facing Catholic hospitals. He knew that there was no out-of-the-box solution.

He tried hard to preserve a Catholic hospital in Pittsburgh, with partial success. The Sisters of St. Francis of Millvale had given control of their hospital, which was renowned for its service to the poor, over to a lay board. They had done so with the best of intentions, believing it would be easier to obtain outside funding. But it had cut the hospital's formal ties to the Church, said Father Lawrence DiNardo, who was then the diocesan vicar for canonical services.

Bishop Wuerl encountered stiff resistance from the board when he set out to return control of the hospital to the sisters. So it took courage for him to attend the meeting where the decision was made.

"That vote took place right in front of the bishop. It was a very interesting moment, but the sisters were back in control," Father DiNardo said. "He wasn't afraid to take a stand. He had no fear about that. He was the bishop. That's something to remember if you want to wear a miter. It isn't all fun and games."

It soon became clear that Pittsburgh's two remaining Catholic hospitals could not survive independently. He spearheaded merger talks that began in the mid-1990s, but they collapsed in 2002. He was able to salvage something by starting talks—completed by his success—for UPMC, the region's largest secular medical corporation, to purchase Mercy Hospital and run it according to Catholic ethical directives.[57]

• • • • • • •

None of these things were easy, because they required building relationships and making appearances throughout the Pittsburgh area. Cardinal Wuerl is, by nature, an introvert whose idea of a good time is reading historical novels. Yet the society pages in the Pittsburgh newspapers were filled with mentions of his appearances at socially prominent gatherings.

There were countless Catholic fundraisers, including annual dinners for Catholic Charities, the St. Anthony School Programs for children with intellectual disabilities, and the Chimbote Dinner that supported the diocese's medical mission in Peru.

One that went back to his days as Bishop Wright's secretary was the annual Medallion Ball, a debutante ball honoring young women who do at least 100 hours of volunteer work, with proceeds benefiting the St. Lucy's Auxiliary to the Blind. This was more than token volunteerism. In 2002 a Joan of Arc medallion was given to a young woman with Down syndrome who had volunteered as a teacher's assistant at the Children's Institute, where she had been a patient since infancy.[18] A 2013 recipient was legally blind and had volunteered at a therapeutic horseback-riding program. It was not unusual for some of the girls to put in as many as 800 hours of volunteer work. It was a significant time commitment for the bishop, who would host the girls and their mothers for a tea at his home several weeks prior to the ball. But it built relationships with new generations of Catholics, and non-Catholic friends of the Church, who had already shown that they wanted to give of themselves to make the world better.

· · · · · · ·

By the end of Bishop Wuerl's term in Pittsburgh, the diocese was definitely back on the map. Philadelphia is the archdiocese for all the Latin-rite dioceses in Pennsylvania, but Pittsburgh usually produced what became statewide documents for the bishops on matters from sexuality to the death penalty. The Diocese of Pittsburgh typically provided the staff and resources for many ecumenical and interfaith projects by the wider religious community. The diocese had a major role in collaborations between the religious community and local government, such as an effort to provide violence-stricken communities with after-school programs.

"The Catholic diocese was at the forefront of so much that was happening in Pittsburgh. And he was the leader who was making it happen," Father Lengwin said.

But a leader's job isn't all glory. Sometimes he has to make very painful decisions—decisions that will make people angry, or—perhaps even worse—decisions that will make people grieve.

And the one big problem facing the Pittsburgh diocese was fraught with tension and grief: the diocese was facing financial ruin.

Bishop Wuerl's coat of arms as Bishop of Pittsburgh. Courtesy of the Diocesan Archives of the Diocese of Pittsburgh.

With union members at a Labor Day parade. Courtesy of the Diocesan Archives of the Diocese of Pittsburgh.

CHAPTER 5:
PULLING PITTSBURGH
BACK FROM THE BRINK

Every five years a bishop has to go to Rome to report on the state of his diocese. Once, when Bishop Wuerl was making his visit, Pope John Paul II asked him to name the three things he spent the most time on.

"Parish sacramental ministry, working with priests, and fundraising," Bishop Wuerl answered.

"Fundraising?" said the Pope. "Oh! You must have schools."

As usual, he was right on the money. The diocese was in a financial mess when Bishop Wuerl took it over, and parish schools were one of the biggest contributors to the problems. But more than that, education was always one of Bishop Wuerl's top priorities. To bring Catholic education to the students who needed it most, and to do so when the financial situation in the diocese was exceedingly fragile and was going to take a lot of fundraising.

· · · · · · ·

The financial mess was really nobody's fault. The sudden collapse of the steel industry had left all of Pittsburgh reeling. Costs in the diocese had soared up: to address the local crisis after the steel mills shut down, the diocese created programs to aid homeless and unemployed Pittsburghers—which meant hiring more staff. These acts of justice and charity created a pattern of deficit spending that had lasted for years. The diocese reached into its reserves to make up the difference.

Now those reserves were exhausted, and Bishop Wuerl had hard choices to make about what diocesan ministries and services to cut.

This was not what he would have chosen as his top priority. There were other serious challenges that he would rather have put his time and energy into first, such as outreach to the many fallen-away Catholics in the region. But without a solid financial foundation, there would soon be no diocesan resources to devote to evangelization, social services, or any other ministries of the Church.

Bishop Wuerl addressed the problems by following the principles of consultation and collaboration to which he had committed the diocese. Task forces of volunteer experts from throughout the community would advise him on how to make changes, and in some cases engage in wide-ranging grassroots surveys and listening sessions. He would hire top flight financial staff members from secular corporations who had a desire to put their skills and experience to work for the Church. And he would do his utmost to make difficult—sometimes heart-wrenching—financial decisions within the framework of the Church's teaching to put care for the poor and marginalized first.

· · · · · · ·

In January of 1988, a month before Bishop Wuerl's appointment was announced, the diocese reported that its central administration had ended the previous fiscal year with a $2.6 million deficit, having taken in a little over $13 million but spent more than $15.6 million. That was more than twice the previous year's deficit, and was projected to grow to $3.8 million by June 1989.

Bishop Wuerl held a meeting with his priests to explain in depth the financial situation and to emphasize that there were no more reserve funds to draw on. That way they would understand exactly where he stood in terms of his ability to help them with their own urgent financial needs.

"The need for immediate action is imperative. We no longer have the luxury of time in facing the deficit spending of the diocese," Bishop Wuerl said in a public statement in April 1988.[59]

He appointed an 11-member task force, including lay experts and priests, to advise him on his plan to cut his central-administration budget, and propose long-term solutions to ensure financial stability.

Even before that task force finished its work, he created a new diocesan development office to coordinate and provide guidance for all major diocesan and parish fundraising efforts. Just over a decade later that office would win a national award for its work in stabilizing and supporting ministry in the Diocese of Pittsburgh.

The task force finished its work in January 1989 and within a month the diocese announced a plan to slash the central administration operating budget that was already in place by more than $1.2 million. The goal was to reduce the deficit for that fiscal year to less than $2 million.[60]

Bishop Paul Bradley, now of Kalamazoo, was then a priest in charge of the office for social concerns in the Diocese of Pittsburgh. "They were trying to cut the budget everywhere. I remember going to Synod Hall, and saying you have to cut your budget by $1,000. It was nickel-and-diming, but it was my role to get everyone to do something to make it work."

No diocesan employee was laid off in the effort.

"I saw the strain that put on him," Bishop Bradley said of the effort to cut spending. "He went to every length possible to get it where it needed to be without hurting individuals. That comes back to his compassion. He has a great sense of justice. He's not a fanatic. He's not going to lead a protest. But for him it's not an issue as such, it's a matter of what's morally right."

• • • • • • •

The strain was worth it, though: the efforts were extraordinarily successful. At the end of the 1988-1989 fiscal year, the deficit was

$741,888, far less than the $1.9 million that diocesan officials had hoped for six months earlier and a 73 percent reduction from the previous year's deficit. By the 1989-1990 fiscal year, the diocese operated in the black, showing a $157,857 surplus.

But budget cuts were only part of the story. There were trims to some of the bishop's favorite programs, such as nearly $12,000 cut from the vocations budget of $69,147 for seeking candidates for the priesthood. Plans for an expensive program to advertise Catholic schools were scrapped. But other programs received modest increases, there were some pay raises, and a new project, the Parish Self-Study Program, was created at a cost of $66,000. Overall, spending climbed slightly, from 15.2 million to $15.7 million.

The real secret to turning around the diocesan financial situation was the generosity of parishioners, who increased their gifts to the diocese by nearly $368,000—money that went into the newly established Parish Share Program, which helped support schools and other programs of the diocese. Other sources of increased funding included major gifts and bequests, which more than doubled to nearly $790,000. Income from fees for other services, such as diocesan-run nursing homes and the marriage tribunal, rose $500,000 to $2.9 million. All this had happened despite a stagnant economy. Investment income, the third-largest funding source for the diocese, remained steady at $1.3 million.[61]

The diocese would continue to run modest surpluses throughout Bishop Wuerl's tenure. During some years budgets were able to grow significantly; in other years they were cut back as recession and other problems took a toll. But deficit spending was regarded as a mortal sin.

Fiscal responsibility meant more than ensuring bills were paid, said Father Frank Almade, who was both a pastor and director of the diocesan Department for Social Concerns during Bishop Wuerl's tenure in Pittsburgh. The bishop "knew that fiscal prudence meant he kept control of the Church," said Father Almade, citing a number of dioceses that have declared bankruptcy and come under secular court control in the twenty-first century.

Bishop Wuerl would have viewed that as rendering unto Caesar what belonged to God—and letting Caesar run the Church entrusted to the apostles. "Don Wuerl would *never* allow that!" Father Almade said.

· · · · · · ·

Though there was belt-tightening all around, there was still work to be done—and that work still needed money. As he began his second year as shepherd of Pittsburgh, Bishop Wuerl re-launched an endowment drive for the Diocese of Pittsburgh Foundation. Interest on the endowment was to be used for pastoral, educational, and human-service programs, ranging from the education of priests to ministry to persons with disabilities.

Raising funds for such projects meant the bishop had to spend a good deal of time and effort asking people for money—something the seminaries don't give classes in. "There ought to be a boot camp for begging, but there's not," Cardinal Wuerl said years later.

Ambrose Murray, who directed the diocesan Extra Mile Education Foundation, recalled that the bishop's contacts in Pittsburgh's spheres of influence were stellar and wide-ranging, and the bishop never deliberately burned a bridge. "He could pick up the phone and talk to anybody in town, and that includes anybody in the business community. And he did," Mr. Murray said. "I think that every business leader of major importance had some sort of relationship with him, whether they were supporting something, whether they were advising him or marshaling forces to get something done."

It didn't hurt that as bishop of the Catholic diocese, he led the largest institution in Southwestern Pennsylvania. But people had genuine respect for him, in part because he had respect for them. "He was never reticent about seeking advice. He realized he didn't have all the answers, and there were people who could provide a perspective he wouldn't get any other way," Mr. Murray said. "When he is in a room with people, he is attentive and he participates, and he will make a quip every now and then that loosens things up. He knows everybody. He remembers everybody. If something difficult is going on with someone and he knows about it, he will be over to say, 'I'm sorry this is going on.'"

· · · · · · ·

Early in Bishop Wuerl's tenure, the diocese adopted an employee personnel policy that spelled out expectations and payscales for different jobs. "I thought it was very good," said Father Almade, who did his doctorate on just wages for lay Church employees. "We're only implementing it on the parish level now. I always thought that one of the mistakes was not ordering parishes to copy it from the beginning. A lot of the [financial] problems weren't at the diocesan level, where there were pay scales and clarity. They really tried to treat people wonderfully and in a systematic way. He handled those things justly. It was in the parishes where you had the problems."

The biggest financial challenges were tied to demographics and schools. Many parishes in the diocese had been built in an era when Catholic immigrants flocked to Pittsburgh for jobs in the mills. The model back then—fed partly by bigotry against and between new immigrant groups—was to establish ethnic parishes, where Mass would be held in the language of the old country and people could keep familiar ethnic traditions and pass them to their children. The result was that in some mill-town communities there were as many as six to eight parishes within a few blocks of each other.

After World War II, with the ethnic neighborhoods still thriving in Pittsburgh and the baby boom at its height, there was a push for every parish to have its own school, at least for kindergarten through eighth grade. Catholics invested heavily in these schools, which were staffed almost entirely by sisters at nominal cost to the parishioners.

That system, which had produced generations of faithful Catholics, suffered multiple blows in the 1970s.

First, the baby boom went bust. With the advent of the birth control pill and the increasing influence of media culture, many young Catholics never grasped the teaching that children are a gift from God, and strictly limited the size of their families.

Catholics also became less likely to send the children they did have to Catholic school. The percentage of Catholic children enrolling in first grade at a Catholic school dropped from 52 percent to 35 percent between 1967 and 1987.[62]

At the same time, tremendous changes were taking place among the communities of sisters that had staffed the schools. Vatican II had challenged them to seek the charism—gift or mission—for which their community was founded long ago and return to it. Often that charism wasn't related to teaching middle-class children. Sisters left the classrooms for mission fields among more marginalized people, and many sisters left the convent altogether. While more than 1,200 religious sisters and brothers had taught full-time in diocesan schools in 1974, just 149 did so in 1994. At the same time, their compensation had grown from little more than token payment to a respectable package of $20,000.[63]

Then the steel mills closed. Young people moved out of the mill towns in search of work, settling either in the suburbs or in other parts of the country. Between 1963 and 1998 the number of students in Catholic schools dropped from more than 130,000 to fewer than 39,000.[64]

The result was that the number of children available to attend many of these schools dropped dramatically at the same time that costs soared because lay teachers had to be hired at a living wage. Some schools had closed quickly. Others had hung on because the local Catholics loved them, but they were unsustainable. Many parishes in newly impoverished communities ran up hundreds of thousands of dollars of debt in a desperate effort to keep the schools open. In most cases, the lender was the diocese, to whom they owed money for insurance and other costs, and which made low-interest loans to them out of savings that better-off parishes kept on deposit.

Bishop Wuerl asked the same committee that he had appointed to address the deficit in his central administration to address an even higher cumulative debt among dozens of parishes. In June 1988, auxiliary Bishop John McDowell reported that the task force had documented a total of $5.6 million owed by 48 of the 333 parishes, and promised to come up with a plan to help them.

He praised the pastors for having tried to do the right things, maintaining ministries to neighborhoods and families that needed support more than ever after the breadwinners lost their jobs. "These pastors have done an extraordinary job," said Bishop McDowell, who died in 2010. "Some of them are holding schools together that are unbelievable."

They had lost, on average, 20 percent of their members when the mills closed, and some had lost far more than that, he said.

One member of his task force was highly critical of the previous diocesan administration, which he said failed to intervene when pastors ran up huge debts and also allowed the pastors to hide the true financial picture from their parishioners. The Rev. Donald McIlvane, a priest known for his social and political activism, praised Bishop Wuerl for trying to address the issues head-on. "These parishes should cut back in spending," said Father McIlvane, who died in 2014. "It's not only mismanagement, it's poor religion. You're supposed to pay your bills if you are a Christian.[65] The rescue plan was announced in February 1989. Bishop Wuerl told the pastors that he would outright forgive the $1.1 million that they owed directly to the Diocese of Pittsburgh for insurance and the Parish Share Program. Low-interest loans from the diocese would help them pay off the rest.

That program helped many of the parishes, and the 1992-1994 reorganization of parishes in the diocese, with a similar consolidation of schools, helped to make many parishes more financially stable. Nevertheless, a decade after the original debt-forgiveness program, parish debts had soared to $26 million in 55 of the 218 parishes in the diocese.

In 2000 came the Great Jubilee, which Pope John Paul II had called as a celebration of Jesus' 2,000th birthday. In the Bible a Jubilee was a year of celebration and gratitude to God, when debts were forgiven and slaves were freed. To honor the Jubilee, Bishop Wuerl enacted another round of debt forgiveness.

Earlier that year Bishop Wuerl had asked the priests at deanery meetings what they would think of a large debt-relief program. They were enthusiastic, and the bishop asked his financial services depart-

ment to design one. It had been refined through consultation with
the Priests' Council, diocesan Finance Council, Pastoral Council,
and other consultative bodies.

Then-Auxiliary Bishop David A. Zubik was in charge of organizing the program, and he said its goal was more spiritual than it was
financial. Referring to the pope's letter on the need for forgiveness
during the Great Jubilee, he said "What we want people to see, based
on the pope's letter, is that if we can tangibly say to a parish, 'You are
forgiven,' it can enable each one of us to ask if there is some personal
way to forgive someone, where a relationship has been broken or a
misunderstanding has occurred."[66]

·······

Schools would remain the most severe source of financial challenges to parishes, and therefore to the diocese. The Catholic schools
of the Diocese of Pittsburgh were the fourth-largest school system
in Pennsylvania.[67] In 1988 parishes were spending half their income
to subsidize their schools. This was despite the fact that tuition had
risen from nothing in the early days to $200 in 1968 to $1,223 in
1988 in elementary schools, and to $2,393 in the high schools.[68]

In 1991, the year the diocesan central administration finally balanced its spending, $4 million in subsidies to some of the most fi-
nancially strapped schools was the single largest expense on its budget.[69]

There would have to be changes to the way schools were funded,
Bishop Wuerl told a gathering of parents, teachers, school administrators, and pastors in 1988. "The diocese is on the verge of financial
exhaustion under the present structure," he said.[70]

The most obvious first step seemed to be closure of some inner-
city schools where there were few Catholics, and most of the students were African-American Protestants. These schools were among
the largest financial drains on the diocese and on the struggling
parishes that sponsored them. Other bishops of urban dioceses were
closing many such schools.

But when the Pittsburgh parents caught wind of such talk they pleaded with the pastors to keep the schools open, because they were islands of hope for their children in a hostile environment.

Both Bishop Wuerl and Father Douglas Nowicki, the diocesan Secretary for Education, listened. The bishop and the priest—who would leave to become archabbot of St. Vincent Archabbey in Latrobe, Pennsylvania—decided they had a moral obligation to look for an alternative.

"They said, if we really are serious about serving the community, especially the poor, then we ought to do this," said Ambrose Murray, who some years later became executive director of what became the Extra Mile Foundation.

"Bishop Wuerl was so fair-minded. His thinking was 'If we can't help these kids, then what are we?' That was something the Church should do."[71]

A few years later, Bishop Wuerl talked about why he felt he had to save those schools. "Many of them don't have a lot," he said of the Extra Mile students. "They come from needy and modest backgrounds. They're disadvantaged in a real sense, and these schools are the one bright spot in their lives. The diocese shares their hope that this life is going to get better for them."[72]

The diocese recruited John Marous to see if he thought it might be possible to get community support for a separate foundation that would support Catholic inner city schools for mostly non-Catholic students whose families could never afford to pay full tuition. Marous was a deeply committed Catholic and up-by-the-bootstraps Pittsburgh native. He was chairman of Westinghouse, which at the time was a major international corporation based in Pittsburgh.

"And John said 'Certainly,' and began to look at corporate leaders they could recruit to lead this charge," Mr. Murray said.

The leaders they recruited ranged from Jack Donahue, the intensely Catholic founder of Federated Investors, to Stanley Gumberg, a Jewish real-estate mogul who cared deeply about bettering the lives of underprivileged Pittsburghers through education.

Mr. Marous insisted that, in order to make their pitch to donors, they had to be able to show hard figures demonstrating that children from economically and socially distressed backgrounds who attended these Catholic schools did better academically than their peers who attended public schools. So the diocese commissioned the Institute for Practice & Research in Education at the University of Pittsburgh to study the schools' graduates for the prior 10 years. It found that, whether they went on to public school—which about two thirds did —or to a Catholic high school, no graduate of the three schools ever had to repeat ninth grade. Their graduation rate from high school was 92 percent, compared to 82 percent for other public-school students. This was despite the fact that about 70 percent of the students were from single-parent homes with incomes below the federal poverty line.[73] By 2008 this disparity had grown to a 94 percent graduation rate for Extra Mile Students and a 64 percent graduation rate for public school students. It was a mark of Bishop Wuerl's fundraising ability that many large donations came in from non-Catholics.

The year after the Extra Mile Foundation was created, John G. Rangos, Sr., who was an active layman in the Greek Orthodox Church, announced that he, along with his Chambers Development Company and a related foundation, would give $500,000 to the Extra Mile Foundation. Mr. Rangos called the Catholic schools "a gem in a sea of discontent."[74] At the time the average ninth-grader who had attended diocesan schools tested at a twelfth-grade level in reading, and was nearly two years ahead of the national average on standardized tests. Other major donors included Jews such as Stanley Gumberg and relatively liberal Episcopalians, some of whom were known to disagree with the Catholic Church on significant matters. They believed in what Extra Mile was doing for black children in some of the city's most blighted and violent neighborhoods, but they were also responding to Bishop Wuerl's charisma, said Ambrose Murray. It wasn't just that people in Pittsburgh were awed by a Catholic bishop, he said. "It was all him. They respected him for his mind. They respected him for his mission. They respected him for his style. He was a consensus builder without being bowled over by the consensus."

If a group of top corporate executives on the board thought some-thing should be done one way, but it wasn't consistent with the social principles or canon law of the Church, Bishop Wuerl knew how to explain so that people accepted it and didn't leave in a huff, Murray said.

The Henry Heinz Endowment put up a $1 million matching grant, which was soon met with money from other foundations. Heinz and the others would continue to be generous. In 1998 the Heinz Endowment gave $2 million to Extra Mile.

By the time Bishop Wuerl left Pittsburgh for the Archdiocese of Washington in 2006, the Extra Mile Foundation had provided $23.6 million for subsidized grade-school tuition, and a newer Crossroads scholarship had given $4.25 million to send Extra Mile graduates to Catholic high schools.[75] The high-school graduation rate for Extra Mile students would rise to 94 percent, with nearly 90 percent going on to college, and some of the others to the military or vocational school.[76]

The figures shifted over the years with inflation, but parents of Extra Mile students paid a fraction of the normal cost of Catholic-school tuition. They were also required to volunteer at the school.

Along the way the foundation garnered support from some very prominent people. In 1999 former United States President George H.W. Bush gave the keynote address at the tenth-anniversary cele-bration for the Extra Mile Foundation.

"This is exactly the type of thing that makes America work," he told 500 people at the $400-per-plate dinner in Pittsburgh's Carnegie Music Hall. "This is the source of our national strength."[77]

• • • • • • •

One of Bishop Wuerl's most important efforts to stabilize the schools was creation of the Bishop's Education Fund within the Diocese of Pittsburgh Foundation. It provided direct tuition subsi-dies for individual students whose parents couldn't afford the full bill.

The bishop went to many major donors to build the fund. In 1994 a prominent Catholic businessman, John Connelly, pledged $10 million, which at the time was the largest donation ever made for Catholic school scholarships in the United States.[78] His company suffered serious financial setbacks along the way, and despite his best efforts was unable to fulfill the entire pledge. Still, the endowment continued to grow.Mr. Connelly's gift became a substantial "starter" fund to encourage others. A May 1995 dinner inaugurated a drive to endow the Bishop's Education Fund with $20 million so the interest could be used for tuition assistance. Within a month Bishop Wuerl had raised $14 million. The following year the massive donations from wealthy Catholics were supplemented by even more sacrificial offerings from average parishioners through an annual collection. A number of especially significant offerings for the fund, amounting to $10,000 each, came from the Federation of Pittsburgh Diocesan Teachers.

In 1997 the diocese launched an annual Catholic Schools Night at a Pittsburgh Pirates baseball game, with proceeds from each ticket going to the Bishop's Education Fund.

A highlight of the occasion was watching the bishop throw out the first pitch. It had been a long time since he had played ball on the streets of Mount Washington, so he practiced in the backyard of his residence. "The weekend before I was supposed to go do that, I went into the backyard and threw the ball a couple of times. Of course, there was no one there to catch it, so I had to go retrieve the ball. It was just to gauge the distance," he said.

And still, major donors continued to supplement the endowment, In 1999 retired Mellon Bank chairman Frank Cahouet and his wife Anne pledged $1 million over ten years.[79]

In its first year the Bishop's Education Fund made $250,000 in direct tuition grants to parents of 1,875 Catholic school students. By 1999 that rose to $500,000.

Between its foundation in 1995 and Bishop Wuerl's transfer to Washington eleven years later, the fund distributed nearly $5 million in assistance to the parents of more than 23,000 students.[80]

• • • • • • •

Around the country, other bishops took note: Pittsburgh was showing them how to put a diocese on a sound financial footing.

Father Almade wasn't sure that the bishop's accomplishments were appreciated as much in his own diocese. "I think that Wuerl's fiscally prudent administration of the diocese was noticed by a few priests, and appreciated and admired by an even smaller number of priests," he said.

Many overworked parish priests complained about "too many priests in the chancery" without appreciating how hard those priests were working to relieve the burdens on parishes, and with an under-standing that only another priest could bring to the situations there, he said. "Most priests are blind to what actually happens in the chancery or downtown. In this regard, I don't think Wuerl ever got the appreciation he deserved."

If Bishop Wuerl's financial acumen was not always noticed, perhaps it was because there were bigger stories to tell. If the Catholic Church was to survive in Pittsburgh, spiritually and financially, there would have to be some painful reorganizing. And the bishop who took on that job would be in the spotlight for a long time—for better or for worse.

St. Paul Cathedral, Pittsburgh. Photo by "Father Pitt."

St. Francis de Sales Church in McKees Rocks was one of six ethnic parishes in a radius of a few blocks. The parish was merged into St. John of God parish. Photo by "Father Pitt."

CHAPTER 6:
HOME PARISHES, HARD DECISIONS

"The Bishop can't be an abstraction."

That was Bishop Wuerl's firm conviction as he addressed the difficult problem of adjusting the diocese to the changes brought on by the loss of Pittsburgh's steel industry. People in every parish had to know not just that there was a bishop, but who that man was—what he was like, what he was trying to do, and what he could do for them.

On the wall of an anteroom to his office, Bishop Wuerl kept a map charting every parish in the six-county Diocese of Pittsburgh.

"He and I would regularly look to see where he hadn't been recently, and where he should go again soon," said Father Robert Grecco, his administrative secretary for seven years. Any occasion would do, whether it was the celebration of a parish anniversary or to comfort parishioners after a tragedy. He would carefully research each parish before the visit, so he would know the right things to say in his homily.

"There was no bishop before him who had that kind of contact with the parishes," said Bishop David Zubik, who served in diocesan administration and later succeeded Bishop Wuerl as bishop of Pittsburgh.

The notion of a bishop visiting for anything other than a confirmation "was not part of the Catholic culture," said Father Lawrence DiNardo, currently the general secretary of the diocese, who grew up at a parish outside the city. "In my time there as a youngster, a teenager, and a young adult, no diocesan bishop ever came. Confirmations were done by bishops from other dioceses. The first diocesan bishop that ever came on the property was around 1975, when the pastor died. By that time I was already ordained a priest."

But Bishop Wuerl understood that the life of the Church is in the parishes, and that it was critical for parishioners to put a human face on the office of bishop. His connection with them had to be personal and spiritual, not theoretical or bureaucratic. He knew that the relationship had to be strong to withstand painful tests ahead.

· · · · · · ·

One of Bishop Wuerl's first tasks had been to review studies of the impact on parishes of the massive population loss that had followed the closure of the steel mills. The diocese had lost enough Catholics to fill 26 large parishes, and faced an even more devastating loss of older priests to retirement.

"I said we will continue evaluating all of this, but we are not going to make any major adjustments or conclusions until I have had a chance to visit the parishes. The people need to see their bishop and know that he cares about them," he recalled.

"The bishop can't be an abstraction. The term 'diocese' or 'archdiocese' is an abstraction. It doesn't mean a lot to people. When you say 'church,' they think of their parish. If you say 'diocese' the only thing they think of is their bishop. The bishop is the figure of unity for the diocese."

Father Frank Almade, now a pastor in New Castle, recalled priests scrambling to make sure everything from the music to the reception afterward was perfect. But parishioners were awestruck to meet their bishop, speak with him after Mass, and even take a photo with him. In fact, it was a recent innovation even for priests themselves to be that approachable. Until a few years earlier, "it was considered Protestant to greet people after Mass," Father Almade said.

Bishop Wuerl visited to install new pastors, dedicate buildings, honor parish anniversaries. In 2005 he celebrated Christmas Mass at a parish whose pastor had fallen ill.

Many Pittsburghers treasure mementos of his visits.

The flight he now takes from Washington to Pittsburgh requires bus transport from the terminal to the plane. On the bus one day a young man several rows behind him called, 'Hey you're Bishop Wuerl, Right? You confirmed my mother. She still talks about it. We have a picture of it on our refrigerator.' And someone else said, 'Bishop, you were at our church for our fiftieth anniversary.'"

More voices chimed in. "I think a third of the people on the bus had some contact in some way or another over the years," he said.

He was especially attentive to visits after disasters. "I wanted to let them know that that you are not here by yourself," he explained. "The whole Church is with you. And the bishop is the symbol of that."

In 2001, the charred shell was still smoldering when he arrived at a the former St. Joseph Church in Harrison, where St. Joseph High School stored all props, scenery, and costumes for its award-winning plays.

"It's just stuff," he told the drama department leaders, who were watching in shock. "It's important stuff. But what's most important is that nobody got hurt." He then sloshed down the water-logged street, thanking firefighters.[81]

In September 2004 the Pittsburgh region caught the tail end of a hurricane, with a once-in-500-years flood. In addition to the aid that Catholic Charities offered to all victims, Bishop Wuerl authorized a special collection to aid fifty-one damaged parishes, where restoration costs were conservatively estimated to reach more than $12 million.[82]

The worst destruction was in Carnegie, where Father Joseph Luisi, pastor of St. Elizabeth Ann Seton and a scuba diver, had helped to rescue two teenagers trapped in the raging torrent. His was a merged parish with nine buildings, of which six were inundated with water that rose above the pews.

When the water receded, Bishop Wuerl arrived in his black clericals, wearing bright yellow boots loaned by a concerned firefighter. He asked Father Luisi to take him through the damaged buildings by flashlight.

"The power was off and we were gingerly stepping through because there were sinkholes and floating debris in the basement. We had to be careful not to step on rusty nails," Father Luisi said. Bishop Wuerl "is a good shepherd. Shepherds are supposed to take care of their flock. That's what good leaders do. They show that they care and they help to motivate others, to inspire others. They help to bring resources where they are needed, and that's what he did."

He also came when the disaster was the fault of someone repre- senting the church.

· · · · · · ·

If a priest was removed due to accusations of sexual abuse, Bishop Wuerl visited to preach and answer questions. In 1998, one of the most respected pastors in the diocese, the Rev. Walter Benz, was ac- cused of embezzling as much as $1.3 million from two parishes. Fa- ther Benz died of a degenerative brain disease before he could be charged. But Bishop Wuerl visited both affected parishes the Sunday after police announced that charges were pending.

He spoke of his own heartbreak at learning that a pastor he had trusted to mentor newly ordained priests had betrayed them all.

When Jesus created the Church, the bishop said, he chose human beings to be his brothers and sisters, and chose some of them to be priests. "He gave each of us, you and me, the power to make choices, even bad choices. Anyone can fall from grace. The Church is both human and divine.... Sometimes the human part is all too human. But you must remember, as I have to remind myself, the divine part of the Church is always there. Christ continues to work through his priests, even one who is less than perfect."

He promised to be with the parishioners "in your suffering and in prayer."

At St. Mary Assumption in Glenshaw, where Father Benz had last served, he greeted every parishioner, kneeling to speak face to face with children. Most parishioners thanked him for coming.

"I thought he did a really good job," said Karen Banze, who was pleased that he seemed more concerned about their spiritual welfare than their financial situation.[83]

He never avoided parishes where people were angry with him.

"Many times he went right into the fire," Father Grecco said. "He installed a pastor in a parish where they weren't happy with him about the difficult removal of another pastor. He could easily have sent the dean but he didn't. He wasn't looking for a fight. He wanted to be there because he knew there were people who wanted the bishop to be there. Sure, there were some people who blew up at him, but he handled it quietly and patiently. I never saw him lash out at someone who lashed out at him. He would be able to stand and listen."

And there would be plenty of lashing out when the time came for the most difficult job of his tenure as Bishop of Pittsburgh.

• • • • • • •

It was officially the program for diocesan "reorganization and revitalization." It was intended to reduce the number of buildings that parishioners needed to maintain, and to ensure that each parish had at least one priest, so that resources could be mobilized for spiritual renewal. In the course of two years, Bishop Wuerl tried to adjust a system that had taken 100 years to build.

A century earlier, when immigrants swelled the Catholic population, the diocese created "ethnic parishes" to preserve their language and customs. In some industrial communities as many as eight Catholic churches were located within a few blocks, each parish speaking a different language and clinging to different old-world traditions. Those parishes continued long after the grandchildren of the immigrants spoke perfect English and moved to the suburbs or the Sun Belt. Many who attended the ethnic parishes no longer lived nearby. With most ministry confined to Sundays, there was little or no outreach to newcomers in the neighborhood.

And in addition to nearly empty parishes, the diocese faced a steep drop in the number of priests. While there had been 567 active diocesan priests in 1966, the projected number for 2005 was 393.[84] Those priests were now clustered in old industrial communities, but most parishioners were in the suburbs. In 1990, six neighboring parishes in Pittsburgh's East End had a weekend Mass attendance of about 1,750, while seven parishes in the northern suburbs drew about 14,500.[85]

That same year, Bishop Wuerl dedicated a new church at St. Ferdinand in Cranberry, a rapidly growing northern suburb. A decade later, St. Ferdinand's seven weekend Masses were standing room only. The reorganization created two brand-new thriving parishes in the North Hills region.

Ss. John & Paul, which Bishop Wuerl founded in 1994, more than doubled in seven years from 700 families to 1,700. Its first pastor, Father Daniel DiNardo, is now the Cardinal Archbishop of Galveston-Houston in Texas. Under his successor, Father Joseph McCaffrey, the parish topped the charts in a pilot survey of parish vitality conducted in multiple dioceses by the Catholic Leadership Institute.[86]

That was the joyful work of reorganization. The painful realities became clear shortly after Bishop Wuerl was installed and went to a small ethnic parish to offer the funeral Mass for its beloved pastor. As the grieving parishioners filed out, several asked when he would send a new priest. As Cardinal Wuerl remembered years later, "I realized, 'I don't have a priest to send here. What will I say to these people?' I had seen all these studies and demographics, but this experience said to me that this isn't a theoretical issue. It's a human, pastoral issue. How do I find a way to take care of all these little parishes?"[87]

· · · · · · ·

He began to place the small parishes under the care of a nearby pastor. But the priests told him they couldn't manage two parishes if they had to maintain two parish councils, two finance councils, two liturgy commissions, two of everything. It was impossible to keep nearly identical Mass schedules.[88]

In October 1988 his first pastoral letter, "New Beginnings in a Long Walk Together," outlined the need for reorganization and issued a call for renewal. Since 1976, he explained, registered parishioners had dropped by 113,000, the population had aged dramatically, and unemployment now ranged from 16 to 25 percent. About one in six of the 333 Catholic churches had lost 45 percent or more of its members.

"Yet we continue to staff nearly the same amount of parishes that we did ten years ago. Some consolidations are going to have to take place," he wrote.

He compared it to downsizing that older couples go through after the children leave home, yet their new, smaller home is filled with the same love that they shared in the large one.

"Love is like that. It grows. It is not limited to any set of four walls," he wrote.

"We can face the future with great confidence. Christ will not abandon us, any more than he was absent from the lives of our parents, grandparents, and those who founded this diocese."

His predecessor had intended to call a diocesan synod to talk about parish restructuring, but Bishop Wuerl sought an alternative. "He wanted to make the process as collaborative as possible among the faithful. A synod is much more controlled, it involves smaller number of people," said Father Lawrence DiNardo, who was diocesan chancellor at the time.

His first step was to survey 40,000 Catholics about the vitality of their parish. The surveys, which were mailed in 1989, covered 32 aspects of parish life, ranging from whether visitors were welcomed to the quality of adult religious education. The final section asked for recommendations on what to do if a community had four parishes, but the bishop could send only three priests.

Every parish had to engage in a self-study on all of these issues, using census figures to make projections regarding future development or decline. It was a pioneering effort at widespread, grassroots consultation rather than reorganization by edict.

"At one time we had well over 10,000 people working on committees across the diocese. We had laypeople reviewing all the data,"

Cardinal Wuerl recalled. "We got some free coverage in the secular media with stories of how many people had left the area, how many jobs were no longer there. That was all part of the study. One of the newspapers ran an editorial saying that maybe the county should consider doing the same thing."

If a parish fell below minimums in categories such as registered members or annual baptisms, it would have to reorganize.[89] One priest for every 2,200 Catholics in the diocese became the guiding statistic.[90]

At town-hall meetings across the diocese, parishioners heard the data and began to share their vision for the future. After two years, in 1991, the determination was made that 272 out of the 332 parishes needed reorganization.

• • • • • • •

Critics of the reorganization would claim that it was about money, that the bishop closed churches to cover the diocesan deficit or for some other purpose. But all of the money from closed parishes went to the parish into which the congregation merged, so the money would follow those who had given it. Others complained that the healthy bank account of their little parish ended up in the hands of a debt-ridden neighboring parish. "The bottom line of a parish is not its bank account. The bottom line in a parish is whether it is a vibrant faith community doing all the things a parish ought to do," Bishop Wuerl said in 1994. "Financial issues were usually the least important. I have said to parishes that, if their bank account is the problem, then give it to the poor and merge joyfully."[91]

The reorganization "was a fundamental challenge to every parishioner and every priest. You were for it or against it," said Father Frank Almade, who led his parishioners through one merger and later served one of the most challenging merged parishes. "The level of skepticism was very high among many people, some of whom should have known better, and it was also high among some priests. I decided I was with him. He was on the side of the angels in addressing the problem, which was that people had moved out of the city and there were fewer and fewer and fewer kids in the city parishes. They were in the suburbs, and we needed to create parishes there."

Bishop Wuerl, he said, "did what the previous four bishops had refused to do: deal with the demographic changes in western Pennsylvania. That took real courage. We were the first diocese to do a diocesan-wide reorganization and, as many have pointed out, we set a pattern that guided a lot of other people."

• • • • • • •

The first round of mergers included 63 parishes in nine clusters. It produced one brand-new parish in an overcrowded suburb, closed 15 buildings and consolidated 56 parishes in depopulated communities into eight new ones that each used two or more church buildings for worship.[92]

Ethnic heritage quickly emerged as a flashpoint for resistance. ("Ethnic concerns slow decision on parishes," read a headline in *The Allegheny Bulletin,* July 13, 1992.) In response, Bishop Wuerl created a diocesan Commission on Cultural Diversity to ensure that every tradition a parish practiced prior to the mergers would be maintained. Priests were given cultural-sensitivity training.[93] Bishop Wuerl offered to meet with any group unhappy with the decisions. "I met with them at least to let them say why they thought all the research and all the studies and all the consultation was wrong," he said.

But he did feel their sadness. At one parish after a difficult meeting he sat on the steps of the church with parishioners.

"One of them said, 'We know we cannot keep this church open. We're not dense, but it just hurts.' And I said 'I know, that's why I'm here.' And one of the others said, 'We know that, we know that,'" Cardinal Wuerl recalled. "I cherish those moments in my memory and in my heart. That is why the bishop has to be visible and present."

In many places, especially those with a pastor who had carefully led the people through the process, there was acceptance—even joy if the change wasn't drastic. At St. Hedwig, a Polish parish in the former mill town of Duquesne, parishioners burst into applause several times as the Rev. Dennis Colamarino read Bishop Wuerl's letter announcing that the parish would merge with a neighboring one, but both buildings would remain open.

"This is great! Now we have two worship sites to enjoy. Both churches are beautiful," said Pat Maiolo, a member of St. Hedwig.[94]

But an organized group of protesters, led by an attorney who belonged to a schismatic Latin Mass society, filed fourteen lawsuits claiming that Bishop Wuerl had no authority over any property in Pennsylvania because he answered to a foreign ruler—the pope.[95]

· · · · · · ·

Legally, the lawsuits had no merit—as courts would decide. But they were dividing the diocese. After such stricken reactions to the first round of reorganization, Bishop Wuerl eased off in some later situations. "Once the lawsuits started, he thought the good of the Church was being undermined by dissension and disunity," Father Lengwin said. His concern about the lawsuits wasn't financial. He had staff attorneys, and knew that the law was on the side of the diocese. "His concern was that the role of the bishop is to preserve unity. When that was falling apart, we slowed down a lot more," Father Lengwin said.

Also, the bishop had realized that many priests weren't able to provide the kind of leadership necessary for major change.

"We believed that our pastors were on board and only discovered later that many were not," Father Lengwin said. "They were telling us one thing and telling the people another. Our struggle was always to help the people have a clear understanding of what we mean by 'Church': that it is more than our parish. It includes our diocese and the universal Church."

In the final round of reorganization, while his staff had advised seven to twelve closures, he approved only one of them.[96] Along the way, a number of reluctant parishes weren't forced to merge immediately, but were told to work toward that over the next several years.[97]

By 1998 all of the lawsuits had failed in court, and parallel efforts to have the Vatican overturn the mergers likewise failed.[98]

Some other bishops who closed churches had their decisions overturned in Rome. Bishop Wuerl succeeded because he understood the relationship between the parish church and the universal Church, and argued that case theologically with Vatican officials, said Archbishop Bernard Hebda, now coadjutor of the Archdiocese of Newark, who was Bishop Wuerl's priest secretary in the early days of the reorganization and later held an important canon-law post in Rome.

"Bishop Wuerl saw it in terms of the principles of the relationship between the work that a bishop is supposed to do, the responsibility he has been given for making local decisions, and what the Holy See should be doing to help the bishop do that," Archbishop Hebda said.

"Some people would talk about it just in terms of practicalities—the number of priests, the number of people. But Cardinal Wuerl was always able to focus on it as a way of ensuring that we would be able to do the work that Christ was asking his Church to do."

The most basic questions in the reorganization were "What makes for a good parish? What makes for a good community?" Archbishop Hebda said. "He was great at making flow charts and things to figure out how to do this. He knew where he wanted us to be and was committed to moving things forward in that way. He was willing to do that even when it was going to involve some pain for him personally."

The official process of reorganization came to an end in March 1994, with each parish expected to devise a long-term plan for spiritual renewal. Their number had fallen from 332 to 218 using 294 church buildings. Two brand-new parishes were created in the suburbs.[99] Overall, 163 parishes and missions had been dissolved and merged into 56 new parishes, and the number of weekend Masses dropped from 835 to 573. Although some parishioners moved from the parish where they were raised to the one closest to home, weekend Mass attendance remained steady at about 350,000.[100]

Many people who were initially angry changed their minds. Barry Arlet, who became the first parish council president in the three-parish Guardian Angels merger in Pittsburgh's West End, told the

Pittsburgh Post-Gazette that he looked for ways to resist the merger. Later he was thrilled to see 150 teenagers in a brand-new youth group and Masses packed as they hadn't been for decades.

"It's like when I was a kid and the ushers would be saying 'We have room for two more over there,'" Mr. Arlet said.[101]

Bishop Wuerl's proactive response to demographic changes created promise of "stability and solidity for parishes that, financially, had been living on the edge," said an editorial in the *Post-Gazette*. "It holds promise for worshipers that their spiritual needs will not only be met but richly and consistently addressed. It holds assurance for the community that the church will remain a strong player in improving the human condition in Pittsburgh."[102]

Without the mergers, seventy-five parishes would have had no priest by 1995, Bishop Wuerl said. It would be 2006 before Pittsburgh had its first parish without a resident pastor, and 2015 before it had more.[103]

• • • • • • •

Not long after the reorganization Bishop Wuerl went into a US-Air Club, where a man asked if he would speak with his mother, who was in a wheelchair awaiting her flight. When the man mentioned her parish the bishop's heart sank, as it had closed in one of the most contentious mergers.

"I was bracing myself to get blasted for closing that church. But she was so sweet. She started to say 'Bishop, about that reorganization, I don't understand...' and I thought, 'Here it comes!' And she said, 'What took you so long?'"

Bishop Wuerl's longtime staff members unanimously agree that, of all the difficult projects he undertook in Pittsburgh, the reorganization took the greatest toll on him.

"It took a great deal of courage to do the reorganization. It's a sign of a leader to recognize what needs to be done and move forward," Bishop Zubik said. "Some people would have said that it's not realistic, that no one has reorganized an entire diocese at one time. But he knew it was the right thing to do."

Bishop Wuerl admitted to the pain he felt in closing parishes. But the alternative, he said, was worse. "There is no way I could have sat by and just watched parishes die. It would have torn me apart."[104]

He had created parishes that used multiple church buildings be- cause he believed that, over time, the pastor and parishioners would ask him to close what they no longer needed. That began to happen within a year, and continued over two decades.

· · · · · · ·

Bishop Wuerl's goal had always been renewal. In a pastoral letter "Future Directions," written in the middle of reorganization, he compared the pain of closing parishes to the pain of childbirth that vanishes with the joy of a new baby. The parishes that emerged from reorganization must focus on spiritual growth and outreach to the fallen-away, he wrote. He created a Diocesan Committee on Spiri- tual Renewal and urged all laity to exercise their baptismal call to serve Christ and the Church.

He urged Catholics to "invite back to Mass someone you know who has drifted away from the practice of his or her faith."

That renewal didn't happen as quickly as Bishop Wuerl had hoped for, but the reorganization laid a foundation for evangelization tak- ing place now, Bishop Zubik said.

"He was a visionary to say that eventually this is going to take place," Bishop Zubik said. "We are seeing the fruits now of all that took place twenty years earlier. His dream is coming true."

Cardinal Wuerl at a Child Protection Mass in Washington. Catholic Standard *photo by Jaclyn Lippelmann. Used with permission.*

CHAPTER 7:
"I'M THEIR BISHOP AND I NEED
TO RESPOND TO THEIR PAIN"

In 2002, when the Catholic Church in the United States was shamed by bishops who had protected child molesters in the priesthood, Bishop Donald Wuerl of Pittsburgh stood out as one who had swiftly removed perpetrators and stood up for victims.

Just months after becoming bishop of Pittsburgh in 1988, he rejected his attorneys' advice and met with victims. Seeing the damage to their lives and their faith, he made zero tolerance the policy of the diocese. He stood that ground even when the Vatican's highest court ordered him to reinstate a priest who he believed to be guilty. In 2002 in Dallas he led the floor fight that established zero tolerance as a national policy.

Bishop Wuerl was "one of the first bishops out front on this," said Father Lawrence DiNardo, his longtime canonical adviser who is now general secretary of the Diocese of Pittsburgh. "He got the ball rolling on this issue and the absolute need of establishing clear and precise procedures to deal with it in as transparent a way as possible."

Once he decided to eradicate abuse, "he was relentless," said Bishop Thomas Tobin of the Diocese of Providence, a former chancery staffer and auxiliary bishop of Pittsburgh. "He jumped in and took charge."

Without knowing it, Bishop Wuerl had already promoted changes that were later credited with diminishing abuse. The Vatican seminary study he had worked on in the 1980s led to much better preparation for celibacy. In 2011 the landmark study "The Causes and Context of Sexual Abuse of Minors by Catholic Priests in the United States 1950-2010" credited those changes with a drastic drop in clerical sex abuse.

"Over the past twenty-five years, a remarkable intensification of human formation and deeper understanding of the importance of its role are evident in almost every seminary," the report said. "Over the same period, the total number of accusations of sexual abuse of a minor by a Catholic priest has fallen from 975 for the period of 1985 through 1989...to 73 for the period of 2004 through 2008."[105]

"It's not enough that you tell these young men to pray," Cardinal Wuerl said of the study's recommendations. "There have to be explicit classes, programs, formation processes to talk to them about human sexuality and about what celibacy will entail and then integrate that into their prayer life, spiritual life, and practical life. "That, I think, is one of the reasons we had a much better formation system after that study was done. But we weren't thinking about child abuse. We were just thinking about healthy celibate living."

• • • • • • •

When he was ordained a bishop in 1986, Bishop Wuerl knew of a few isolated cases of pedophile priests, including one years earlier in Pittsburgh and a highly publicized one in Louisiana. But "there was no awareness of how widespread it was," Cardinal Wuerl recalled.

Especially after the Louisiana case, "we were being told by psychologists and institutions that you can send this person for treatment and he can overcome his problem," he said. "Many bishops didn't understand that this was anything other than a moral problem.... It was clear that we didn't realize the horrible impact on the victims."

Setting a zero-tolerance policy in Pittsburgh wasn't just a case of administrative smarts, said Father Ronald Lengwin. "He had an in-credible sense of good and evil," he said.

When Bishop Wuerl was appointed to Pittsburgh, three priests were on administrative leave for sexually molesting two brothers. Their parents had initially asked his predecessor only to remove them from ministry. But, after reflecting on their moral duty to pro-tect others, in October 1988 they pressed charges and filed suit.[106]

Bishop Wuerl summoned his close advisors and attorneys to dis-cuss whether he should visit the family. "The almost unanimous ad-vice was to follow the legal advice, which was the accepted wisdom of the day. It was that, if you had been sued, you shouldn't go," Father Lengwin said. But Bishop Wuerl, he continued, "said, 'You know what? I'm their bishop. I'm their bishop and I need to respond to their pain.' And he decided he was going, and he went."[107]

A bishop must respond as a pastor, Cardinal Wuerl explains. "The lawyers could talk to one another, but I wasn't ordained to oversee a legal structure. As their bishop I was responsible for the Church's care of that family, and the only way I could do that was to go see them."

For fourteen years afterward he said only that he had met the vic-tims. But some members of his staff spoke off-the-record of how he had returned the next day vowing to do everything possible to ensure that such a crime would never again happen on his watch. In 2002, when the sexual abuse scandal was nonstop news, a reporter asked him to tell the story and, after a few days' consideration, he did.

He had asked their pastor to arrange a meeting.[108] That decision "was a movement of the Holy Spirit, and I will forever be grateful for the guidance to do that." The parents invited him to dinner at their home. Then-Father Zubik went with him.

"You can't be part of a meeting like that without realizing the hor-rific pain and damage that abuse causes," Bishop Zubik remembered. "That family was particularly close, not only to each other, but ex-ceptionally close to the Church. To experience the betrayal that they felt from representatives of the Church, from individuals they had trusted their kids with—you can't describe it."

Cardinal Wuerl recalled that "the family could not have been more gracious, especially considering what they had experienced. They were such a good witness to the faith for me at that point. I left them convinced I would never reassign a priest who had abused someone. They should never have a chance to do that again."

Stories of the next day in the office became legend in the Pittsburgh chancery.

"It changed him. It just changed him in many ways in terms of how his response was going to be," Father Lengwin said. "We were going to be much more pastoral than we were in the past."

Bishop Wuerl held a mandatory meeting to inform all priests that sexual contact with a minor was not simply a sin that could be forgiven, but a crime that would result in permanent removal from ministry and possibly prison. The priests were also told that if they received any allegation against a Church employee or another priest, they must report it to the chancery.

"He asked us to be very conscious and sensitive to whatever was going on in the parish, the school or daycare center, to be on the alert for such things," said Father Philip Donatelli, then a pastor in the diocese.[109]

Father DiNardo's most vivid memory was "that the silence of the priests cannot be tolerated," he said. "Bishop Wuerl's point of view was that you need to understand that it's not in the interest of the Church or the interest of the priesthood to be silent. If you know something, you need to tell us. The priesthood is a very small, selective group of people who all know each other. He was saying that we cannot protect people who are hurting other people. That was revolutionary."

The diocese settled the lawsuit. Two of the priests went to prison and never returned to ministry. Charges against the third were dropped because the statute of limitations had expired. Bishop Wuerl, however, forced him to retire and he was forbidden to say Mass for anyone other than nuns in the convent where he was assigned to live.[110]

Bishop Wuerl had addressed the arrests in his diocesan paper the week they became public, saying that he was creating a committee of experts to consider diocesan policy on response to allegations. In 1989 that panel of experts—which later included the parent of a victim—became the Diocesan Review Board. Bishop Wuerl would make decisions in abuse cases only after hearing their evaluation and recommendation.[111]

Fred Thieman, an Episcopalian and former U.S. attorney for Western Pennsylvania, chaired many review-board meetings. The board had "extreme independence and the freedom to be as objective as we wanted to be," he said. "We were given the freedom to reach whatever decisions we wanted to reach, based on the best evidence."

Bishops had no guidelines in 1988. And there was little support from Rome for removing abusive priests, according to an analysis that Nicholas Cafardi, dean emeritus of the Duquesne University School of Law, presented in his book *Before Dallas*. The 1983 Code of Canon Law had been drafted to give priests rights that would protect them from the arbitrary decisions of bishops. But little attention had been given to protecting the faithful from dangerous clergy. Consequently, bishops could not remove abusive priests without a Church trial, and none had been held for that purpose in living memory. The Church's statute of limitations was very short, and there was a "catch 22" involving mental illness. Bishops would argue that perpetrators should be removed because pedophilia was a mental illness, but canon law forbade penalizing a priest for mental illness, and removal from ministry was a severe penalty.

A document from 1962 about priests who were sexual predators should have made it easier to remove perpetrators through the Vatican's Congregation for the Doctrine of the Faith. But it was issued only in Latin, to bishops who were told to keep it confidential, and was quickly forgotten.

"By the time the crisis first broke [in Louisiana] in 1984, the bishops who got [that document], even if they understood it when they got it, were dead and gone," Cafardi said.[112]

Bishop Wuerl didn't know about the 1962 document, but he was aware that he faced resistance in Rome. Knowing that he might not be permitted to remove every abuser from all ministry, he created a possibility that a priest who had received treatment and been approved for ministry by psychiatrists could serve in a restricted setting that involved no contact with children, while living under close supervision. It was used briefly in one case, but the priest was removed after more allegations came in.

"When decisions had to be made, we were breaking new ground," Father DiNardo said. "How do you restrict a person's faculties when you don't have the penalties canonically? Everything related to...the sexual abuse scandal has to be contextualized in the time and place they occurred. From hindsight, there are things we do that are easier now because of the changes in the rules. But at the time it happened it wasn't so easy. You were sticking your neck out more."

• • • • • • •

In 1993, while the diocese was dealing with several complex cases and encountering resistance from Rome, the bishop released a written policy on clergy sexual misconduct. It covered not only child sexual abuse, but other abuse of power for sexual gratification, including non-consensual sex with adults and consensual sex with parishioners or employees. While some situations might not require permanent removal from ministry, that was the prescription for child sex abuse.

The policy explained the review board, the assumption of zero tolerance for abuse of a minor, and the strict conditions under which an offender would have to live and work if the Vatican insisted he must be kept in ministry. It announced the appointment of a qualified layperson to track complaints of misconduct and to assist those who brought such complaints. It also established a pastoral team to assist parishes where accused priests had served. In a section that would be strengthened later, it said the diocese "encourages and supports the complainants to report the matter" to the police, and that the diocese may decide to inform the police of allegations in cases where the victim has not done so.

At the time, Father Lengwin said, the diocese was trying to be sensitive to people—especially adults reporting abuse from long ago —who did not want to go public.

Bishop Wuerl was simultaneously working through the bishops' conference to urge Rome to change Church law so that abusive priests could be removed swiftly and permanently. "The foundation [of the canons] is that when you are a priest you are a priest forever, and that a bishop can remove you from an assignment, but he can't remove you from ministry without grave matter and a canonical trial. If the bishop does this through administrative action, it can be only for a brief period of time," he said. "So what we needed to do was to get the law changed so that a priest could be removed not just from an assignment, but from ministry."

Such changes in Church law would be a long time coming.

In 1993 the bishops created their ad hoc Committee on Sexual Abuse and heard from the Rev. Canice Connors, then head of the St. Luke Institute, a psychiatric hospital for Catholic clergy and religious. He recommended steps bishops could take to be more responsive to victims and more vigilant in preventing future abuse. But Bishop Wuerl was among those who criticized his insistence that some perpetrators could be returned to limited ministry.

Although the guidelines were optional, "we all agreed in 1993 that we were not reassigning them. I just assumed everybody else was following that," Cardinal Wuerl said. "By that time it was clear that you are putting kids at risk if you reassign them."[113]

One reason he worked so hard on the issue was the case of Father Anthony Cipolla, which defined his response to abuse and eventually began to change the way Rome responded.

· · · · · · ·

In November 1988 a nineteen-year-old former seminarian filed suit, saying that Father Cipolla had molested him from the age of twelve. In remarks he would later repent of, Bishop Wuerl challenged the young man's version of events. It was the only time he publicly questioned an accuser's story.[114]

The bishop would eventually deem the case credible.

He learned through that experience "to be much more open to listening to a victim, even if all the circumstances don't add up immediately," he said. "We learned that, when an allegation comes in, you turn it over to the public authorities. Because they are the ones who can investigate whether a crime has taken place. We can't."

Cipolla never was tried or convicted, and has always maintained his innocence.

Despite the bishop's initial skepticism, he immediately sent Father Cipolla for evaluation. He was never returned to ministry.

The attorney for the former seminarian had unearthed a detailed detective's report from 1978, when Father Cipolla was charged with molesting a nine-year-old boy. The priest had admitted having the naked child on the bed in his rectory, but claimed to have been giving him a medical exam. A decade later in his appeals to the Vatican, Cipolla would instead claim that the mother was confused, and that the "exam" was a catechism quiz.

The mother's sworn deposition stated that she dropped the charges under pressure from her pastor, Bishop Vincent Leonard, and Cipolla's attorney.[115]

In March 1993, the Vatican's highest court, the Supreme Tribunal of the Apostolic Signatura, ordered Bishop Wuerl to return Father Cipolla to ministry. Instead, the bishop filed a petition for the court to take the case back—a move that was almost unheard-of.[116]

Decisions of the Signatura are supposed to be secret. They are written in Latin and sent via diplomatic pouch to the bishop. But Cipolla's canon lawyer in Rome faxed the decision to the priest's civil attorney, who immediately called a reporter. The bishop's copy was still in transit.

Some attorneys and victim advocates who want to claim that Cardinal Wuerl was lax on predators have tried to explain away the Cipolla case as a single instance in which he was grandstanding to burnish his reputation with the media. However, when the reporter who received the decision—a co-author of this book—called the diocese to say she had a copy, Bishop Wuerl was furious. His staff vigorously downplayed the significance of the case and the courage that it took to send the case back to the Signatura.

The verdict praised Father Cipolla. It made no mention of his pending civil trial. It discounted his 1978 arrest because the boy's mother withdrew the complaint. Bishop Wuerl was excoriated for using the wrong procedure to try to ban Cipolla from ministry, and for trying to force the priest into a psychiatric hospital. The tribunal said that Bishop Wuerl had improperly used the canon on mental illness—which it said was only for psychosis so severe that the priest was disengaged from reality.

The ruling ordered Bishop Wuerl to accept Father Cipolla as a priest in good standing, give him an assignment, allow him to say Mass publicly and to wear a Roman collar and other clerical garb.

Father Lengwin, the bishop's spokesman, said from the outset that he would not return Father Cipolla to ministry anywhere, at least while a civil trial was pending, and that the bishop planned to reopen the case because it was based on "inaccuracies."

"In our view, nothing has changed. We will be appealing the decision of the Signatura as provided to us by canon law," Father Lengwin said.[117]

The decision from Rome "both scared and paralyzed the other bishops," said Nicholas Cafardi. "They felt that if Rome would not support them in the removal of abusive priests from ministry, what was the point of doing it?" Bishop Wuerl was "to the best of my knowledge, the only one who actually appealed a [Vatican] decision returning an allegedly abusive priest to ministry. He does stand out. He took on the Roman canonical system and said they had got it wrong. That took a lot of courage."[118]

The conflict was between a pastoral approach and a purely canonical one, Cardinal Wuerl said. "When we realized how flawed the decree was, you have to respond. It wasn't as if we were all standing around and said, 'Let's take on the Holy See.' One thing led to another and then to another. As it turned out, we were right."

So eager was the bishop to send the case back to Rome that he called a meeting at his home to discuss it on the morning after the Blizzard of 1993. Roads were closed and at least one priest walked there through four-foot drifts.

Bishop Wuerl "had this dogged determination. When something happened he wouldn't rest on it until he could begin to get a solution. He had to put something in motion," Bishop Tobin remembered.

It seemed clear that the court had lacked key facts, including the pending civil trial. The reason was that, under Vatican rules at the time, the diocese wasn't represented at the hearing. Instead, the case against the priest was handled by the Vatican's Congregation for Clergy. That procedure would change as a result of Bishop Wuerl's efforts.

The day after the meeting at his home, Bishop Wuerl flew to Washington to present the papal nuncio with his petition to reopen the case. That appeal suspended the earlier verdict, meaning that Father Cipolla remained banned from all ministry and from presenting himself publicly as a priest. Bishop Wuerl also asked for the diocese to be represented at any future rehearing.[119]

"If he really felt that something was the right thing to do, as he did in the Cipolla situation, even if it bothered some people on the other side of the pond, he did what was right," Bishop Zubik said. "He knew his theology, he knew his history, and he knew he needed to be able to defend the Church that was entrusted to him."

That meant standing up for the rights and authority of diocesan bishops, Bishop Zubik said. "You need to be treated with respect, according to your responsibilities. That wasn't happening in the Cipolla case. He wasn't being respected as the head of a diocese, and they weren't communicating with the diocese, they weren't communicating with him."

Six months later the diocese made a pre-trial settlement with the former seminarian. Father Cipolla's attorney protested.[120]

For more than two years while Bishop Wuerl waited for a rehearing, Father Cipolla repeatedly defied the ban on ministry. He was discovered concelebrating Mass on the Catholic cable channel EWTN, leading pilgrimages, conducting retreats, and serving as a cruise-ship chaplain. Pittsburgh sent warning notices to every other diocese in the country.[121]

In October 1995, the Signatura reversed itself and ruled that Bishop Wuerl had been right to remove Cipolla from ministry.

· · · · · · ·

"In a case with international implications for how the Catholic Church responds to priests who molest minors, the Vatican's highest court has declared that Pittsburgh Bishop Donald W. Wuerl acted properly when he banned an accused child molester from ministry," said the story in the *Pittsburgh Post-Gazette*. "The decision of the Supreme Tribunal of the Apostolic Signatura represents a stunning reversal of an earlier high-court ruling that had rocked the Catholic Church. Canon lawyers compare the about-face to the U.S. Supreme Court taking the same case back and reversing its own decision.

"The earlier ruling had said that a priest had to be insane before he could be removed from ministry on mental health grounds, and had ordered Wuerl to reinstate the accused priest, the Rev. Anthony Cipolla. The new decision, which could have bearing on hundreds of sexual molestation cases in the U.S. alone, gives bishops much more leeway to deal with sexually abusive priests."

The first ruling said a priest could be removed for mental illness only if he was so psychotic that he was divorced from all reality. The second, given after the Signatura sought an authoritative definition of the canonical term "psychic defect" from the Vatican office that interprets the Code of Canon law, said it meant any mental condition that could harm the faithful.

"If there is anything that stands in the way of providing for the salvation of souls, not just on account of insanity but...because of... some general mental disorder, it can constitute an impediment to the exercise of the ministry of clerics," it said.[122]

The former seminarian who had filed the lawsuit in the Cipolla case struggled for years with depression, anger, and sexual-identity issues. Most of the money he received in the settlement went to lawyers or to assist relatives, and was soon gone. But he pursued therapy, came to accept himself, vowed not to be controlled by anger, and enjoyed his professional life. On several occasions he publicly credited Bishop Wuerl with acting to protect vulnerable children. Because of those statements he is slandered online by a few individuals who have an agenda to portray Cardinal Wuerl as a villain in cases of sexual abuse.

In 2002 Bishop Wuerl successfully petitioned for Pope John Paul II to involuntarily laicize Cipolla, who had continued to disobey the ban on his ministry.[123]

Close observers believe that Bishop Wuerl stepped on powerful toes when he sent the case back to the Signatura, blocking his advancement for the remainder of that pontificate.

"I think he knew it was going to hurt him," said Sister Margaret Hannan, his longtime chancellor. "He was so politically astute that he knew sometimes that his decisions were political suicide, but he had such a vision and such a strong faith and such spiritual depth that he would go forward because of his love for the people and for the Church. He was willing to take personal hits."

His actions showed selfless courage, Father DiNardo said. "If there are people out there who think that Bishop Wuerl's whole goal in life was to do whatever he can to please the Holy See and move himself forward in the Church, this was a good, shining example that maybe their judgment of him is mistaken."[124]

• • • • • • •

Although other dioceses weren't fighting pitched battles with the Vatican over the right to remove child molesters, Bishop Wuerl believed the other bishops understood the problem and were trying to do the right thing. In early 2002 he was working on revisions to the diocesan policy that would end promises of confidentiality to victims and require all allegations be given to the civil authorities. That was when news broke about a sex-abuse case that had been covered up in the Archdiocese of Boston, followed by similar reports from many other dioceses.

"I just assumed that everybody was doing what we would do. When the Boston situation erupted, it was a shock," he said.[125]

Too many bishops, he said, had relied on psychiatrists and lawyers, rather than on their own pastoral judgment. "A scientist's decision or a doctor's decision or a technician's decision is a very valuable piece of information. But that is only one piece of the puzzle. You wouldn't be a bishop if all you needed was a treatment-center professional to tell you how to deal with clergy," he said at the time.[126]

That spring he and his staff reviewed the files of all 464 living diocesan priests for old allegations that might have been forgotten with the passing years.

Bishop Wuerl then announced he was "raising the bar" of protection for parishioners. If a case came down to a credible accusation against a credible denial, with no other evidence, he would choose to err on the side of child safety and remove the priest at least until a better determination could be made. The priest could appeal. As a result, he said, he removed "several" priests.

He would not identify them because of the uncertainty surrounding their cases. Some were believed to involve contradictory situations in which a third party claimed that a priest had molested someone else, but the alleged victim denied it.[127]

That policy "did not mean that the priest would be thrown out of the priesthood if it was a question of one person's word against the other," Cardinal Wuerl said. "But we err on the side of any victim in the sense that we put the priest on administrative leave and begin the whole study of an investigation. We let the civil authorities do that. If there was no way of getting beyond that, then we would find some assignment for the priest that would not jeopardize a young person. But actually we never removed anyone on the basis of just one person's word against another. We did say that if we were going to err, we would err on the side of the victim. But our goal was not to err at all."

While he tightened standards for action in abuse cases, Bishop Wuerl also publicly proclaimed the integrity and sacrificial service of the vast majority of priests.

In his homily to all the priests of the diocese at the Holy Thursday Chrism Mass in 2002, he received a standing ovation for saying that the crimes of a few cannot obscure the faithful ministry of the many. He placed blame for the scandal squarely on bishops.

"What has led us to where we are today in the scandal around a number of priests who have abused minors is not so much the abhorrence of the moral failure itself but added to it, the sense of failure on the part of Church leadership to respond adequately to this sin, which is also a crime," he said.[128]

In mid-April 2002 he met with Allegheny County district attorney Stephen Zappala to discuss their respective roles in responding to allegations of abuse. A statement from the district attorney indicated that one of the bishop's concerns was to ensure that, if all allegations were turned over to the district attorney, accusers would not be attacked or humiliated.

"The Diocese of Pittsburgh has always collaborated with my office when necessary, and part of today's conversation focused on the mechanisms that my office has in place" to respond to complaints, Zappala said. "I am confident that if a situation arises that would require involvement on the part of my office, the diocese will communicate that information to me. I assured the bishop that, depending on the nature of the referral, a person being presented as a victim will be treated with sensitivity and their information will be handled in complete confidence."[129]

Bishop Wuerl then announced that henceforth the diocese would report all allegations, no matter how old or questionable, to the appropriate civil authorities.[130]

. . . .

Shortly before the summer meeting of the U.S. Conference of Catholic bishops, draft rules for responding to allegations were circulated to the bishops. The proposed norms—which the bishops intended to have codified and enforced by the Vatican—would allow a priest with one past offense to return to ministry if he was not diagnosed as a pedophile, if he had received treatment and if restoration was approved by a lay review board that had offered the victim a hearing. The proposed policy would not have banned such a priest from parish ministry.[131]

Bishop Wuerl announced that he would oppose any policy that returned an offender to ministry, especially parish ministry. "If you are going to make a mistake, make it on the side of the young people. Err in defense of the flock, not the shepherd," he said.

The exception for a single instance was unreasonable because no one knew if other victims had remained silent, he said. "Who is doing the counting?" he asked. "I believe that it is essential to be able to assure the Catholic faithful that there is no priest in a parish assignment against whom there is a credible allegation of abuse of a minor."[132]

At the Dallas meeting, 700 people from the media outnumbered bishops more than two-to-one.

The meeting opened with gripping testimony from adults who had been victimized by clerics when they were children or teens. They spoke of suicidal depression, rage, damage to their relationships, and rejection by the Church when they came forward to seek justice.

That "gives us the perspective we need to draft our document—the perspective of those who are suffering," Bishop Wuerl said shortly afterward.[133]

The following day he broke with his usual practice of working behind the scenes and led a floor fight that resulted in a zero-tolerance policy.

He stepped up because, going into Dallas, "there was no leadership offering any direction," he remembered years later.

Against strong opposition, he won approval to define sexual abuse as "contacts or interactions between a child and an adult when the child is being used as an object of sexual gratification for the adult. A child is abused whether or not this activity involves explicit force, whether or not it involves genital or physical contact, whether or not it is initiated by the child and whether or not there is discernible harmful outcome." At Vatican behest this language was later modified in the charter and norms, but it remained the definition for the researchers from John Jay College of Criminal Justice, whom the bishops commissioned to study the crimes.

The Church's definition of abuse must be based on Christian morality, which is broader than the definitions in civil law, Bishop Wuerl said. "Whatever the sexual abuse is has to be included in our definition of sexual abuse, whether or not it is covered by civil law.

What we have been talking about all along is something that is im-moral—and may also be a crime."[134]

He also had a critical role in a floor fight over reporting, arguing that bishops must, at a minimum, immediately tell civil authorities about any allegation in which the alleged victim was still a minor. Some bishops only wanted to report allegations that they had first investigated and found credible. Bishop Wuerl convinced the major-ity that the bishops can judge only fitness for ministry, while civil authorities must determine whether a crime was committed. "I be-lieve where we have erred in the past is appropriating to ourselves the decision of whether or not to report the allegation because we have decided it is not credible," he said.[135]

The charter established a National Review Board to oversee the bishops' response to allegations of child sexual abuse and to commis-sion studies by leading experts on criminology about the scope and causes of child sexual abuse by priests.[136]

Before he left Dallas, he was at work on a pastoral letter to address the sexual-abuse crisis.

Concern for victims must be the first response of the Church, he wrote in "To Heal, Restore, and Renew." "I again renew my invita-tion to anyone who has been abused by a priest to meet me so that I might express the depth of my sorrow that this has happened and the sincerity of my desire for reconciliation."[137]

• • • • • • •

The next step was for Rome to make the charter binding on the bishops of the United States by translating it into canon law for this country. "We need Rome's authority to bind every bishop in the United States to follow these norms," said Bishop Wuerl. "That is what we did not do in 1992-1993."[138]

The norms faced strong opposition from some canonists.[139] Some Vatican officials saw the sex-abuse crisis as a problem trumped up by the media in "English-speaking countries." "This is where Cardinal Ratzinger was of such help. He understood the need for the bishops to be able to remove abusive priests because it doesn't allow for rehabilitation," Cardinal Wuerl said of the future Pope Benedict XVI, who was then head of the Congregation for the Doctrine of the Faith. "There is always forgiveness, but there are always consequences and you have to live with the consequences—one of which is that you can't minister any longer."

One provision of the Dallas Charter required outside auditors to determine whether each diocese had complied with the charter. On its first audit in 2003, the Diocese of Pittsburgh received a commendation for "the overall high quality of diocesan response to the spirit and words of the charter."[140]

• • • • • • •

Bishop Wuerl fought hard to create some system of accountability for bishops who failed to protect children. Four months after the bishops adopted the charter, he was named to the committee that was supposed to find ways for bishops to hold other bishops accountable. He acknowledged that the committee had no canonical teeth. Its members, he said, would work with brother bishops "on the level of fraternal support and fraternal encouragement because, canonically and legally we can't get involved in other dioceses."

He said at the time that he could not imagine any diocese that would refuse to carry out the charter, and indicated that any bishops who did would be publicly shamed when the USCCB released their names.[141]

In November 2002 by a vote of 249-2, the USCCB adopted that committee's "statement of commitment" to hold each other accountable to the charter, and to apply it to themselves in the same way they would apply it to their priests. It also included an apology.[142]

Within a year, the charter seemed to be influencing Rome more than Rome had influenced the Charter. The Vatican issued new rules that allowed the Congregation for the Doctrine of the Faith to laicize a priest against his will and without a Church trial if the evidence was clear and the wrongdoing was egregious. Furthermore, the judgment could not be appealed to the Vatican's court system.[143]

Throughout Bishop Wuerl's tenure in Pittsburgh, the diocese offered to pay for psychotherapy for victims, and other related ex-
penses such as parking or babysitting. He made financial settlements
in only the three cases that fell within the statute of limitations.[144]

But after the Boston scandal, a team of Southwest Pennsylvania
attorneys filed lawsuits concerning seventeen former priests on behalf of thirty-five people whose claims fell far outside the state
statute of limitation. The alleged perpetrators had either been removed from ministry years earlier, were dead, or, in one case, had
moved to another diocese a quarter-century earlier, with no record of
sexual abuse. That priest was among those who had never previously
been reported to the Diocese of Pittsburgh.

Many were cases in which the diocese had long since acknowledged
credible allegations. In some the accused priest had been criminally
convicted amid publicity. Other claims, however, were more questionable. One involved a priest—whose ministry had been restricted
for reasons other than child abuse—who was never at the parish in
question during the alleged victim's childhood.[145]

In an effort to overcome the statue of limitations, the plaintiffs'
attorneys argued that the offense wasn't the molestation, but a conspiracy to conceal the fact that priests molested children. Therefore,
they argued, the statute of limitations wasn't triggered until the victims realized there was a conspiracy in 2002.[146]

The diocese argued that the suits' conspiracy claims were based on
publicity about other dioceses, not what had happened during
Bishop Wuerl's tenure in Pittsburgh.[147]

John E. Murray, Jr., then the president of Duquesne University,
was the lead writer of a letter to the editor that was also signed by
two prominent attorneys and a former chief judge of the U.S. District Court for Western Pennsylvania. "How do you defend yourself
against lawsuits based on claims that occurred 40 years ago?" the letter asked. "Bishop Wuerl is renowned for his policy of reporting any
illegal act to civil authorities over many years. Depriving he diocese
of a statute of limitations defense based on allegations of offenses
that occurred decades ago make it prohibitively difficult to establish
an effective defense."[148]

The Allegheny County Court of Common Court of Common Pleas accepted a test case and a hearing was held, but ultimately the case was dismissed due to the statute of limitations.

After Bishop Wuerl was transferred to the Archdiocese of Washington, the interim administrator, then-Auxiliary Bishop Paul Bradley, made a $1.25 million settlement with thirty-two of the accusers. The money for what was called an "outreach fund" came from insurance and was distributed by an independent arbitrator. The diocese also agreed to continue to pay for counseling as part of the settlement. There was no legal need for the diocese to settle, since the courts had ruled the cases could not go forward.

Alan Perer, a local attorney who with his wife and law partner Diane, had represented the plaintiffs, expressed regret that their clients did not get their day in court. Nevertheless he praised the diocese for acting voluntarily. "We think it is a fine and good and moral gesture," Mr. Perer said.[149]

That settlement fund was in the works before Bishop Wuerl left Pittsburgh.

He had always resisted financial settlements in cases that were too old to be brought to court, because there was no way to verify who was telling the truth. The diocese would pay for counseling—sometimes for psychiatric hospitalization—because both the true victims and those who brought what seemed to be dubious claims were clearly in need of such assistance, he said.

"My primary concern was that, if someone has been harmed, then we will try to help make them whole with counseling and pastoral assistance," he said.

On the other hand, many accusers had claims that were highly credible, and had suffered greatly, he said. He did not want to try to sort out who had a credible claim and who did not, both because it was impossible and because he believed that someone who makes a false claim has a serious problem and is in need of help. The independent arbitrator, a retired judge, would assess each case and try to make fair awards.

Both the scandal and the charter left priests feeling vulnerable. A survey commissioned by the U.S. bishops' conference showed that only 42 percent of priests believed their bishop would give them a fair hearing if they were accused. Just 27 percent believed that accused priests had been treated fairly.[150]

Father Frank Almade, a pastor during Bishop Wuerl's tenure in Pittsburgh, credited him with taking responsibility when other bishops didn't. If priests were afraid, "that was not a Bishop Wuerl problem," he said. "In every profession there is a chance of someone making a false allegation. But ninety-eight percent of them aren't false, and are not motivated by money. Bishop Wuerl was on the side of the angels, whether he gets credit for it or not."

Because of what he did, Father Grecco said, priests in Pittsburgh could hold their heads up. "He saved the face of the priesthood during those dark days. He was always saying that there are good priests in this diocese. We can still go out there with our collars on and not worry about being ridiculed because our bishop did the right thing, no matter how difficult it was."

Throughout his years of addressing the issue of child abuse, he received support and encouragement from Cardinal Joseph Ratzinger, then prefect of the Congregation for the Doctrine of the Faith and later Pope Benedict XVI. Bishop Wuerl was elated in 2001 when the authority for judging cases of sexual abuse and for removing offending clerics was transferred to the Congregation for the Doctrine of the Faith.

"Cardinal Ratzinger was of such help. He understood the need for the bishops to be able to remove abusive priests," he said.

In 2005, Cardinal Ratzinger became Pope Benedict XVI. Just over a year into his pontificate, Pope Benedict appointed Donald Wuerl Archbishop of Washington DC.

It had been a well-run archdiocese, especially regarding sexual abuse. In 1986, under Cardinal James Hickey, the Archdiocese of Washington became one of the first to adopt a written child-protection policy. By the time Archbishop Wuerl arrived, the archdiocese was equipped to do its own fingerprinting of all employees and volunteers, so that the archdiocese would be notified immediately if anyone in its fingerprint database was arrested.

One of his first steps was to review all of the policies and procedures related to child sexual abuse to make sure that they followed or exceeded the charter, said Auxiliary Bishop Barry C. Knestout. "We really tightened up a few things in terms of how we do background checks and how we make sure those are effective," Bishop Knestout said, explaining that they now use a national database, instead of those limited to archdiocesan territory. "He is involved every step of the way when we do have an accusation, with regard to how we respond to both the victim and the accused. He has met with those who have been victims. He responds pastorally."

In 2008 Pope Benedict made Washington the first stop on his visit to the United States. It was in Washington that he held the historic first meeting between a pope and survivors of child sexual abuse by a priest.[151]

Under Pope Benedict, the Vatican issued universal rules for cases of child sexual abuse, They fell short of the zero-tolerance policy in the U.S. bishops' Charter for the Protection of Children and Young People, but granted some of what the U.S. bishops had asked for in the 1990s, such as increasing the statute of limitations.[152]

Pope Francis has taken steps to address child sexual abuse that Cardinal Wuerl has advocated since the Dallas Charter of 2002. In 2014 he appointed a commission to advise him on the universal Church's response. In June 2015, as this chapter was drafted, the Vatican announced the creation of a new tribunal to judge bishops.

"Pope Francis has taken a couple of really significant steps," Cardinal Wuerl said. "He has met with victims. He has made it clear that nothing he is doing is going to, in any way, go back on everything that has been done. He has confirmed that zero tolerance is a legitimate position. He is a forgiving person, but I don't see him stepping back from the provisions that have been made to protect young people."

Looking back on how difficult it was to remove abusive clergy twenty years ago, Cardinal Wuerl said, "I think the Church can be very proud of where she is today."

Within the U.S. Conference of Catholic Bishops he has remained an advocate for keeping the victims front and center, said Archbishop Gregory Aymond of New Orleans, who has served as chair-man of the U.S. Bishops' Committee on the Protection of Children and Young People. "In diplomacy and in informal discussions he has been extraordinarily supportive. He has been a consistent voice, not only for the protection of children and young people, but for healing and the pastoral care of the victims and survivors."

Cardinal Wuerl has led by example, said Monsignor Ronny Jenk-ins, general secretary of the U.S. Conference of Catholic Bishops and previously the canon lawyer who advised them on implementation of the child-protection charter and norms. "He really understood, as a shepherd, what this meant for children, for the faithful, for the Church. In Pittsburgh he fought very strongly to institute strong measure of protection and to address the injustices and the priests who had offended. He didn't just announce something, he did it."

Praying with students at St. Augustine School, Washington. Catholic Standard *photo by Rafael Crisostomo.*

At an interfaith gathering in Washington. Catholic Standard *photo by Michael Hoyt.*

With Rabbi Walter Jacob, rabbi emeritus of Rodef Shalom congregation in Pittsburgh. Courtesy of the Diocesan Archives of the Diocese of Pittsburgh.

CHAPTER 8:
EVERYBODY'S BISHOP

A while ago, a letter came to Cardinal Wuerl from a woman in Pittsburgh who wasn't Catholic, but had seen something in the news about his work with Pope Francis.

"She wrote that 'I always thought of you as everybody's bishop,'" he said.

That impression wasn't an accident. It was the product of years of work in reaching out to people of all faiths. Bishop Wuerl really did think of himself as everybody's bishop, because to him to be a Christian meant to be sent to everybody.

• • • • • • •

On a warm and blissfully tranquil September evening in 1994, a USAir 737 carrying 132 souls crashed on its approach to the Pittsburgh International Airport, killing everyone on board. Many were from Pittsburgh. The entire city was plunged into shock and mourning.

The mayor called Bishop Wuerl and asked him to hold some kind of public memorial. The bishop agreed—as long as all of the city's major faith traditions were represented and took part in leading it. The mayor agreed, and the bishop's staff handled most of the organizing.

The resulting prayer service in Downtown Pittsburgh's Market Square drew thousands. There were prayers from rabbis, Muslims, Buddhists. One of the most haunting moments was a recording from an Evangelical Free Church outside of Pittsburgh, on which one of the crash victims sang about going to heaven.

Bishop Wuerl preached on life after death and healing after devastation.

To walk anywhere in and around Pittsburgh since the crash "is to know the numbness of sorrow and the sense of powerlessness before death," he told the silent crowd, which included many loved ones of the victims. "We are not here to explain this loss away, but rather to be with those who grieve, to stand quietly with you as a pledge of our care and our concern.... Know also that, in faith, we ask God, who loves each of us, to grant you consolation and comfort. And may the God of life and love grant to those whom death has taken from us a place in the lasting kingdom of peace, of light and eternal love."[153]

That service was emblematic of Cardinal Wuerl's engagement with the community beyond his own church throughout his ministry. He has built close relationships with community leaders from all backgrounds, and with religious leaders of all faiths. He has worked with them whenever possible to bring healing whenever there has been a disaster or serious division.

"The reason we were able to organize that so quickly and meaningfully and beautifully and that it was so well attended, was that that was part of our history in this community," Cardinal Wuerl recalled, mentioning interfaith and ecumenical events dating back to the era of Bishop Wright thirty years earlier.

Bishop Wuerl had also held a memorial service at a Catholic parish in the community where the plane had crashed, a community that was home to many flight crews and airport workers.

"Death need not be proud today," he told the mourners. "For in death, for believers, life is changed, not taken away.... But even the person with the strongest faith knows that today he's making this walk a little more alone.... Reassure one another that even this tragedy cannot separate us from the love of God."[154]

His long-term response was to spearhead the creation of an interfaith chapel at the Pittsburgh International Airport, and assign a priest full-time to care for both airport workers and travelers.[155]

Whenever religious leaders and religious communities can work together, it strengthens the witness of all of them, he said. "There is so much bleaching out of religion from what is called the secular marketplace today," he said. "But this should be the marketplace for all of us. We are all part of the public square. People of whatever faith and people who have no faith, people whose interests don't include a religious perspective. We are all a part of this."

. . . .

On the morning of his appointment as bishop of Pittsburgh, Bishop Wuerl had addressed the entire community.

"To all who live in this area I offer my hand in friendship and in a spirit of collaboration. It is my sincere hope that all of us—members of other Christian churches, our brothers and sisters in the Jewish community and other religions, and all men and women of good will —can continue to work together to keep this a most livable community."[156]

That's how he was raised, he said. Although the neighborhood where he grew up was so Catholic that the parochial schools outnumbered the public schools, he played sports with Protestant children. His first boss, at the drug store where he worked in high school, was Jewish.

"I got to know his family very well," he said. "They were your neighbors. They worshiped differently than you did, but they weren't strange people. They were your friends. I found that very helpful as I went to seminary."

Because Cardinal Wright had been an architect of the regional ecumenical organization Christian Associates, and had worked hard to build good relationships with the Jewish community, Bishop Wuerl already knew many local religious leaders when he was named to Pittsburgh.

Relationships with the Jewish community were especially important to him, in part due to a painful history of anti-Semitism that the bishops of the Church had condemned during Vatican II.

Because Christianity flows from Judaism, the time he spent conversing with rabbis enriched his understanding of his own faith, he said. "When I was a young priest I began what developed into really strong relationships with people like Rabbi Walter Jacob at Rodef Shalom Congregation and Rabbi Alvin Berkun at Tree of Life," he said. "There's a richness in seeing your own identity from the perspective of people who live in that tradition."

Some of the relationship-building was more symbolic, but significant. In 1992 he was the keynote speaker at a Holocaust observance co-sponsored by the United Jewish Federation, the Holocaust Center of Greater Pittsburgh, and South Hills Interfaith Ministries. In 2000 he was the keynote speaker at Pittsburgh's American Jewish Committee dinner, and the same group gave him its Community Service Human Rights Award for interfaith bridge-building in 2006. In 2002 he co-chaired the Jewish National Fund dinner in Pittsburgh. Pittsburgh's Jewish community planted a forest in Israel in his honor.

In 2005 Bishop Wuerl was instrumental in arranging a papal knighthood for Rabbi Jacob, an honor rarely given to non-Catholics.[157] At the same time, Rabbi Jacob invited Bishop Wuerl to formally install him as titular head of a new Jewish seminary in Germany.[158]

· · · · · · ·

But these symbolic gestures, valuable as they are, were not only symbols. They were signs of real, substantial cooperation between the religions.

Under Bishop Wuerl's leadership, the Diocese of Pittsburgh became the only one in the United States to have a rabbi regularly teach religion classes in all of its high schools. It was intended "to provide a perspective in which our young Catholic people will see the relationship they have with the wider community, and especially with the Jewish community because of our ancient historic religious roots," he said in 2005

The rabbis taught about the basics of Judaism, and also about centuries of Christian persecution of Jews. Although the Church has never officially taught that all Jews were collectively responsible for killing Jesus, that was a widespread popular belief until it was officially condemned at Vatican II. Rabbi Berkun, who said that teaching religion classes at Central Catholic High School in Pittsburgh was one of his greatest joys, was pleased that most students in the twenty-first century had never heard the epithet "Christ killer."

And that, said Bishop Wuerl, was a tribute to all the work that had been done since Vatican II. "The fact that they haven't heard of the animosity that used to exist says to me that we have been successful in eradicating that antagonism."[159]

In 1999 Bishop Wuerl, together with Rabbi Berkun, was responsible for the creation and dedication of the only Holocaust memorial on Vatican property. They headed a group that raised $30,000 for a 7-foot bronze menorah cast by Israeli sculptor Aharon Bezalel. It was erected on the grounds of Wuerl's alma mater, the Pontifical North American College, where American seminarians study. Bishop Wuerl was then chairman of the board of the seminary.[160]

Four years later they teamed up again to erect a scaled-down four-foot replica of the Vatican Holocaust memorial at St. Paul Seminary in Pittsburgh.[161]

Perhaps the most spectacular event connected with his work on Catholic-Jewish relations in Pittsburgh was a 2004 concert at the Vatican, for Pope John Paul II in honor of the twenty-fifth anniversary of his pontificate, by the Pittsburgh Symphony Orchestra. Conducted by the pope's favorite maestro, Gilbert Levine, who is Jewish, the performance also featured a Muslim chorus from Turkey singing alongside Pittsburgh's Mendelssohn Choir. The concert focused on the place of the prophet Abraham in Judaism, Christianity, and Islam, and was a plea for peace and reconciliation between members of the three faiths.

"The history of relations among Jews, Christians and Muslims is characterized by lights and shadows, and unfortunately, has known painful moments," Pope John Paul told the audience of 7,000. "Today we feel pressing need of a sincere reconciliation among believers in the one God."[162]

Bishop Wuerl spoke at various times in various synagogues. In 1999 Rabbi Berkun invited the bishop to address his congregation after an anti-Semitic extremist opened fire on a Jewish day care center in California. "As Jews, we felt very isolated and vulnerable. He came and brought a message of hope," Rabbi Berkun said.[163]

• • • • • • •

That was also what Bishop Wuerl did for the whole community, including the Islamic community, after 9/11. Not only was there the shock that the rest of the nation felt about the attacks on the World Trade Center and the Pentagon, but a fourth hijacked plane, apparently destined for the U.S. Capitol, crashed in a neighboring diocese, about an hour outside Pittsburgh, when its passengers tried to take it back from terrorists.

In the hours after the attacks, Bishop Wuerl asked all parishes to keep their doors open for private prayer. At St. Mary of Mercy, next door to his office in Downtown Pittsburgh, the Blessed Sacrament was exposed for several hours so Downtown workers could come in and pray. At St. Paul Cathedral on the evening of the attacks a Mass for peace was held.

"We pray in a special way for everyone touched by this tragedy, especially the victims of these horrific actions and their families," Bishop Wuerl said in a statement. "In this time of national catastrophe and shattering violence, we must remember that our only security is in the living God."[164]

Throughout that period of grief and fear, he was an advocate for the Muslim community of Pittsburgh, warning against any kind of bigotry against them based on generalization and paranoia. On September 20, as he had after the crash of Flight 427, he was a key figure in organizing an interfaith memorial service in Market Square. Eighteen leaders from various branches of the Christian, Jewish and Islamic faiths offered prayers. During the service a rabbi and an imam who had long been engaged in interfaith dialogue, embraced.

"Good trees must bear good fruit," Bishop Wuerl said. He called for "compassion, mutual respect and peace among peoples."[165]

When Bishop Wuerl was transferred to Washington, D.C., five years later, representatives of the Islamic community expressed fervent thanks for his leadership. "The Muslim community of Pittsburgh is grateful especially for his outreach after 9/11," said Farooq Hussaini, who represented the Islamic Center of Greater Pittsburgh. "When we were being persecuted and didn't know where to turn, he came to a press conference on the 13th of September 2001. That made us feel he cares."[166]

One week after the attacks he prayed a special blessing at PNC Park when Pirates baseball resumed amid fears that large gatherings would be targeted by terrorists.[167]

Cardinal Wuerl recalled the players from both teams with caps off and heads bowed. "I always in those situations said a prayer that everyone could say 'Amen' to," he said, which meant avoiding praying specifically in the name of Jesus or of the Trinity. "I would always begin 'Good and loving God' and remind everyone that we are called as children of the same good and loving God to pray for and respect one another. And we prayed for all who had died."

But in addition to the attacks on the whole country, the bishop had to respond to much more personal violence much closer to home.

· · · · · · ·

The year 2000 was an especially violent one in Pittsburgh and surrounding communities.

In January eight-year-old Taylor Coles was shot dead along with her father and another man in a popular Pittsburgh restaurant. She had been a student at Holy Rosary, one of the Extra Mile schools, and the bishop went to celebrate Mass.

He told the children that they were not alone, and that their family, their school, their church and their community were there to support them.

"You can change the world. All of us working together can," he said. "It begins in the heart. It begins in the heart of each one of us. Never give up hope. Never give up hope in yourself. Never give up hope in what you can accomplish. Never give up hope that when all of us band together we can make the world a much better place."[168]

That spring, within weeks of each other, two mentally ill men— one white and one black—committed mass murders out of racial, ethnic, and anti-Semitic hatred against those who differed from them. Bishop Wuerl immediately held special Masses to pray for the victims, their families, and the affected communities. He also delivered a high-profile speech at Tree of Life Synagogue on the need for gun control—one of many times he felt compelled to address a difficult issue, regardless of the backlash he might suffer.[169]

· · · · · · ·

But there were many happier occasions when Bishop Wuerl also made himself visible as a community leader.

At the annual blessing of the boats that ply Pittsburgh's three rivers, he spoke of Jesus calming the storm on the Sea of Galilee.

"May Christ, who calmed the waters, bring all of us to the harbor of life and peace," he prayed.[170]

He broke some new ground ecumenically, in 1992, becoming the first Catholic to serve on the board of Westminster College, a Presbyterian Church (USA) school with a strong history of evangelical missions.

The next year he became the first Catholic bishop to visit Pittsburgh Presbytery when he spoke at an ecumenical worship service that preceded one of its meetings. "Study alone will not overcome the forces that keep us apart. But the heart, open to the Spirit, can lead us into the mystery of the [unity of the] Church," he said.[171]

His relationships with the Evangelical Lutheran Church in America and the Episcopal Church were especially close.

In 1996 the Catholic and Episcopal dioceses and the Lutheran synod signed a covenant of cooperation that could lead to shared social and educational ministry. It stemmed not just from theological conviction, but from a close friendship between the three bishops.

"In many cases we have two or three social programs in the same neighborhood, trying to reach the same people in need. We will look at how we can best cooperate and reduce overhead," Bishop Wuerl said.[172]

In 1989 he became the first Catholic bishop to address the South-western Pennsylvania Synod Assembly of the Evangelical Lutheran Church in America. He had just returned from a trip to Iceland, where Pope John Paul II had made a pastoral visit and where a friend of his was the bishop. "It was alarming to me, but you will be happy to hear the population is ninety-five percent Lutheran," he said. But "just as there is one Christ, there can only be one body of Christ in the world today. All the other difficulties...were introduced not by the will of Christ...but by humans trying to live out that unity."[173]

In 1999, when the Vatican and the Lutheran World Federation signed a joint declaration on the meaning of justification—the central doctrine over which the Protestant Reformation began in the sixteenth century—the Catholic Diocese of Pittsburgh and the Lutheran synod celebrated together.

"If we can agree on justification, then there is nothing we cannot agree on," he preached from the pulpit of the First Lutheran Church of Pittsburgh on Reformation Sunday that year. "I believe that the last time we were in church, someone was at the door with a hammer," he said, referring to Martin Luther posting his famous list of 95 doctrinal disputations on the cathedral door in Wittenberg, Germany.[174]

That was not the only celebration. There were others at the time of the signing, and another to celebrate the fifth anniversary. Bishop Wuerl took the lead in suggesting and promoting all of them.

"If I had called the meeting, I don't know if anybody would have come," said Bishop Donald McCoid, who was then the ELCA bishop of Pittsburgh and who remains a good friend of Cardinal Wuerl. "His generosity and ability to initiate things really helped people become aware of the significance of this."

On every possible occasion he worked cooperatively, with an ulti-
mate goal of seeking unity, with Protestant and Orthodox Christians.
In 1993, when Billy Graham preached a crusade in Pittsburgh,
Bishop Wuerl had a representative on the executive team for local
planning and encouraged his priests and parishes to participate.[175]

Building strong ecumenical relationships is good for the Catholic
Church, he said. "It opens us up to the rest of the community in a
way that we are all able to do things together that, individually, we
simply couldn't do. There is a bearing of witness that we can only do
together. Our witness is diminished when we are divided."

It's possible to work with other people, organizations and religious
bodies with whom you have serious differences over theological and
social issues, he said. "When you are working with other groups, you
have to agree on what you want to work for. If that doesn't compromise your principles and values, you can do that. You aren't going to
get a lot done if you say, 'I'm never going to work with anybody who
doesn't completely agree with me.'"

That applies even to organizations, such as a number of Protestant
denominations, that support legal abortion, he said.

"Everybody knows that the Catholic Church is opposed to the destruction of unborn human life. That doesn't come as a surprise to
anybody. But it doesn't stop people who want to work with us in trying to provide shelter for the homeless."

In the early 1990s, Bishop Wuerl teamed up with the Presbyterian
Agency on Aging and four local hospitals to open a twenty-two-bed
AIDS hospice in what had been a personal-care home operated by
the Catholic Diocese of Pittsburgh. The Corpus Christi Residence
was the only one in western Pennsylvania that was meant primarily
for those with AIDS, at the time when the disease was a swift and
certain death sentence. Bishop McCoid joined Bishop Wuerl in an
ecumenical service of dedication when it opened after a $1 million
conversion in 1994.[176]

After a wave of publicity about arsons at black churches, Bishop
Wuerl took the lead in raising money from congregations across the
ecumenical spectrum in Pittsburgh to help them rebuild. He co-
chaired the effort with the Rev. Robert Russell, pastor of Trinity

AME Zion Church outside of Pittsburgh.[177] The relief fund in South Carolina had just $18,000 in it when the check for $120,000 arrived from Pittsburgh.[178]

In 2000, when misunderstanding of a Vatican document led to widespread reports that the Church was consigning non-Catholic Christians to hell, the bishop rushed to correct that impression, and explain the sources of confusion. "This says we are all in some way, either through baptism or profession of the revelation of the word of God, related to each other. Those are elements of the true Church that we share," he said.[179]

· · · · · · ·

Christian Associates, the regional ecumenical organization that Bishop Wright had had a key role in founding, included every bishop or his equivalent in a ten-county region, and was large and unwieldy. Bishop Wuerl longed for something more personal and more nimble in its response to community needs.

One night he had dinner with his good friends, Lutheran Bishop Donald McCoid and Episcopal Bishop Alden Hathaway, and floated the idea of what would soon become Christian Leaders Fellowship. This was a monthly gathering of bishops and their Protestant counterparts in each other's homes for prayer, Bible study, and mutual support. Through those meetings and private conversations, "I truly, truly felt a friendship and bond with Cardinal Wuerl that was on a personal level, but also on a level where we were able to do some very important things in the life of our churches and in the life of Christian cooperation in Southwestern Pennsylvania," Bishop McCoid said.

Christian Leaders Fellowship was able to take the lead when something needed to be done quickly, such as organizing an ecumenical prayer service after a disaster. This group began popular traditions in Pittsburgh, such as the Holy Saturday blessing of the city from the overlook atop Mount Washington. Until the cost became prohibitively expensive, the group rented a major concert hall each year in Pittsburgh for a Christmas concert that kept the focus on Christ.

Bishop Wuerl effectively seconded some of his staff to assist Christian Leaders Fellowship in organizing these events.

"It wasn't something that was done for the Catholic Diocese of Pittsburgh. It was done in a way that everybody felt a part of things," Bishop McCoid said.

Each year in January the members of Christian Leaders Fellowship went on retreat together. One night at St. Emma's Retreat House the roof sprung a leak due to a clogged drain. When they spotted a nun headed down the hallway carrying a ladder, Bishop Wuerl and Bishop Hathaway jumped up and told her they would take care of it. As they climbed up on the roof and began working, Bishop Hathaway said to Bishop Wuerl, "Let's pray that neither one of us falls, because the other one will be blamed," Cardinal Wuerl recalled. "Then we had to stop working because we couldn't stop laughing."

"The fellowship that we had was extraordinary," said Bishop Robert Duncan, who succeeded Bishop Hathaway at the Episcopal Diocese of Pittsburgh, but later led the majority in that diocese out of the Episcopal Church and into the new, more conservative, Anglican Church in North America. Most of the regular participants in the breakfast stood for traditional orthodox understandings of the Bible and the creeds, even if they disagreed on other issues. "What was sometimes said at the breakfast table was that we all have more in common with one another than we had with many people in our own traditions."

After Bishop Duncan was elected to head the Episcopal Diocese of Pittsburgh, Bishop Wuerl obtained permission from Rome for his consecration to be held in St. Paul Cathedral, which had more than twice the seating capacity of the Episcopal cathedral. Bishop Wuerl's personal gift to Bishop Duncan for that consecration was a pectoral cross—which all bishops must wear—that Bishop Wuerl had personally designed and commissioned in Rome. At the top of the cross was an image representing the Holy Spirit guiding the Church and angels protecting the Church. At the center were images representing the priests, and on its arms were representations of deacons and the laity.

"It was an extraordinary gift" representing both friendship and respect for a different Christian tradition, Bishop Duncan said, "It is the cross I wear to this day."

And it was blessed by a saint.

"He told me that he had taken it to the Holy Father to have it blessed," Bishop Duncan recalled. "That was Pope John Paul II, and when Bishop Wuerl presented it the Holy Father said 'Donald, you're not asking me for another auxiliary [bishop], are you?' He said no, that this was for the Anglican bishop, and the Holy Father wasn't too worried about that."

While Christian Leaders Fellowship kept the focus on Christ, Bishop Wuerl also made every effort to cooperate with non-Christian groups when possible. One such celebration, held around Thanksgiving when Pittsburgh had its annual Light Up Night festival, was "Spiritual Light Up Night." It brought representatives of all the major faith groups to a church in the city's popular shopping area, the Strip District, for prayer.

Cardinal Wuerl recalled one year when the decision had been made to illuminate the outside of the church as the mayor read a decree encouraging young people to be of service for good in their neighborhoods.

"Just as I threw the switch, a light snowfall started, so when the light went on it illuminated the gently falling snow and it was beautiful," the cardinal said. "The mayor forgot that his mike was on and he said, 'How did you do that?' He meant it as a joke, and everyone started to laugh. I said, 'It was grace, your honor, it was grace.' But it shows you the ease of relationships in this city, both interfaith and ecumenical."

Community leaders of all kinds knew that they could call on Bishop Wuerl in times of trouble. At no time was that more important to him and to the Pittsburgh region than in 1994, when gang violence was taking the lives of Pittsburgh teens and young adults on an almost daily basis. At the behest of U.S. Attorney Fred Thieman, Bishop Wuerl joined about 40 others on the Youth Crime Prevention Council, including U.S. Senator Harris Wofford, philanthropist Teresa Heinz, and Pittsburgh Mayor Tom Murphy.

Its goal was to identify high-risk neighborhoods for youth and create and coordinate programs designed to keep them out of trouble, avoiding both duplication of services and poorly designed responses that would fail to effectively counter the appeal of gangs. Bishop Wuerl quickly became a leading member of the group, and was the one who held it together a few years later after Mr. Thieman left his post as U.S. Attorney, said Mr. Thieman, who is not Catholic.

Mr. Thieman had not met Bishop Wuerl until the attorney organized the retreat for community leaders that launched the Youth Crime Prevention Council. "He was totally encouraging and excited about it," Mr. Thieman recalled.

But that evening the bishop received a call about a devastating fire at one of his churches. "He came and apologized that he had to leave early to get to the parish—but that was a good introduction for me to the multiple facets of shepherding while also trying to be involved with community issues. From them on, he was one of the strongest supporters of this initiative. And he held such stature in the community that he incredibly helped my efforts to do things. Through the process we became good friends."

Bishop Wuerl brought "convening power, passion, and integrity" to the entire effort, Mr. Thieman said. "It wasn't simply that he would lend his name to something. He would pick up the phone, get personally involved, and make sure the right people were at the table."

While the U.S. attorney also has influence, "there is a difference between getting together out of respect for power and coming together around a commitment to the issue itself. That is where Bishop Wuerl really elevated it to another level through his moral integrity. He was not fulfilling an expectation or role. He was clearly personally committed to the cause of justice for young people."

The bishop also put his spiritual resources to work. In March 1994 he called on Catholics to spend three days in prayer, fasting and doing good works in order to halt gang violence. He opened the effort with a special Mass at St. Mary of Mercy. "We know that one way to reduce and even eliminate violence is through a change of human hearts," he said. "Prayer is one of the ways in which hearts are touched."[180]

Esther Bush, executive director of the Urban League of Pittsburgh, was so impressed with the bishop that she recruited him for her own board after serving with him on the Youth Crime Prevention Council.

"It's not just what he says, but how he says it in terms of making you think about what's the right thing to do, especially in a situation where the conversation might be somewhat heated," she said. After Mr. Thieman was no longer the U.S. attorney, "the bishop just stepped in and very quietly kept us all together and made us work."[181]

Three years after the council was founded, violent crime by youth in Pittsburgh had plummeted, dropping 18 percent in 1996 and more than 15 percent the year before that. The Youth Crime Prevention Council's efforts to target high-risk neighborhoods with high-quality services received a significant share of the credit.[182]

· · · · · · ·

Everyone agreed that the Youth Crime Prevention Council was doing good work. But sometimes the bishop had to step into painful, contentious community situations.

In 1996 recurring tensions over treatment of black citizens by a predominantly white police force ran high after a white officer who was being dragged at high speed by a stolen car he had pulled over, shot and killed two men in it. Mayor Tom Murphy called for a rally in Market Square to try to bring all sides together for reconciliation, but the crowd was bitterly divided.

An African-American city councilman was booed when he spoke of widespread distrust of the police by many black citizens, and said the best way to support the police would be to establish an independent review board to evaluate accusations of wrongdoing.

Bishop Wuerl was the next speaker up, and he commented on the boos by asking, "If anything, our gathering tells us we need God's grace, don't we?" He warned against the dangers of pre-judging any-one.[183]

Later that year he would receive a Racial Justice Award from the YWCA of Greater Pittsburgh for his efforts to root racism out of parishes and Catholic schools. More than 3,000 people received racial awareness training though the diocese, including all of the teachers.

In April 1997, before the Ku Klux Klan held a rally in Downtown Pittsburgh, Bishop Wuerl joined a phalanx of community and religious leaders who held a press conference urging citizens to attend an alternative "Unity Rally" instead.

It would begin with a Mass at St. Mary of Mercy Church, followed by an ecumenical prayer service.

"Racism is an evil that we speak out against...hatred ridicules what God has taught us in sacred scriptures: that we should love our neighbors as ourselves," Bishop Wuerl said at the press conference.[184]

There were signs later that the prayer bore fruit, Later that summer one of the Klan leaders, who had identified himself as Catholic at the time of the rally, renounced his membership in the racist organization. He cited his desire to enter fully into the life of the Catholic Church as a reason for his change of heart, saying he had never been confirmed and he realized in Pittsburgh that his chances of ever being so were gone. "You would not believe how bad I felt after the Pittsburgh rally," he said. "I've got to try to make things right."[185]

Bishop Wuerl "has always said that the role of the Church is to change hearts. If this is truly a conversion, he would certainly applaud that. This is what the church hopes to accomplish," said Father Lengwin, the bishop's spokesman.

• • • • • • •

When Bishop Wuerl left Pittsburgh for Washington, D.C., Mike Clark, a news anchor at WTAE, Pittsburgh's ABC affiliate, wrote a column describing coverage of a trip to the diocesan medical mission in Chimbote, Peru, where he watched the bishop embrace people who were ill with unknown diseases, blessing them and assuring them of God's love.

"Bishop Wuerl has been receiving lots of credit for his business acumen in straightening out the financial situation in the diocese," Clark wrote.

"But I'll remember him most for simply letting us all know we have all been called to a holy life, no matter who we are."[186]

Cardinal Wuerl still returns to Pittsburgh, where his brother lives and where a seminary classroom was converted into a modest apartment for him. He says he can always spot a Pittsburgher, because they inevitably address him as "Bishop-Wuerl-oh-I'm-sorry-I-meant-Cardinal-Wuerl."

He tells them that he's happy to answer to "Bishop."

Courtesy of the Diocesan Archives of the Diocese of Pittsburgh.

A BISHOP AMONG BISHOPS

It's fair to say that no bishop ever received a rougher introduction to the bishops' conference in the United States than Bishop Donald Wuerl.

At forty-five, he was extremely young for a bishop and, unlike most rising stars in the Catholic hierarchy, he had no obvious patron or "archangel" to steer a path for him. His mentor, Cardinal John Wright, was long dead. And though Archbishop Hunthausen, the ordinary of his archdiocese, was personally kind and supportive of him, they were on opposing sides of a pitched battle over authority in the archdiocese—and many bishops perceived the young auxiliary of Seattle as a symbolic threat to their own authority. The conflict over his assignment in Seattle was national news and media mobbed the meeting where the bishops would discuss how to respond.

"There were some who were just unhappy that I was there because they saw it as a lack of approval of the direction of things there—which it was," Cardinal Wuerl said. "A few were never able to get beyond the personal part of that—which is why I have such high regard to this day for Archbishop Hunthausen. It was never personal for him. We both realized it was an institutional issue. And so we were able to move forward. But there were some who just made this personal, instead of putting some distance between the issue and the personality. There were some who were unhappy with me because I wasn't demonstrative enough. There is a maxim that truth is great and it wins out. Cardinal Wright used to say, 'Sometimes it takes centuries.'"

Bishop Michael Pfeifer of the Diocese of San Angelo, Texas, had only been in the bishops' conference slightly longer, and was saddened to see the young bishop under so much pressure. "We had never seen so many reporters as there were at that meeting. I think poor Bishop Wuerl was suffering a lot, because he was looked at as an outsider coming in," Bishop Pfeifer said.

But by sheer talent, hard work and the grace to forgive and move on, he quickly became one of the most respected bishops among his peers.

"He really blossomed. He was always so respected for having great leadership qualities and being a great teacher." Bishop Pfeifer said. "When he speaks at the conference he is very focused on the Church and what the Church teaches and believes. He has written a lot. He has been on countless committees. He showed what kind of leader he was when he was named the bishop of a diocese. His outstanding qualities came to the fore. I look at him like the suffering servant, like Jesus. Ultimately, through his suffering, because he did what the Lord called him to, we've all been blessed by his leadership. He is a very intelligent man, very gifted, very knowledgeable."[187]

A somewhat older auxiliary, Bishop Peter Rosazza of Hartford, arrived at the meeting in strong support of Archbishop Hunthausen, and opposed to the pope's effort to make him cede some of his authority to Bishop Wuerl. But he couldn't help feeling sympathy for his fellow auxiliary. "Poor Donald Wuerl was like red meat in there," he said of the stormy meeting. "Nobody knows him. Very few people knew who he was or the quality of the man. Little by little people got to know who he was and the greatness of this man. I was very impressed with his theological knowledge. He's also a very personable guy. I've always liked him and found him easy to talk to. He's open, and he often has a mediating role. He is someone who is good at getting a group that brings both sides together."

Despite the anger and uproar, "I was invited my first year to be on the Committee on Doctrine. And I've been on committees ever since," Cardinal Wuerl remembered.

He examined, thoroughly in advance, every issue the bishops planned to address.

"He went to those meetings well prepared. When all of the documentation arrived I was responsible to go to each office for their comment, so they could help him prepare," said Father Robert Grecco, Bishop Wuerl's administrative secretary in Pittsburgh.

His first bishops' conferences as the ordinary of Pittsburgh found him taking a lead on some difficult issues. The Congregation for the Doctrine of the Faith had sent the bishops a paper for comment, which essentially undercut the teaching authority of national or regional bishops' conferences. He planned to speak to it that June in Collegeville, Minnesota, and his prepared response was nuanced. Other issues came up, however, and the discussion of that document was put off till November.

At the November meeting, Bishop Wuerl had a critical role in the debate. A committee made up of former presidents of the bishops' conference had deemed the paper so poorly researched and agenda-driven that they wanted to ask the Vatican to take it back and start over. The phrase they used for this came from Vatican II, and meant a worthless draft: "*Schema non placet*"—literally, "the draft is not pleasing."

Bishop Wuerl would lead the opposition to that effort. "While other bishops spent yesterday afternoon debating budgets, agricultural policy and other matters, Wuerl was hunched over a yellow legal pad drafting amendments to the bishops' proposed response. He believes that the committee of bishops issued an ultimatum when it was merely asked to join a dialogue," said a story in the *Pittsburgh Press*.

The committee had criticized the paper as defensive and negative, but that was also an accurate description of the proposed response, he said in an interview at the time. "I recommend that we accept the [Vatican's] invitation to dialogue and that we put our response into pastoral terms. I don't recognize in [the proposed response] the pastoral tone in which bishops usually speak. I could live with almost everything [in the proposed response] if they would just get rid of that 'non placet.'"[188]

In the end the bishops passed, 205-49, a toned-down version of their rejection of the Vatican document—just two votes over the two-thirds majority required. Many of the amendments had come from Bishop Wuerl, but both sides agreed that they had more to do with tone than substance. The committee had agreed to the proposal of Bishop Wuerl and some others to strike a paragraph that called the Vatican's draft "defensive, negative, and unobjective." But while it dropped the offending phrase "schema non placet," it kept an English-language request to destroy the draft and start again.

The committee that drafted the proposed response included Bishop Wuerl's old friend, Cardinal Bernardin of Chicago, and the prelate who had confirmed him, Cardinal John Dearden of Detroit. It was unsettling to criticize so many people whom he respected, he said. "You're speaking against twenty years of conference leadership," he said. "But in the conference, if you take a reasoned position that is well thought out, even if you don't necessarily win, the fact that you took that position is respected."

· · · · · · ·

If Bishop Wuerl seemed to be holding down the conservative position regarding authority in that debate, during the same meeting he was the anchor for what most observers would have identified as the liberal position in another document on the authority of bishops. He served on a committee that had drafted guidelines for a bishop to use if there were questions about the theological orthodoxy of a theologian working in his diocese.

"This is intended to minimize what we sometimes call witch hunts—people who call into question the orthodoxy and integrity of other people," he said.

Because theology is complex, nuanced, and constantly developing, a perfectly orthodox theologian may sometimes say or write something that strikes others as unorthodox, he said. The paper proposed ground rules for dialogue between a bishop and a theologian, who may well conclude that there is no problem with the theologian's proposals. But if, after extended dialogue, the bishop believes that real problems exist, the paper offered a full spectrum of responses, from continued study of the controversial proposal to issuing a warning that a particular theological proposition is in conflict with the Catholic faith.[189]

An earlier draft presented the year before had come under fire from more conservative bishops at the meeting because they believed it failed to recognize the innate teaching authority of the bishop. This time the objection would come from Rome. The committee that Bishop Wuerl served on hastily withdrew the paper after a fax arrived from the Congregation for the Doctrine of the Faith, saying that the document failed to assert the bishop's authority over the theologian. "An attitude which tends to equate bishops and theologians appears to inspire the whole orientation of the document," it said.

Bishop Wuerl was clearly frustrated, but attributed the problem to a lack of clarity in his committee's text. But the discussion was deferred for six months.

"I hope I live long enough to see this paper published," he sighed.[190]

That prayer was granted in June 1989, following extensive conversations between the committee members and officials in the Congregation for the Doctrine of the Faith. It passed 214-9.

Bishop Wuerl's endorsement of the paper was critical to its passage, said Father Leo O'Donovan, then a staff theologian at the USCCB. "The fact that [Bishop Wuerl] supports it so strongly now is, I think, very reassuring to a lot of bishops."

But what stopped the argument among the bishops in its tracks was when Cardinal John O'Connor of New York—a champion of conservative theology—and the more liberal Cardinal Joseph Bernardin of Chicago both endorsed it.

Cardinal O'Connor described it as "primarily a call to civility and charity. And that makes it clear that ultimately every decision must be made by the bishop."

Cardinal Bernardin said he already used a similar process in Chicago. "The document will bring serenity and a certain sense of peace" to bishops and theologians, he said.

"The two of them represented two wings, two very substantial viewpoints, in the conference," Cardinal Wuerl said. "Always during the coffee break there would be a lot of discussion, so that if we were not going to go forward with the way we are doing this, we have to find some middle ground that everybody can be comfortable with. There would be all these conversations going around, so that everyone knew by the time we went back in the room that if Cardinal Bernardin said, 'I've been rethinking and I think we should have some rewording...,' everyone knew that was as good as we were going to get."

Cardinal Bernardin, he said, was very much a role model in his effort to build consensus across the full spectrum of the Church. "I have always admired the pastoral way in which he approached problems," he said when his longtime friend was near death. "He was always attempting to keep as many people as possible in tune with the Church and on board with the Church, even when they were having a difficulty with some aspect of the life or teaching of the Church."

Cardinal Wuerl himself now holds that mediator role in the bishops' conference.

"He has always had a sense of the big picture," said Archbishop J. Peter Sartain of Seattle, who has known Cardinal Wuerl for forty years. "He always recognizes what it means to be part of the body of Christ, each of us in his or her own way, and how the parts can only relate to each other."

He is "the center of the conference," Archbishop Sartain said. During committee meetings, "when a variety of thoughts were expressed by a variety of people around the table, he is able to summarize and bring the discussion to a conclusion while sort of bringing everybody's thoughts into the summary. He does that with respect and affirmation, but then encapsulates it in a way that fairly represents what people have said, and relates what is said to Christ and the teaching of he Church." When he is dealing with people whose point of view differs greatly from his own, "he does it respectfully. He never puts anybody down. He brings people into the conversation by affirming what they've said and sometimes gently leading it to a different direction."

· · · · · · ·

Bishop Wuerl's willingness to speak with anyone and to hear all points of view made headlines when, during a retreat for U.S. bishops in California, he met with a group of men who had resigned from active priesthood and married. The married men belonged to the Corps of Reserved Priests United for Service (CORPUS), and asked for an official liaison to be appointed from the bishops' conference to their group, and to have a married priest address the bishops' conference. CORPUS advocates a married priesthood, but Bishop Wuerl said at the time that the meeting was not to discuss the requirement of celibacy in the western Church.

He had held the meeting, he would later explain, at the request of the conference president, Archbishop Daniel Pilarczyk of Cincinnati. He was the logical choice because he was then chairman of the committee on priestly life and ministry.

The meeting was a rare occasion when he received a public statement of praise from the liberal, independent Association of Pittsburgh Priests. They commended him for having "treated your brother priests in a Christian way."

In October the *New York Times* reported that Cardinal Antonio Innocenti, prefect of the Congregation for Clergy, had written to Bishop Wuerl about the meeting in July. Bishop Wuerl told local media in Pittsburgh that the inquiry from Rome was just that: an inquiry about what had happened. The cardinal had seen news reports of the meeting and wanted to ask what had transpired. Bishop Wuerl sent a reply and enclosed a memo that the conference president, Archbishop Pilarczyk, had written to the other bishops to explain why the meeting was held and what was discussed. He pointed out that that a month after the letters were exchanged, Pope John Paul II personally appointed him to the Synod of Bishops on the Priesthood.

"I didn't see the letter so much as a criticism as I did a request for information," he said.[191]

One of the married men who met with Bishop Wuerl, Anthony Padovano, had known him years earlier when both were active priests. "Bishop Wuerl was both courageous in going ahead with this

dialogue and in how he was demonstrating a collegial style of leadership. I know that is not only dear to his heart but is a style of leadership that the Church officially called for at the Second Vatican
Council," Padovano said.[192]

The bishop did not apologize for the meeting. "I remain firmly
convinced that the only way you begin to make headway with people
who share other views is to listen to them and talk with them—let
them explain their position while I explain mine," he said after the
story claiming Vatican criticism ran in the *New York Times.* "I believe that remains a necessary part of any type of resolution of problems."[193]

· · · · · · ·

As one newspaper headline put it, Bishop Wuerl was a "whirlwind"
at meetings of the bishops' conference. One reporter charted his
schedule for one meeting in 1993.

He flew in from Rome on a Sunday morning and went immediately to a meeting of the Committee on the North American College, the American seminary in Rome. He left that early to chair a
meeting of the Committee for Liturgy and Worship of the National
Shrine of the Immaculate Conception. That committee worked
through dinner. From there he retreated to his room to read a six-
inch stack of documents on issues the bishops would discuss that
week,

On Monday after six a.m. Mass he went to the Committee on the
Structure and Mission of the Bishops' Conference, which was preparing a reorganization of the conference that would occur several
years later. From there he went to an eight-thirty meeting of Sapien-
tia Christiana, which supervised schools that grant Vatican-approved
degrees in theology, canon law, and philosophy.

Immediately after that came the first meeting of the general assembly of bishops. That was also nonstop work, as he used the coffee
breaks to talk to other bishops about issues they would vote on later.
Lunch was spent with the Committee on Doctrine, whose projects
then included updating ethical directives for Catholic health-care fa-

cilities and a study of feminist theology. The meeting broke for Mass at the National Shrine of the Immaculate Conception, and from Mass he went to a reception hosted by Catholic Relief Services, which sought to update the bishops on its humanitarian work world-wide. He left early to study the documents for the next day's meeting —but did so while watching the last quarter of Monday Night Football. His beloved Steelers won 23-0.

Tuesday began with six a.m. Mass and more committee meetings. During the general session he was elected chair of the Committee on Priestly Formation. A working lunch was followed by an executive session. He never breathed a word of it, but other sources said the main topic was the concern of nuns that they would have no voice at an upcoming Synod of Bishops in Rome—a synod that would be primarily about the life and ministry of Catholic sisters.

After the executive session ended, he met with the subcommittee that would produce a ten-year-update of the bishops' celebrated letter on the nuclear arms race. They spent most of the night vetting dozens of proposed amendments. But inclusive language in the liturgy dominated the next day's meeting, where he had a key role in ending a bitter debate by proposing that a disputed translation be sent to the bishops' committees on doctrine and liturgy for evaluation before any vote was taken on it.

He had the evening free, and spent it catching up on reading. Thursday's meeting ended with an executive session. But he stayed on after most other bishops headed home in order to attend more committee meetings.[194]

• • • • • •

One of the most challenging assignments Bishop Wuerl worked on was a reorganization of the bishops' conference itself, to move the control from full-time staff members to the body of bishops and to make sure that projects were chosen according to five-year priorities that the body of bishops had voted on. At the November 1993 meeting, for example, he attended a meeting of the "Committee on the

Structure and Mission of the Bishops Conference" immediately after six a.m. Mass.

He was deeply concerned that the bishops' agenda was driven not
by the bishops, but by the personal interests of staff members. After
being elected chair of one committee early on, he went to a meeting
and discovered that the agenda he had prepared in consultation with
the committee was not on the table, and another was in its place.

"The staff said 'We prepared this one because these are the things
we need to talk about.' I said, 'I beg your pardon.' The fact is that
they were used to running the meeting, because chairs came and
went. At a certain point, the bishops said that we need to get back in
control of the conference and the bishops need to set the agenda."

The chairman of the committee that was supposed to present the
new structure to the bishops for a vote in November 1996 was Cardinal Joseph Bernardin of Chicago. But Bernardin's cancer took a sudden turn for the worse shortly beforehand, and he asked Bishop
Wuerl to present the plan in his place. The cardinal would die while
the bishops were meeting.[195] Cardinal Wuerl remembers the process
of working on that plan, especially all of the consultation, as one of
his favorite projects. But it was also exhausting.

When he rose to present it, he said he had two action items.

The president corrected him, saying there was just one.

"I said, 'No, there are two. One to vote on this and the other that
this committee go out of existence. We do not want to be the ones to
have to try to implement this for he rest of our lives."

In the end there was overwhelming support for the restructuring,
and the conference has continued to operate the new way for nearly
twenty years.

"I think ninety-five percent of the bishops embraced the idea that
all of us together set the priorities," Cardinal Wuerl said. "Personally, I think it's a much healthier conference than thrity years ago
because the bishops set the priorities. The staff are now becoming
more and more accustomed to working together, and the leadership
shares the vision of the reform. They don't even think of it as reform. This is who we are."

· · · · · · ·

It is not unusual for Cardinal Wuerl to stand at the podium to present a paper, but it is very unusual for him to lead a floor fight. His influence is most often exerted during coffee breaks, as he consults and persuades his colleagues to come together.

"At the coffee break you are not just listening to someone speak. You are interacting with other people," said the cardinal, who drinks his coffee black, but mixed with half decaf. "In our conference I always thought coffee breaks were the time when you spoke to people and said, 'If you are really going to move forward, don't you think we have to find some middle ground?' Coffee breaks are when you do that."

Bishop Zubik has found his methods to be distinctive: "Unlike some of the other boys in the conference, when he gets up to speak, he doesn't get up to speak to be noticed, but because something needed to be said. You will seldom see one of his green cards go up."

Bishop Bradley of Kalamazoo added that the cardinal's methods are effective: "When he gets up to talk, everybody sits up and listens. Whether people like him or don't like him, it's not a matter of personality. His reputation is such that if he is going to say something, it's worth listening to."

· · · · · · ·

Over the years Cardinal Wuerl has mentored many bishops, both in his own diocese and beyond. In fact priests and auxiliary bishops who served in Pittsburgh during his administration now hold positions as diocesan bishops, archbishops, and cardinals.

Among them are Cardinal Daniel DiNardo of Galveston-Houston; Archbishop Bernard Hebda, coadjutor of Newark and apostolic administrator of St. Paul-Minneapolis; the late Bishop Nicholas Dattilo of Harrisburg, Pennsylvania; Bishop Thomas Tobin of Providence, Rhode Island; Bishop Edward Burns of Juneau, Alaska; Bishop Bradley; and Bishop Zubik.

Their presence in the hierarchy speaks to "a hidden treasure of Western Pennsylvania, the quality of our priests here," Cardinal Wuerl said. "We're just workers. We don't need fireworks. They do their job. I like to think it shows I just had the right sense to pick the right people."

His mentoring extends well beyond those who served in his administration. Bishops from across the nation seek his advice, and he often reaches out to new bishops. He jokes about having gone from one of the youngest bishops in the conference to someone who has been there so long that others seek him out for institutional history lessons.

Because of his early years in Rome, he has always had knowledge of how to navigate and respond effectively when there is a conflict or misunderstanding with someone at the Vatican, said Jesuit Father Thomas Reese, the author of books on the institutional Church.

When Bishop Wuerl—along with many other bishops—was under attack from theologically conservative activists who believed he was promoting an unorthodox strain of feminism and systematically closing parishes that were faithful to Church teaching, he would send the articles to Rome before the activists themselves did.

"Wuerl is sophisticated. He understands the Vatican. He knows who to talk to. The bishop who has never worked in Rome probably doesn't know which office to respond to—and the people in Rome don't know him. Wuerl is known and respected in Rome. When [activists] start accusing him, they lose their credibility," Father Reese said.[196]

When then-Father Thomas Tobin was named an auxiliary bishop, Bishop Wuerl asked him to come along on a previously scheduled trip to Rome. "One of the things he did," Bishop Tobin remembered, "was to take me shopping at Barbiconi's," a famous dealer in ecclesiastical vestments in Rome. "He helped me buy a cassock and my first miters and surplices—the things that you need. He arranged for us to meet and have Mass with Pope John Paul—and I have a neat picture of Pope John Paul putting the pectoral cross over my shoulder with Bishop Wuerl standing in the background. I have a picture of a saint giving me the pectoral cross."

That, Bishop Tobin said, "was just the beginning. I think what he really taught me, aside from the ceremonial parts of being a bishop, is about being a diocesan administrator. Just by watching him he taught me some great skills about how to run a meeting, how to appoint committees, how to deflect any controversies that might arise during the meeting in some gentle way. He is a master at that kind of administration. Whatever I learned was from seeing that in action."

Cardinal Wuerl enjoys mentoring, and knows how valuable it can be. He's glad to assist others, he said, because "there really isn't a school for being a bishop. We sort of learn by osmosis." "One of the first things we talk about is prioritizing your time, and to remember your duty is to maintain the unity of the Church. There are a lot of different approaches to living out the faith, but what holds us together is the creed, the Mass, the sacraments, our love of God and our discipleship in Christ."

Making personal prayer time a high priority is a prominent feature of his advice. Another is "don't be afraid of work," he said.

· · · · · · ·

Cardinal Wuerl remains a team player even on the rare occasions when he had lost a battle. In the early 1990s he was a strong supporter of liturgical language that used gender-inclusive words in reference to human beings generically or groups that included both men and women. But when it was clear that Rome would not support it, he backed off. Although he considers the overall translation of the Roman Missal unwieldy, he not only kept his silence, but wrote a book, *The Mass: The Glory, The Mystery, The Tradition,* to explain and promote the revised texts of the Mass.

The tide had turned in 2001, with the publication of *Liturgiam Authenticam,* which forbade inclusive references to humanity and demanded a more literal translation from the Latin—no matter how awkward that sounded in English. At that point he no longer spent public political capital trying to force the issue on the floor in the bishops' conference, although he voiced approval for efforts to address the matter more quietly in Rome.[197]

"If you look at the long list of committees he has served on and the length of time he has served on those committees, it bespeaks an incredible dedication to the work of the conference," said Archbishop Gregory Aymond of New Orleans. "I think that not only his fingerprints but his heart prints are deeply embedded in the conference."

At a meeting at the USCCB headquarters, Msgr. Ronny Jenkins, the General Secretary, introduced Cardinal Wuerl to the staff, noting his long involvement with the conference. Msgr. Jenkins noted that Cardinal Wuerl has been the chairman or member of of eighteen standing committees, nine ad-hoc committees, and the task force that reorganized the Conference. He added that the committees on which Cardinal Wuerl has served as chair include the Committees on Doctrine, Education, Evangelization and Catechesis, Priestly Life and Ministry, Priestly Formation, Laity, and the North American College, Rome. Cardinal Wuerl's service on Ad-Hoc committees includes among others the Ad-Hoc Committees for the Catechism of the Catholic Church, Health Care Issues, Defense of Marriage, and Religious Liberty.

· · · · · · ·

Not only in the United States, but also in the global Church, there were signs that his brother bishops appreciated Donald Wuerl's hard work in every kind of committee and meeting. Especially after Benedict XVI was elected Pope, Bishop Wuerl found himself at the center of important councils and committees at the Vatican.

He brushed off predictions that all of those posts meant he would soon be leaving Pittsburgh for a large archdiocese or for Rome.

"All that shows is that they are scraping the bottom of the barrel. They had run out of people to do those things, so I was tapped," he said.

In this case, however, he was wrong. On May 16, 2006, Bishop Wuerl was appointed Archbishop of Washington, D.C.

Pope Benedict XVI visits Washington. Catholic Standard *photo by* *Michael Hoyt. Used with permission.*

Cardinal Wuerl greets parishioners at St. John Baptist de la Salle Parish *in Chillum after dedicating the new altar inside the church.* Catholic Standard *photo by Jaclyn Lippelmann. Used with permission*

Davide Kusherner, 7 years old, removes Cardinal Wuerl's mitre after White Mass at St. Matthew the Apostle Cathedral on Sunday, October 26, 2014, in Washington, DC. Photo by Leslie E. Kossoff/LK Photos. Used with permission.

CHAPTER 10:
ARCHBISHOP OF WASHINGTON

While Pittsburgh had been in crisis when he inherited it, with the Archdiocese of Washington Bishop Wuerl—now Archbishop Wuerl —found a different situation. The archdiocese had been well run for decades under Cardinal James Hickey (1980-2000). Cardinal Theodore McCarrick arrived and in his five-year tenure carried out a very successful major development campaign. There were a few trouble spots and room for growth, but Archbishop Wuerl was at the helm of an archdiocese poised for renewal.

"He came in and took all the good work that had preceded him and he built upon it and took it to a new level," said Jane Belford, his chancellor until 2014. "He was able to look at something, make projections, and say, if we continue in this way, where will be in two year or five years? Where do we want to be? And he would figure out how to get there."

Ms. Belford was already on the staff when he arrived, but he continued to bring women into leadership as he had done in Pittsburgh. When the *Washington Post* asked Ms. Belford what it was like to be a woman in a workplace filled with priests, she said she had worked at secular corporations that were more male-dominated. "Cardinal Wuerl's senior financial adviser is a woman, the head of communications is a woman, his spokesperson is a woman, his general counsel is a woman.... With regard to jobs and leadership, Cardinal Wuerl probably has more women in his cabinet than President Obama."[198]

In his first formal meeting with the pastoral staff in Washington, "the first thing he spoke about was the three C's: consultation, collaboration, communication," said Auxiliary Bishop Barry Knestout, who was a pastor when Archbishop Wuerl arrived, but was soon recruited for pastoral administration and was made a bishop in 2008.

Communication, Bishop Knestout said, meant using every avenue available, from traditional pastoral letters to live-tweeting important Church events.

Archbishop Wuerl started with a small communications department and added a digital media specialist and a recording crew that produces videos and TV commercials without paying tens of thousands of dollars to outside contractors. He himself participated in online chat sessions to communicate directly with his flock when controversies came up.

All that communicating is hard work. But Archbishop Wuerl is willing to do that work.

• • • • • • •

"His ability to stay focused and his capacity to work are immense," said Father Mark Knestout, pastor of St. Bartholomew parish in Bethesda, Md., and the brother of the auxiliary bishop, "He makes a great deal of sacrifice of his own personal needs and individual time. He spends his time working for the good of the Church."

Board members of the nonprofits affiliated with the archdiocese were surprised that he attended the meetings.

One of the most remarkable things about him, given the demands of his schedule, is that he keeps those appointments, said Pat Clancy, a member of the Archdiocesan Finance Council and a retired banker. "The cardinal is one of the most disciplined human beings I've ever known. The benefit of that is that it allows for great order. He doesn't cancel meetings. Usually when people are in positions like that, their schedule is subject to change frequently. But when he says he is going to do something, he does it."

That goes far beyond showing up at meetings.

"He faces the tough decisions," Mr. Clancy said. "He often brings people together who can help him see the various facets of a particular issue, and he listens intently. He has an incredible memory. If he is at a meeting and he hears something that was last brought up two years ago, he remembers it very clearly. He'll ask, 'That was a problem two years ago. Why is it still a problem?'

"He's not flashy. He doesn't come in and say, 'Here is what we are going to do.' He listens and thinks things through. Over time he keeps addressing the issue until it is fixed."

• • • • • • •

In 2008 the Archdiocese of Washington held its first annual "All Are Welcome Conference on Faith, Deafness, and Disabilities." The next year the cardinal brought together disparate programs for different disabilities into a new Department of Special Needs Ministries to serve those who are deaf, blind, physically or intellectually challenged, and mentally ill.

In 2009 he also instituted the White Mass, an expression of love and support for children and families affected by physical and mental disabilities. The children and young people whose lives are celebrated wear white robes. They do all of the lay roles, including serving at the altar and reading the scripture.

He recalled a young man with a significant intellectual disability who had worked long and hard to read a short passage from St. Paul. A priest walked him to the ambo and, when the vast crowd caused the boy to hesitate, the priest guided his hand to the text.

"He started to read, and I thought 'I will probably lose it,'" Cardinal Wuerl recalled. "And of course the people in the front rows were all pulling out their handkerchiefs. He did it haltingly, but beautifully. And when he was done he turned to me and smiled and nodded. It was like, 'See? I did it.'"

The cardinal wanted to "jump up and embrace the kid. As he started down to his seat people applauded. What that must have meant to him."

. . . .

In Washington, Archbishop Wuerl inherited a well-established Catholic Charities Health Care Network with a mission of providing medical care to the poor, but he has endeavored to improve services. In 2011 existing services for women with crisis pregnancies were unified under Catholic Charities as "Sanctuaries for Life." It offers seamless assistance to well over a hundred women and their children each year, with medical care, childrearing support and life-skills training.

In June 2014 the District of Columbia Department of Behavioral Health gave its first ever five-star rating to Catholic Charities of the Archdiocese of Washington for its services to people with mental illness. This was part of an annual review that the department does with all service providers it contracts with.[199]

"We are now recognized in Washington as the agency to go to for those needs," the cardinal said.

In addition to the large public ministries, he often responds privately to individuals who are suffering. Most of those moments are unknown to all but those present, but a few fall into public view.

On Christmas Day, 2008, Archbishop Wuerl had just celebrated Mass for 3,000 people in the Basilica of the National Shrine of the Immaculate Conception when he was told that the night before, a parishioner in College Park, Md., had been robbed and beaten nearly to death in the church parking lot. After walking though the basilica's cafeteria to speak briefly with people who were enjoying a free Christmas meal, he rushed to the hospital where the man lay in critical condition. There he prayed and gave him the Sacrament of Anointing of the Sick.

"I wanted to show some solidarity with the parish and the family and with his wife, just to let them know that we are with them in prayer, we are with them in this very difficult time," he told the Washington Post, which gave significant coverage to the gruesome Christmas crime. The victim survived, but lost sight in one eye.

"Christmas came precisely to help us beyond things like this, to help all of us live in a way that an event like this wouldn't be part of our experience," the archbishop told the reporters. "And when it is, how to respond."[200]

. . . .

A highlight of Archbishop Wuerl's ministry was the visit of Pope Benedict XVI in 2008.

The pope's acceptance of his invitation was an answer to prayer. He hoped it would renew the interest of inactive Catholics and invite non-Catholics to learn more about the faith. He wanted it to be a joyful celebration of faith.

But planning for a papal visit can be an administrative nightmare. Venues for tens of thousands of people must be booked, and security must be cleared with several levels of law enforcement. Millions of dollars must be raised to pay for it.

The single most difficult issue with planning, he said years later, is that once the papal nuncio confirmed that Pope Benedict had accepted the invitation, he was told not to tell anyone. "So you're told the pope is going to come, so you can make plans. But you can't say that," he said.

He pulled together a small team, led by Auxiliary Bishop Knestout. The others were archdiocesan chancellor Jane Belford, Michael Kelly, former chief financial officer of AOL-Time Warner, and Cardinal Wuerl's priest secretary, Father Carter Griffin, who is now seminary vice-rector and vocations director of the archdiocese.

The cardinal himself asked ten major donors to raise $4.5 million for the visit and an additional $1 million gift for Pope Benedict to distribute it to poor people worldwide.

The rest of the logistics were in the hands of his team, whom he met with daily. Nationals Park, a baseball stadium where they planned to hold the papal Mass, was still under construction. Kelly had the task of approaching the owners.

"I said, 'Mike, you can't tell the Lerner family why we want the park.' But they aren't where they are because they can't connect the dots—which they did," Cardinal Wuerl said.

He recalled a meeting at the papal nunciature between his team, the nuncio, and the Secret Service. They had to find a room large enough to spread the enormous map on the floor and examine potential routes. At one point the Secret Service agent asked how many steps there were from the curb—where the pope would exit the Popemobile—to the doorway of the National Shrine.

The archbishop dispatched Father Griffin to count them.

Pope Benedict would visit the White House, hold Mass at Nationals Park, and meet with the bishops in the shrine.

The transformation of the brand-new ballpark into an open-air cathedral was the most challenging part. Two days beforehand, five hundred workers installed flooring over the infield. A platform for the altar was built at center field, with a cover that stood seventy-five feet high. Dress rehearsals were held for the 570-voice choirs, celebrity soloists and volunteers.

Starting at six a.m., a hundred priests were available to hear Confessions, while a private Mass was held at eight a.m. to consecrate tens of thousands of hosts. Priests and Eucharistic ministers stood ready throughout the stadium to distribute them to 55,000 people in little more time than it would take in a large cathedral.[201]

The only misstep occurred when Pope Benedict was seated at the altar and realized he had left his gift to Cardinal Wuerl in the team manager's office, where he had vested. He ordered his priest-secretary to retrieve it—despite layers of security between the manager's office and the altar.

The cardinal learned later that the pope's secretary turned to another priest who turned to the closest Secret Service person and asked him to bring the vestment to the altar, despite the agent's protest.

"The only thing I knew was that here was this man running [toward the altar] and jumping over the barrier. I thought he had to be Secret Service, or else they would have tackled him," he recounted.

"But everything went like clockwork," he said of the overall visit. His personal highlight came after that Mass when, in a break with protocol, Pope Benedict invited him to ride with him in his car.

As they got in, he said, the pope told him that the Nationals Park liturgy "was a true prayer."

Monsignor Georg Ganswein, the pope's secretary commented on how silent the crowd was during Mass.

"I couldn't resist saying, 'Monsignor, they go to Mass,'" Cardinal Wuerl said. And the pope laughed.

At the time of this writing the Cardinal was celebrating the visit of Pope Francis in September 2015.

• • • • • • •

The visit of Pope Benedict brought the whole archdiocese together. But Catholics ought to feel united all the time. How can a large and incredibly diverse archdiocese be reminded, over and over, that they are all one?

One way is by joining together in celebrations. Keeping in mind the charge that Pope John Paul gave him to maintain unity in the Church, the cardinal has always sought occasions to gather the flock for anniversaries of their life together.

With his appreciation for history, he delighted in helping to complete a project that his predecessors had supported: the rebuilding of an historic chapel in St. Mary's City, Maryland, which Jesuit priests had build soon after the first Catholic settlers came to that colony in 1634. In 1704, it had been locked by the county's sheriff by order of the royal governor. At that time, Catholics in Maryland – which had been founded on the principle of religious freedom—could no longer worship in public there.

The chapel was rebuilt at a cost of $3.2 million, and when Archbishop Wuerl dedicated it in 2009, the current sheriff unlocked the door for him, and the archbishop helped push the door open.

The chapel, Cardinal Wuerl said in his homily, is testimony that the early settlers sought to "establish a society, a civil community, in which everyone is free to worship as they chose."[202]

One of the most historic anniversaries was at St. Joseph Church in Pomfret, Maryland, which dates to colonial times. The cardinal celebrated an outdoor Mass, reminding parishioners that their parish is "part of something larger."[203]

• • • • • • •

Both the administrative and the symbolic efforts have been bearing fruit. In 2014, a glowing profile in the Washington Post showed that the archdiocese was thriving. Its annual fundraising appeal was the highest ever, as was the number of converts—1,306—who joined the Church that Easter. Eighty men were studying to become diocesan priests. Gifts and revenue to Catholic Charities had grown from $50 million to $77 million under his watch, while diocesan financial aid to students in Catholic schools rose from $800,000 a year to $5.5 million a year.[204]

Instead of dealing with the effects of a sudden population decline, as he had been forced to do in Pittsburgh, Archbishop Wuerl had to manage significant growth. The Archdiocese of Washington grew from 560,000 to more than 620,000 members in the first nine years of his tenure.

"Our concern is not to amalgamate parishes. Our concern is providing for all the different immigrant groups," Cardinal Wuerl said.

Responding to growth is as much of a challenge as managing decline. Pittsburgh had taught him that segregation of immigrants only reinforced prejudice and fostered disunity. "Now we are asking why don't we invite people, make them feel welcome in our parishes and have Mass there in the various languages?" he said.

Mass is regularly celebrated in more than twenty languages, including Vietnamese, Korean, Chinese, Polish, Portuguese, French, and American Sign Language. The 270,000 Spanish-speaking parishioners account for nearly 45 percent of the archdiocese.[205] Every seminarian is required to learn at least enough Spanish to celebrate Mass. "We have a large number of Latino deacons who can take the homily that a priest has written in English and deliver it in Spanish," Cardinal Wuerl said. For some other groups he has made agreements with bishops in nations including South Korea, the

Philippines, Nigeria, and Ethiopia to send a priest, with all costs borne by the Archdiocese of Washington.

But reliance on priests from overseas isn't the best solution. Many of their home nations have far fewer priests per Catholic than does the United States. Older Catholics remember when the Archdiocese of Washington had many Irish-born priests who had arrived as missionaries, and they are sometimes shocked to learn how times have changed. "Today," Cardinal Wuerl said, "Ireland is desperate for priests."

While more priestly vocations are needed, he said, the United States has one of the best priest-to-parishioner ratios in the world. "We also have something very important, which is the lay involvement in our parishes. The lay involvement that the Second Vatican Council called for is taking place in a very robust manner across the country, as lay people are teaching, running RCIA, and doing volunteer work in parishes.

•••••••

All that success happens partly because Cardinal Wuerl knows his archdiocese well right down to the parish level. Just as it was in Pittsburgh, visiting parishes has remained Cardinal Wuerl's first priority.

On his first Christmas in the archdiocese, he celebrated a children's Christmas Eve Mass at St. Catherine Laboure in Wheaton, Md., midnight Mass at St. Matthew's Cathedral, and then Christmas Day Mass at the Basilica of the National Shrine of the Immaculate Conception.[206]

"It comes fundamentally from a real love, which can't be faked," said Auxiliary Bishop Knestout. "It's expressed in his efforts to reach out and be present in the parishes, and to let people know he's been present through the stories in the *Catholic Standard*" (the official archdiocesan newspaper). Despite the frequent travel required of all cardinals, "it's rare, very rare, that he's out of the archdiocese for an extended period of time. He always comes back in a few days so he can do an event, whether it's an installation of a pastor or to be present to the people sacramentally."

The cardinal is driven to make sure that each parish reaches its unique neighborhood in the most effective way possible, said Father William Byrne, pastor of St. Peter Parish on Capitol Hill and secretary for pastoral ministry and social concerns.

"He was particularly concerned about creating a spiritual home for legislators and others who work on the Hill, especially the young adults," Father Byrne said. "He was very encouraging of my ministry to Catholic members of the House of Representatives. I have a monthly dinner for Catholic members of Congress, and he is very interested in making sure that is thriving."

The dinner typically draws a changing cast of about fifteen members from both sides of the aisle, and the Cardinal wants to make sure it is a partisan-free zone, Father Byrne said.

"We have discussions that transcend the political things. These are always faith conversations," he said.

The cardinal does not intervene in the governance of his parish, he said.

"He is a manager, he is directive, but he is not a micro-manager. He will say, 'Here is a vision; now go make that happen. That allows room for experimentation and initiative, while the mandate is clear.'"

The cardinal, said Susan Timoney, executive director of the archdiocesan Department of Evangelization and Family Life, "is incredibly interested in the life of the local Church,"

She helps parishes use "Indicators of Vitality". The simple questionnaire asks parishioners to evaluate strengths and weaknesses in worship, education, community life, service to those in need, and administration, including financial stewardship. "The whole parish can identify where they want to be in six months to a year, and then the following year," she said.

Dr. Timoney, who has a doctorate in theology, says that she was initially underwhelmed at the simplicity of the questions. However, "as I began to work with the parishes, I saw that every parishioner thought they could answer those questions," she said. "When you begin to reach 100 or 200 responses, you see a pattern. It's clear where people recognize strengths, and their concerns about weaknesses tend to bubble up."

No goal is to take longer than two years to achieve.

"We had parishes that wanted to adopt the secular idea that you have to have a five- or ten-year strategic plan. But that outlives the life of the council members and often the tenure of the pastor and his ability to implement it. So the strategy is to have simple goals that take six months to two years," she said.

The underlying purpose is "to increase our capacity for evangelization," she said. The parish leaders look at demographic shifts in tier community that "may help them to see a new ministry and perhaps let go of another," she said.

· · · · · · ·

The Indicators of Vitality have helped to unite parishes that were seriously divided.

One had received a large bequest, and two factions formed around clashing proposals for how to use it. One wanted to expand the school gym; the other wanted to build a parish center.

"The pastor was finding it really hard to make a decision, because no matter what he decided, one group would be happy and the other would be mad," Dr. Timoney said. "So I suggested that we use the five indicators of vitality in order to first ask the question, 'What is the Lord asking us to do in this place and time to increase the capacity of the parish to serve the community?'"

As the parishioners and parish leaders addressed that question, they realized that they had no adult Bible study, in part because there was no place to gather.

"So they built a lovely new parish center," Dr. Timoney said. "While there were, in fact, people who were unhappy, they were engaged in the process every step of the way, and they themselves saw that the need to expand the gym was not the greatest need. They did not cause any trouble at all."

Another parish had a strong faith history that included sending many young men to seminary. But its neighborhood was changing, and there was discord over how to respond as Mass attendance dropped.

"A lot of people felt it was dying," Dr. Timoney said.

In its heyday the parish had adopted contemporary worship, with guitars. Now a new group of young adults wanted Gregorian chant and traditional devotions, such as Holy Hour.

"The pastor said he didn't know what would happen when he brought the two groups into the room together, because each was blaming the other for all the problems," Dr. Timoney said.

"By an act of the Holy Spirit, the first thing we asked them to do was share what they loved about the parish. It was the first time each of these groups heard that they all have the same love for the parish. One had raised their kids there, and the other wanted to raise their kids there."

One important decision was to change Mass times so that they differed from those of neighboring parishes. The result was fewer Masses, but they were filled.

They welcomed a growing Nigerian immigrant community that had become important in the neighborhood. The Africans held Mass on Sunday afternoons, with a meal and dancing afterward. Soon the Nigerian priest moved into the rectory and was willing to offer Mass for the rest of the parish.

The young Catholics who wanted more traditional devotions became a magnet for other young Catholics who wanted to raise their children in an active Catholic community. In response to their concerns, the parish school changed its curriculum to one based in the classics, which attracted even more young Catholic families. The young families formed an intentional community around the parish and school, so that the parish territory "has become a twenty-first-century version of the 1960s Catholic neighborhood," Dr. Timoney said.

All this heartening success made the archdiocese itself stronger. But Christians do not just cater to their own needs. A measure of how healthy a Catholic community really is how much influence it has on the culture around it.

Some people thought the sharply politicized culture of Washington would make it hard to build up ties outside the Catholic community. But with hard work and sincere attention to the needs of all people, it turns out that you *can* do that in Washington.

Serving hot meals to the homeless. Catholic Standard *photo by Jaclyn Lippelmann. Used with permission.*

On the 9/11 Unity Walk with religious leaders from all faiths. Catholic Standard *photo by Michael Hoyt. Used with permission.*

CHAPTER 11:
YOU *CAN* DO THAT IN WASHINGTON

At his inaugural Mass, Archbishop Wuerl said that the Catholic faith must be lived out in the real world. The Church must "see that the light of the gospel shines on all of the discussions and all of the debates that help to mold our culture and society. The voice of our most cherished values, the voice of the great teaching tradition rooted in God's word and God's wisdom, simply has to impact on our culture, our society.

"The wisdom of God is a thread that needs to be woven into that fabric to create a truly good and just society. This aspect of ministry will bring the Church into relationship with many in the cultural, educational, social-service, and political world. The voice of the gospel must be heard in any discussion that involves human dignity, human solidarity, development and ultimately holiness."[207]

In Washington, Archbishop Wuerl would inherit a wealth of social services, and continue to build on them and bring them together in ways that reduced holes in the safety net. His goal was to see that it was all done in the name of Christ, even when working cooperatively with those who were not Catholic or Christian.

• • • • • • • •

There were striking differences between interacting with the wider community in Pittsburgh and doing so in Washington. In Pittsburgh, for instance, his annual Red Mass was attended almost exclusively by lawyers, local judges or those otherwise engaged in the local justice system. In Washington the Red Mass pews included members of the U.S. Supreme Court and the vice president of the United States.[208]

Not all diplomatic issues he faced in Washington were equally weighty. One of the first was: Steelers or Redskins?

"Fortunately the teams are in different conferences and both apparently need prayers," the archbishop quipped during a Washington Post online chat.[209]

On the question of whether the Washington NFL team should change its name, which is an ethnic slur against Native Americans, he refrained from giving the owners direct advice, while suggesting they should listen to the pain of those maligned by the name.

"The task of the bishop is to call people to do the best they can, to call people to respect others, to call others to apply the principle of 'Do unto others as you would have them do unto you,' and then entourage them to make the right call."

Pressed by a reporter on whether that wasn't a directive to change the name, he said, "I don't like to draw conclusions for other people. You want to encourage them to do the right thing, but it has to come out of the heart."[210]

But the cardinal found the highly politicized nature of Washington frustrating. "In Pittsburgh you could do something with a politician and it wouldn't be considered partisan. You could say, here is a problem—is there any way to get this youth center built in this part of the city? You could have a whole group of people—Catholics, Protestants, and Jews—working on it. And it wasn't considered partisan. In Washington it's far more partisan, or at least it's viewed as partisan." As a result, he said, "you must constantly communicate that your relationship to them is as a pastor, not as a partisan politician...I am finding you can do that in Washington. You just have to demonstrate it more clearly."

After a bruising encounter with the District of Columbia city council over a same-sex marriage bill that would have required Catholic Charities to certify the marital status and provide spousal benefits to same-sex couples, the archdiocese has made efforts to repair and strengthen its relationships with legislators on all levels of government, as well as its relationships with other religious communities, including those that support same-sex marriage.

That fight, during which the archdiocese was largely isolated from many of its longtime partners in the mainline Protestant and Jewish communities, "taught us that some of our relationships with the interfaith community were a little superficial, and we needed to develop more substantive relationships. We've been able to do that under Cardinal Wuerl's leadership," said Michael Scott, director of the District of Columbia Catholic Conference, which represents the archdiocese on public-policy issues in the capital.

The cardinal, he said, is not trying to get them to change their support for same-sex marriage or any other policy, but to recognize that any infringement on the religious freedom of the Catholic Church is a threat to the freedom of all religious bodies to teach and follow their own beliefs.

· · · · · · ·

One clear sign that Cardinal Wuerl has been able to build strong ties with religious leaders who aren't necessarily in agreement with him is his remarkably amicable relationships with multiple competing wings of Anglicanism.

He has excellent relationships with the Episcopal Church and the competing Anglican Church in North America, while serving as the Vatican's point person for the Anglican Ordinariate—an arrangement that allows Episcopal and Anglican male clergy to enter the Catholic Church with their entire congregations. The ordinariate is potentially a rival to both of the other bodies.

His ties to the Anglican Church in North America go back to his close friendship with Bishop Robert Duncan, the former Episcopal bishop of Pittsburgh who became the founding archbishop of the Anglican Church in North America.

Yet he also built a very strong friendship with Bishop John Chane, the now-retired Episcopal bishop of Washington, whose views on matters such as same-sex marriage are very much at odds with Catholic teaching.

Soon after Archbishop Wuerl was installed in Washington he invited Bishop Chane to breakfast. He spoke of the kinds of relationships he had had with ecumenical leaders in Pittsburgh, and said he hoped there could be something similar in Washington, in terms of a regular gathering for prayer, Bible study, and mutual support.

"It was absolutely wonderful from my point of view," Bishop Chane said. "We began bringing together the leaders of the denominations as quite a significant thing, and he was the one who orchestrated it."

On a practical level, Bishop Chane said, the archbishop proposed ways in which their parochial schools could work together, since the Episcopalians had a network of eighteen schools that overlapped territorially with the Catholic archdiocesan schools. That involved everything from shared programs to bulk purchasing, including insurance costs.

Bishop Chane also said he picked up some good governance habits from Cardinal Wuerl, including meeting every few months with his principals "and engaging in personal visitation to the schools to let those in education know they were supported," he said.

In August 2011 an earthquake badly damaged the Episcopal National Cathedral—which had no earthquake insurance because the possibility of a damaging tremor in that part of the country was considered remote.

"The first letter I received with a check in it came from Cardinal Wuerl," Bishop Chane said.

The check was for $25,000.

Cardinal Wuerl also offered the Basilica of the National Shrine of the Immaculate Conception to host a large ecumenical service that had been scheduled for the National Cathedral.

Cardinal Wuerl, Bishop Chane said, has never allowed the issues that divide the churches—and that divide Anglicanism—to divide the two of them. "He has continued the connection between Anglicanism and Roman Catholicism at a time when there were really significant divisions in this country between the two over matters that were really painful for Episcopalians," he said, in a reference to debates over gay ordination and same-sex marriage.

"That was never an issue between us," he said, "We talked about how to do the gospel together, how to be the Church better in a complex and changing world."

Cardinal Wuerl "took a great risk in reaching out to me right off the bat," Bishop Chane said. "I was seen in the Episcopal Church as one of those liberals who was very clear on where I felt the Church needed to be on issues that were divisive. I was present for the conse-cration of [openly gay Bishop] Gene Robinson. I think it took some courage for him to reach out to someone who was radical in the life of Christendom and the Anglican Communion. But that never both-ered him."

Cardinal Wuerl "is very respectful, he is not judgmental," Bishop Chane said. "That doesn't mean that he is weak or that he doesn't have a position. But he is not a finger-pointer."

At that time the Episcopal Church in some dioceses surrounding Washington was embroiled in lawsuits with parishes that had sought to break with the denomination and take their property with them. In the middle of that an Episcopal parish in Maryland approached Cardinal Wuerl about coming into the Catholic Church through the ordinariate. The transition was accomplished without a lawsuit and without rancor.

"You have to be transparent with everybody," Cardinal Wuerl said. "Everybody has to know first of all what your position is and that you respect them, even if you differ from them or they differ among themselves."

In setting up the ordinariate and working for the transition of the parish, "none of those discussions look place without the other party being aware and invited in. I think that is one way in which you sus-tain good relations with everybody."

When the Vatican was getting ready to announce its plan for the global ordinariate, Cardinal Wuerl took a train to New York City to visit Episcopal Presiding Bishop Katharine Jefferts Schori. "That way she could hear about all of this first hand before it was publicly announced," he said.

"There was no intrigue going on. It was transparent. Bishop Jef-ferts Schori could not have been more gracious," he said, adding that she understood that the Catholic Church wasn't actively recruiting Episcopal congregations but responding to Episcopalians who were asking to come in. She pointed out, he said, that there are many for-mer Catholics in Episcopal parishes.

At the same time, he had kept his old friend Bishop Duncan ap-prised of the impending ordinariate so he would not be blindsided by the creation of a structure that might appeal to members of his own church.

"He never surprised his allies," Bishop Duncan said. "Our rela-tionship was such that he could talk about these things and he knew I wouldn't betray him."

· · · · · · ·

St. Luke's Episcopal Church in Bladensburg was largely made up of immigrants from Africa and the Caribbean. Bishop Chane allowed the parish to lease its facility from the Episcopal diocese, with an op-tion to purchase it.

"Cardinal Wuerl and I sat down and talked about it. The issue for me was not whether this priest and his parish were Roman Catholic, Anglican or Episcopal. The issue was how best can this priest and his people serve the community and bring the gospel of Jesus Christ. So we began the conversation on how that might take place."

Those conversations began in secret, but eventually Bishop Chane had to bring it to his advisers and councils. Those groups initially re-sisted the amicable departure and lease arrangement, predicting pub-lic embarrassment to the diocese. Instead, "When the newspapers picked it up they were astounded that there wasn't any animosity," Bishop Chane said.

· · · · · ·

Cardinal Wuerl has also kept up ties to the Jewish community. Each year the U.S. Conference of Catholic Bishops co-sponsors training days for teachers from Catholic schools around the country on how to teach about the Holocaust.

"I try to go over, even if it's just for an hour, to offer support," he said.

When a Jewish man from the Washington area was jailed in Cuba after smuggling in communications equipment to link the island's Jewish community with Jews in the wider world, Cardinal Wuerl participated in an interfaith prayer service for his release. It would take another four years, but Alan Gross was eventually allowed to return home in 2014, even as the Vatican facilitated a move toward normalized relations between the United States and Cuba.[211]

Meanwhile, Catholic schools reached out to other parts of the community that no one else was serving. As in Pittsburgh, the question was how to keep serving those children without bankrupting the school system.

· · · · · · ·

While he continued to build relationships outside the Church, there was a great deal to take care of inside the Church, starting with a schools crisis. More than a decade before Archbishop Wuerl began his tenure there, one of his predecessors, Cardinal James Hickey, had created the Center City Consortium to support and revitalize inner-city Catholic schools. The model was a bit different from the Extra Mile Foundation in Pittsburgh, but the intention was the same. Over eleven years the archdiocese and many donors gave $68 million to support these schools which, like those in Pittsburgh's Extra Mile program, served mostly non-Catholic children whose parents were either on public assistance or numbered among the working poor.[212]

It started with eight schools, then in 2005, just before Cardinal Wuerl arrived, it was expanded to fourteen in an effort to avoid closing more struggling schools. But the fundraising didn't keep pace with the expansion, while enrollment in some of the schools dropped —in part because children could now attend public charter schools for free. A consolidation had reduced the number to twelve in 2006, but soon after Archbishop Wuerl arrived in Washington he realized that the entire Center City Consortium was in danger of collapse. More than half the money that all the parishes of the archdiocese contributed to Catholic education was going to the Consortium schools. The archdiocese had started an endowment to support elementary education—but in 2007 the interest from that endowment covered only the deficit at two of the twelve consortium schools.[213]

Following the model he had long used in Pittsburgh, consultations were held at all twelve of the schools and their related parishes, with participation from over 1,300 people. The plan that emerged to save quality education in those neighborhoods was to convert seven of the schools to independent, secular charter schools and return one to the responsibility and oversight of its parish, St. Augustine, a strong, historic African-American church. That would allow the Center City Consortium to continue to support the four remaining schools under a new name, the Consortium of Catholic Academies.[214]

The decision to turn those schools into secular charter schools caused a brief public furor. Some protested because the schools would no longer be Catholic. Others feared that the archdiocese was abandoning the inner city and the 1,400 students who attended those schools.

A group called Black Catholics United also formed to protest the decision to convert the schools to public charters, saying it "raised questions as to whether there remains a place in the Archdiocese of Washington for African American Catholics."[215] It was those protests, coupled with the willingness of St. Augustine parish to resume responsibility for its school, that reduced the number of proposed conversions to charters from eight to seven.Acting on his commitment to openness, the archbishop visited the parishes to meet with all who were concerned and also participated in a live online chat at Washingtonpost.com, answering questions about Washington's Catholic schools and the charter school conversion. He called the decision a "heartache."

One participant expressed deep disappointment in the decision, quoting the former archbishop, Cardinal James Hickey, who had said, "We do not educate them because they are Catholic; we educate them because we are Catholic." "It sure seems you have chosen to turn your back on the neediest in our community," the participant wrote.

The archbishop responded that the decision placed the children first, because in the past schools in such financial straits would have been closed outright. The possibility of a public charter school gave the archdiocese an alternative that would preserve quality education from many of the same teachers, though with a loss of religious content in the classroom.

"All of us wish we could keep every Catholic school in the nation open, but history has proved that is not possible," he wrote. "I wish more than anyone that these schools could remain Catholic and I am always willing to receive from anyone the millions of dollars it would take to do this. In the meantime, the Catholic response has to focus on the children. That is what this framework does. It puts the children first."

The *Washington Post* had already run an editorial praising the decision, calling it "a bold and creative alternative to closing the schools." Public officials had estimated that the public system would give the seven schools an annual infusion of $16 million, and that the schools had the advantage of coming in with an established track record as excellent educational facilities. With so much money at stake, there was politics and there were delays, but ultimately it was completed.

· · · · · · ·

Meeting the immediate needs of the students was one thing, but Catholic schools needed to plan for a secure future. The cardinal sought to bring features of the Extra Mile model to Washington, reaching out to donors who had not typically been associated with Catholic schools.

"The Extra Mile Foundation is as interfaith as you can get. Everybody is in on it, and their sole purpose is helping those minority kids who are in some of the worst areas of our city get an education. They've been doing it for over twenty-five years," he said.

In his first seven years in Washington he was able to raise archdiocesan support of Catholic schools to $5.5 million a year.

"Most of the giving is from Catholics, but we just established a separate foundation for a couple of our inner-city schools, and that is interfaith," he said. "It is not owned by the diocese. It's a separate entity. The bishop sits on the board and appoints the members, so corporations can give to that and it's not giving to the Church."

Today the four schools in the Consortium of Catholic Academies have a 100 per cent on-time graduation rate and strong test scores. They have also developed innovative programs that meet continuing demographic changes. Sacred Heart School offers bilingual K-8 English/Spanish immersion program, so that all students become fully literate in both English and Spanish.

• • • • • • •

The cardinal has also strengthened Catholic Charities, which became a critical task after the bruising fight with the city council over same-sex spousal benefits for its employees. When its longtime director retired in 2011, Cardinal Wuerl appointed one of his most popular and charismatic pastors, Monsignor John Enzler, as president and CEO of Catholic Charities. At the time, some Catholics were aghast that he would remove such a gifted priest from parish ministry, but the result has been revitalized and expanded services and a new appreciation from the community for all that Catholic Charities does.

"The day I arrived I wanted to visit every city council member personally, and I did that probably in the first four months," Msgr. Enzler said. "What I wanted to say to each of them, particularly to those who had been most tough with us, was that I hope we can discuss issues we disagree on in your office, not in the papers. We both have a real commitment to the poor, and I want to make sure we don't get involved in fisticuffs in the news media. A couple of them who had been really negative towards us respected that and took it seriously."

Cardinal Wuerl, he said, was completely supportive of those conversations.

Within a year, Father Enzler had been named Washingtonian of the Year by *Washingtonian Magazine*. He had built deeper connections to the parishes by getting their members involved in new programs, such as the a "Joseph's Coats of Many Colors" drive to collect winter outerwear for more than 9,000 children and adults, and "Cup of Joe" to provide a bagged breakfast to people in emergency homeless shelters.

His goal is for each parish to have some ministry to the poor in collaboration with Catholic Charities. "It could be a good program, it could be a counseling center, work with those who battle alcohol and drug abuse or maybe with people with disabilities," Msgr. Enzler said.

The cardinal himself has been an exemplar of hands-on work with the poor. "He loves to come and feed the poor. He has been with us a number of times, coming to different shelters and programs. He really does enjoy seeing first-hand what is taking place," Msgr. Enzler said,

Every Wednesday staff and volunteers from Catholic Charities serve dinner from a van to people who are waiting for their transportation to homeless shelter. "Every once in a while the cardinal comes to serve the dinners with us," said Auxiliary Bishop Mario Dorsonville, who is vice-president for mission at Catholic Charities. "And while he is serving the people he is speaking and interacting with them and trying to find the path to grasp the reality of the people of the street."

Those visits are an essential part of the cardinal's ministry, Mr. Scott said. "He doesn't just show up at the shelter or the Catholic Charities event and then go back to the office and see those as different jobs. You can be out every day of the week doing something with the poor, but it has to inform the decisions you're making back at the chancery. And it really does inform him."

· · · · · · ·

Catholic Charities' mental-health services have won accolades from the secular community, but the fact that they exist at all is a credit to Cardinal Wuerl, Bishop Dorsonville said. At the time he came to the archdiocese, those services faced what many people would have considered impossible financial challenges. But Cardinal Wuerl responded to arguments from then-Father Dorsonville and others to invest another two years to see if they could be made sustainable. Last year the Catholic Charities behavioral health program received the first five-star rating that the District of Columbia has given to any behavioral-health provider. Services include crisis intervention, psychiatric clinics, employment assistance, medication management, day services, individual and group counseling, community support, and case management.

In addition to making more counseling and treatment available through outpatient centers "we got it down from a $1 million loss per year to a $250,000 loss per year—which is fine because we are a nonprofit. We can find donors," Bishop Dorsonville said. "We help 1,100 people a year who have mental illness."

One of the programs that Cardinal Wuerl is most proud of began in Msgr. Enzler's former parish and is now throughout the archdiocese: providing respite care for families with special-needs children. Two decades ago, as a parish priest, Msgr. Enzler became aware of the toll taken on parishioners who cared for a severely disabled child. His parish organized volunteers to do everything from involving less severely handicapped children in sports to round-the-clock child care so parents could have a weekend getaway. Many of the "children" were adults who had aged out of government services provided to minors.

When Cardinal Wuerl learned about the program, he looked to expand it beyond that parish.[216] It is now coordinated by Catholic Charities under the name of each town and "Community Resources." "It says we are all part of this community together and special-needs members are also part of our community," Cardinal Wuerl said. Victory Housing, an archdiocesan ministry begun in the 1960s to provide affordable housing to the poor and working poor, has continued to grow under his watch. Today it provides not just subsidized housing but related social services for residents of 2,175 units in 30 communities.

· · · · · · ·

All these initiatives reach people in the Washington community who never set foot in a Catholic church. But a bishop's reach extends farther than his own flock. Merely by being a Catholic bishop, he is a visible part of a global organization with more than a billion members.

And even before he was a bishop, Donald Wuerl was right in the middle of some of the most important movements in the global Church.

Catholic Standard *photo by Rafael Crisóstomo. Used with permission.*

CHAPTER 12:
THE GLOBAL CHURCH

Whenever Cardinal Wuerl visits Rome, he likes to include a visit to the crypt of St. Peter, beneath the altar in the great basilica that bears the Apostle's name. The cardinal makes a particular point of it if he is in the company of some of his priests.

Together, in a space as close as they can get to the bones of the first pope, they recite the Apostles' Creed. It is a sign of their union with Jesus, who chose Peter as the rock on which he would build his Church. And it is a sign of the union with every Apostle, bishop, priest, deacon, and believer who has been united in faith with Christ down through the ages.

The successor of Peter today is Pope Francis, and Cardinal Wuerl is not only united with him in faith and ministry, but has become a close adviser and fervent defender of the first pope from the Americas.

Cardinal Wuerl "has always been a good, clear teacher. But he is filled with such hope about Pope Francis, and he is one of the most articulate interpreters of who Francis is and what Francis is doing. He has come alive with this whole thing," said Father Thomas Rosica, CEO of the Salt and Light Television Network in Canada and an English-language assistant to the Holy See Press Office. "To have somebody like him as the Archbishop of Washington, the capital of the United States, is a perfect fit. My only regret is that he isn't thirty years younger."

· · · · · · ·

More than thirty years ago, Cardinal Wuerl began his ministry in the heart of the global Church, through his work for the Congregation for Clergy. That global perspective has remained with him. It has been further reinforced by the many times when he was elected or appointed to serve in the Synod of Bishops, a regular international gathering of bishops representing each nation of the world, to discuss how Church teaching should be applied in their own time and place.

In 1971, when he was just five years a priest, Father Wuerl provided staff assistance to a synod that Pope Paul VI convened on the priesthood.[217] In 1990, Pope John Paul II appointed Bishop Wuerl a member of the synod on "The Formation of Priests in the Circumstances of the Present Day." It was a logical choice, given Bishop Wuerl's work on the Vatican study of seminaries in the United States. He had been on the ballot to choose elected members in late 1989, but lost to two cardinals, the president of the bishop's conference, and Bishop John Marshall of Burlington, Vermont, who was the head of the study. That group, however, had asked him to accompany them as an adviser before the pope made him one of his thirty-six personal appointees to a gathering of around 240 bishops.Each participant had an opportunity to speak briefly, and Bishop Wuerl intended to speak on continuing academic, professional, and spiritual renewal of priests after their ordination.[218]

In 1997 his brother bishops elected him as their representative to the Synod on America, to discuss the state of the faith in North and South America—considered all one continent by the Vatican. This time his choice of topic was the challenge of spreading the faith in an increasingly secularized society—and making sure that faith in Christ was the context for the Church's social-justice work.

Following the 1997 synod, Cardinal Wuerl participated in the Synod on the Eucharist in 2005, the Synod on the Word of God in 2008, and the 2012 Synod on the New Evangelization, where he served as the Relator General. Cardinal Wuerl also participated in the two Synods on the Family that were held in 2014 and 2015.

The synod, at that point in history, was a tightly controlled process with no real opportunity for debate or discussion during the month-long meeting. That was a point of frustration for Bishop Wuerl, but he found value simply in gathering across national and cultural lines.

No matter what the synod ultimately said about evangelization, social justice, or many other pressing topics, he said, "It will have brought bishops from North and South and Central America together to talk about common problems. And that is something we have never done before."[219]

At that meeting he was the first speaker who was not a Vatican official, and was also chosen to give the first homily at the synod. In it he assured his brothers that God would help them find solutions to the many pressing problems the Church faced in the Western Hemisphere.

In 2005 he was elected again by his brother bishops to the Synod on the Eucharist.

Deeper involvement in the synod process and its reform would continue later, after he became Archbishop of Washington. But meanwhile in Pittsburgh he had other ways of keeping up his global contacts.

• • • • • • •

Missionary outreach was always important, and in Pittsburgh a primary focus was support for the Catholic maternity hospital and related social services in Chimbote, Peru, founded by a Pittsburgh priest, Monsignor Jules Roos, in the year that Bishop Wuerl was ordained a priest. In addition to raising money for the medical mission, Bishop Wuerl traveled to Chimbote in 1991 to celebrate the clinic's twenty-fifth anniversary.

Chimbote was a continuing commitment, but there were many special collections to aid victims of manmade and natural disasters worldwide. In 1990, while attending the Synod on the Priesthood, he was deeply moved by the testimony of bishops from Eastern Europe who were emerging from decades of communist suppression and had no buildings, books, or even paper to use for training new priests. He promptly offered his assistance, well before the U.S. Conference of Catholic Bishops organized a special collection.

"The most moving part of the synod has been listening to these bishops tell their stories, he said. "The only applause that we have had so far is for these bishops from the Ukraine, Byelorussia, Czechoslovakia, Romania, places like that."[220] He would supplement the national collection, as in April 1995, when he presented visiting Cardinal Vinko Puljic with a $25,000 check for relief efforts in war-torn Bosnia[221] More than a decade later, during his final weeks as bishop of Pittsburgh, when Cardinal Puljic visited again, Bishop Wuerl presented him with another $25,000 check, for funds collected from Pittsburghers of Croatian heritage and the diocese itself.[222]

• • • • • • •

Despite his longstanding friendship with Pope John Paul II, it was not until after his death that Bishop Wuerl's influence on the global Church grew rapidly.

Very early in the reign of Pope Benedict XVI, there were signs of great respect for the bishop of Pittsburgh. That fall, at the Vatican's annual "school" for new bishops, Bishop Wuerl was the only speaker who did not hold a job in the Vatican bureaucracy. He spoke about diocesan administration, emphasizing the importance of accountability and openness, especially with regard to money and sexual scandals.

"Accountability, understood as transparency of the exercise of authority, does not mean giving up decision-making authority. It does, however, mean that such apostolic authority is exercised in the context of an informed and consulted local church," he told 110 new bishops.[223]

Two weeks later he was back at the Vatican as an elected participant to the Synod of Bishops on the Eucharist. He was enthusiastic about changes that Pope Benedict had made to the format of the meetings, shortening each bishop's speech by two minutes in order to create an hour of previously unheard-of open discussion at the end of each day.[224]

By the time he returned to the United States he had not only spoken at the school and participated in the synod but had ordained twenty-one American seminarians to the diaconate—an honor usually reserved for a high-ranking Vatican official. At the synod he was the only U.S. representative elected by the 250 other bishops to the council that would help Pope Benedict draft a final document summarizing the most important conclusions that the pope drew from the synod.

He had helped to draft fifty propositions that the bishops sent to Pope Benedict. He had served as the "relator"—a combination of secretary and consensus-builder—for thirty English-speaking bishops from across the globe.

One factor at work in his choice as relator was language skills. He is comfortable in Italian and French, as well as the synod's official language of Latin. It was the first synod at which he encountered bishops who did not speak Italian. His English-language group included people from nations as disparate as Hong Kong, Pakistan, and Uganda.

"The Church is going to have to deal with the reality that, at a practical level, there is no longer any common language. The official language of the synod was Latin, but that is not a conversational language," he said.[225]

A steady drumbeat of rumors about a transfer to an important office in Rome or an important archdiocese in the United States finally turned to fact on May 16, 2006, when Pope Benedict appointed him to the Archdiocese of Washington, D.C. As archbishop of the capital city of the world's greatest superpower, his ability to make a global impact increased exponentially.

Even if it was never officially cited, his influence was clear in the 2007 appointment of Bishop David A. Zubik, his longtime aide and protégé, to succeed him in Pittsburgh. Most informed observers were convinced that that could not happen, because Bishop Zubik had been the ordinary of the Diocese of Green Bay for a relatively short time and had major projects to complete there.

"This is clearly an indicator of Archbishop Wuerl's influence. It shows that Wuerl put in a very strong word for him and the people in the Vatican listened," said Father Thomas Reese.

So no one was surprised when, at the first opportunity after his predecessor turned eighty and was no longer eligible to vote in a conclave, Pope Benedict elevated Archbishop Wuerl to the rank of cardinal. An entourage of more than 400 people from both Washington and Pittsburgh accompanied him to the ceremonies at the consistory of November 2010. They wore repurposed Washington Nationals baseball caps, in which the "W" now stood for "Wuerl."[226]

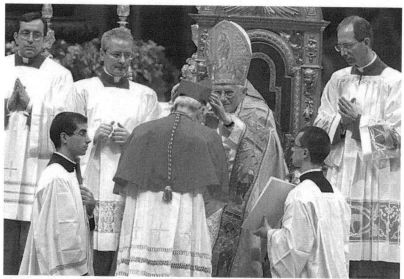

Receiving the red hat from Pope Benedict XVI. Catholic Standard *photo by Paul Fetters. Used with permission.*

Posing with friends after he was named a cardinal. Catholic Standard *photo by Paul Fetters. Used with permission*

Receiving the cardinal's ring from Pope Benedict XVI. Catholic Standard photo by Paul Fetters. Used with permission.

CHAPTER 13:
A CARDINAL AMONG CARDINALS

At the consistory, Pope Benedict reminded the twenty-four new cardinals that they must exercise the kind of self-sacrificial leadership that Jesus did, and that the red robes of a cardinal symbolize a willingness to die "for the increase of the Christian faith, for peace and harmony among the people of God, for freedom and spread of the Holy Roman Catholic Church."[227]

The signs of just how global the College of Cardinals had become were evident in the range of celebrations. Vatican security was frantic over someone in the crowd who sounded a vuvuzela—a plastic horn associated with international soccer matches—during the processional. At both the Mass of elevation and the next day's Mass for the presentation of the rings, Congolese pilgrims there to honor their new cardinal ululated—a high-pitched, throbbing cry of joy.[228]

Cardinal Wuerl's entourage encompassed its own kind of diversity. Both liberal MSNBC commentator Chris Matthews and Michael Steele—then chairman of the Republican National Committee—attended because they considered the cardinal a friend. Dan Rooney, the chairman of the Pittsburgh Steelers and then-ambassador to Ireland, was in the entourage—as an official representative of President Barack Obama, who sent the first-ever presidential delegation to the consistory. The cardinal's barber was there, as was Rabbi Alvin Berkun, a close friend from Pittsburgh.[229]

The cardinal's ring designed by Pope Paul VI, with an engraving of the crucifixion, replaced the bishop's ring that Cardinal Wuerl had inherited from his mentor, Cardinal Wright. Cardinal Wuerl gave that ring, which he had worn every day for twenty-five years, and which had been presented to Cardinal Wright by Pope Paul to honor his participation in Vatican II, to the Diocese of Pittsburgh. Since it had been worn by two Pittsburgh bishops, Cardinal Wuerl said he believed its true home was Pittsburgh.[230]

Cardinal Wuerl celebrated Mass for the pilgrims at the Basilica of St. Paul's Outside the Walls, where the bones of the Apostle Paul are entombed. Peter demonstrated how to follow Jesus while Paul told the world about Jesus, he preached. Pope Benedict was doing both the previous year when he came to that very basilica to call for a "new evangelization."

Catholics must find new ways to bring the gospel to "the many people out there who have heard of Jesus, and then forgotten," he said. "We are supposed to invite them back to the faith.... We are asked to be like Paul," he said. "Every one of us has within us the ability to do what Peter and Paul did."[231]

All cardinals have a figurehead role at a church in Rome, called their titular church. Pope Benedict gave Cardinal Wuerl an especially meaningful titular Church: the Church of St. Peter in Chains. In addition to Michelangelo's statue of Moses, it holds a set of chains that, legend has it, once bound St. Peter.

Some time after Pope Benedict had assigned him the church, the pope brought it up in conversation. "He reminded me that he had given me this church. He smiled and said, 'And I have the other one,' meaning the other one dedicated to St. Peter."[232]

Each cardinal's job is to advise the pope, both when they gather as a college, and through various Vatican offices—formally known as congregations—that the pope appoints them to. Cardinal Wuerl's appointments were significant from the start and have only grown more so.

When he was elevated to the College of Cardinals, Pope Benedict appointed him a voting member of the Congregation for Clergy—where he had once worked and had been a consultant since 1984—and to the Congregation for the Doctrine of the Faith, as well as to the Pontifical Council for Promoting Christian Unity, which oversees ecumenical relationships and also the relationship between the

Catholic Church and Jews.[233] Since his election Pope Francis has appointed Cardinal Wuerl a member of the Congregation for Bishops, the Pontifical Council for Culture, and the Administration of the Patrimony of the Apostolic See. These congregations and councils—meaning gatherings of cardinals and bishops—function as powerful committees or boards that oversee and set policy for the work of the Vatican.

• • • • • • •

Pope Benedict had already begun to make changes to the synod, with more opportunity for smaller group discussion and less time listening to hundreds of speeches that could just as easily have been read. But the 2012 Synod on the New Evangelization was a breakout event. Pope Benedict named Cardinal Wuerl the "relator" for the synod. This is a critically important role, involving organizing the work and summarizing the ideas of the synod, in order to produce final recommendations to the pope. To be chosen as a relator is a sign of great respect from the pope, and allows all of the cardinals to gain experience working with the chosen cardinal. Cardinal Karol Wojtyla was relator of a synod not long before his surprise election as Pope John Paul.

Among those the cardinal made a deep impression on at the Synod on the New Evangelization was Archbishop Gustavo García-Siller of San Antonio.

"The regular hours for the synod were very intense. He worked into the night to put together all of those reports on a daily basis," Archbishop García-Siller said. "People trusted him a lot. As we were preparing ourselves he gave us very good direction, but also very practical."

Cardinal Wuerl was able to explain some timing of the inner workings—so that, for example, someone could make sure that a speech was likely to be delivered on a particular day at a particular time.

"He is very wise and practical," Archbishop García-Siller said. "He knows how things work."

• • • • • • •

Something no one was prepared for was the first resignation of a pope in 600 years. On February 11, 2013, Pope Benedict announced he would step down at eight p.m. on February 28, citing deteriorating strength that he believed was limiting his capacity to fulfill his ministry. One result was that the cardinals would have significantly more time to prepare for an election, and without either the grief or the elaborate preparations and ceremonies of a funeral.

Cardinal Wuerl was among eleven cardinals from the United States eligible to vote in the conclave. After leading more than 2,000 people in a Mass of thanksgiving for the ministry of Pope Benedict, he left immediately for Rome.

This was the first conclave in which there was speculation by journalists who were experts on the Church about the possibility of an American pope. The Italian media, in particular, were taken with Cardinal Sean O'Malley of Boston, in the Capuchin robes that are a witness to the life and teachings of St. Francis of Assisi.

John Allen, the most authoritative American journalist covering the Vatican, wrote that if the cardinals were indeed open to a pope from the United States—an idea long dismissed because of an aversion to a pope from any superpower—then Cardinal Wuerl would most fit the profile that many cardinals were looking for. He cited Cardinal Wuerl's Vatican experience, his ability to confront Vatican bureaucrats about bad decisions, and his gift for building consensus among Church leaders.[234]

Already, in homilies before he left the United States, Cardinal Wuerl had spelled out what he believed were the top qualities needed in the next pope. First and foremost it was to engage with those who had left the Christian faith and become secularized and lead them back to the Church.[235]

He expounded on that in interviews and homilies in Rome. When the new pope is introduced to the world, he said in a homily at St. Peter in Chains, "He needs to step out onto that balcony and he needs to say, 'Christ is with us. We need to listen to him. He has the answers to the questions of the human heart. He shows us a better way to live than the secular world can offer."

In an interview he dismissed the idea that administrative skills would be the top priority of the cardinals, despite several scandals and a wide impression of chaos in the Vatican bureaucracy. While the need to clean up problems in Rome was real, he said, "I don't think I would necessarily put that as my first reason for choosing someone. A good evangelizing pope can always pick someone to oversee the curia. He can pick someone with administrative skills."

The focus of the conclave, he said, must be "the ability of the Church to bring the gospel once again to those who think they know what the gospel says and to whom they believe it has no meaning." That would require multiple channels of communication, especially in the new media that link so much of the world today, particularly among young people.[236]

. . . .

The cardinals would enter the conclave a month after Pope Benedict announced his resignation and twelve days after he stepped down. Prior to the conclave 150 cardinals gathered to make speeches about what they hoped to see in the next pope, but only 115 were under 80 and eligible to vote.

By numerous accounts, Cardinal Wuerl made a significant impact on the pre-conclave meetings by lobbying successfully for an extended coffee break, during which the cardinals could talk informally about their priorities and possible candidates. His predecessor in Washington, retired Cardinal Theodore McCarrick, was too old to vote, but was reportedly telling many people that if there was a deadlock among leading candidates, they should seriously consider his good friend Cardinal Jorge Mario Bergoglio from Buenos Aires.

Cardinal Wuerl had argued for the coffee break because, when there is a need to find middle ground, he said, "coffee breaks are when you do that."[237]

. . . .

It was apparent from the moment that Pope Francis stepped onto the balcony, with his simple greeting of "Brothers and sisters, good evening," that he would be a very different pope from his predecessors.

He asked the crowd for their silent blessing before he gave his. And, when he left the balcony, he refused the limousine and rode back to the Vatican guest house on a bus with the cardinals.

Cardinal Wuerl had worked with Cardinal Bergoglio at two synods, but had also asked many others about him during the pre-conclave meetings, where the Argentinian had made a favorable impression with a talk on the need for the Church to stay focused on its spiritual message.

He was chosen, Cardinal Wuerl said, "because every one of us is called to a relationship with God and we were looking for someone whose life says that."

With Pope Francis, "I think we are going to see a call to gospel simplicity. I think we are going to see a call to faithfulness to the rigorous demands of the gospel," he said hours after the election. "St. Francis of Assisi is the saint who tried to live literally the demands of the gospel...with complete and total trust in God. I think that is what Pope Francis will call us to do."[238]

There was evidence of that the next day when Pope Francis returned to his hotel in downtown Rome—actually a residence for visiting clergy where he had stayed many times—to personally pay his bill and bless the weeping staff members. Then he celebrated Mass for the cardinals, but even this tradition had a different tone. In it he warned that unless the Church gives a powerful witness to Jesus Christ, it becomes just another NGO—a non-governmental organization, just an ordinary nonprofit philanthropic corporation.

"The whole style of the Mass was in itself a message," Cardinal Wuerl said. Pope Francis discarded many trappings and formalities that set popes apart from other bishops, he said. Instead of vesting in a private area, he did so with the cardinals and wore simple vestments.

"It was just like I would do at the cathedral. When you are vesting with the priests, you are also talking with the priests around you. Many times they take the opportunity to ask a question or raise a point. He was doing the exact same thing," Cardinal Wuerl said.[239]

He announced he would not live in the papal apartments, but in the same Vatican guest house where the cardinals had stayed during the conclave.

It soon became clear that Pope Francis was serious about both evangelization and internal reform at the Vatican. He very quickly created a council of nine cardinals from archdioceses worldwide, to meet with him every two months to help set priorities for the Church.[240]

Eight months into his papacy, his nuncio to the United States, Archbishop Carlo Maria Vigano, delivered an address at the U.S. Conference of Catholic Bishops, saying that Pope Francis "wants bishops in tune with their people.... He wants pastoral bishops, not bishops who profess or follow a particular ideology."

Already there were prominent Catholics, including some bishops, who expressed concern that Pope Francis was straying from Church doctrine and discipline. Cardinal Wuerl was beginning to emerge as his greatest defender in the United States. The cardinal cited personal friends who had long fallen away from the Church and were returning to Mass because Pope Francis spoke to their hearts.

"It's the same teaching," he said. "It's just being said in a way that is more approachable."[241]

• • • • • • •

Cardinal Wuerl has been a loyal follower and defender of every pope he has served under, but with Pope Francis it's as if he has been allowed to be the bishop he always wanted to be. "Many, many people have told me he has come to life under this pope," Father Rosica said.

His communication skills are now being put to work across the global Church, starting with the interviews he did for major networks on the night Pope Francis was elected.

"The media love to speak with him and deal with him because they know they will get a hearing," said Father Rosica, who has asked him to take some very difficult interviews on issues of global concern to the Church. "The first way that he communicates is with his very person. He respects the person with whom he is speaking. That says everything. Even with a tendentious situation his gentlemanly style invites conversation."[242]

In June 2014 he gave an interview to a Protestant magazine, *Plough Quarterly*, which is published by a community of evangelical pacifists. In it he spoke of how often non-Catholics, including leaders of other churches, speak of their admiration for Pope Francis. "All over the world, Christians and other people see in him something wonderful. It's not some new teaching; he is saying he same thing that the church has been saying for 2,000 years. But with him, people see someone doing it.... They look at him and say, 'This is the way it should be.'

"I was in an ecumenical and interfaith gathering...and Christians of different faith communities spoke as if Francis were everybody's pope. What struck me particularly was the remark from one interfaith participant: 'You know, he is showing all of us religious leaders how we are supposed to live our lives.'"[243] In the fall of 2013, Cardinal Wuerl wrote several essays for the Jesuit magazine America, interpreting Pope Francis. In one on Pope Francis and the New Evangelization, he wrote that the interviews and talks Pope Francis has given echo his talk to the cardinals in the pre-conclave meetings "to speak to the issue that people are struggling with; but first and foremost to bring them an experience, a sense of God's love."[244]

As attacks on Pope Francis have come from the Catholic right—often from those who were stalwarts in defending the authority of previous popes, and the need for Catholics to respect what they say—Cardinal Wuerl has mounted defenses of Pope Francis in his blog, "Seek First the Kingdom."

On March 11, 2015, he reflected back on his experiences as a seminarian during Vatican II.

At the time, he said, he heard stories of great divisions within the council, and asked Bishop Wright if they wouldn't weaken the church, especially when the issues at stake were "settled Church practice and teaching." Even one of his professors had warned that Pope John XXIII might be leading the Church astray.

Bishop Wright, he wrote, reminded him of the discussions, debates, and formulation of new language at the Council of Nicaea. The Second Vatican Council "was doing...what bishops in communion with Peter have always, in one format or another, done. They have gathered to speak with clarity, listen with humility, and be open to the Spirit. Speaking about how best to proclaim and live the Gospel is not a threat to Church unity. The challenge comes from those who will not accept the validity of the discussion, want to impose their own views as if they alone were in possession of the one true faith, and call into question the fidelity of everyone else."[245]

• • • • • • •

There was a great deal of media attention in late 2013 when Pope Francis named Cardinal Wuerl to the Congregation for Bishops. He replaced a respected canonist whom the media tagged as far more "conservative."

John Thavis, a veteran Vatican correspondent for Catholic News Service, remarked that the appointment of Cardinal Wuerl is "yet another sign that the new pope wants people in sync with his pastoral vision of the Church, and in particular with his views on what makes a good bishop."[246]

When a diocese opens up, the papal nuncio in that country begins a confidential consultation process to bring up names of bishops or priests who might be good to appoint. When he has collected the information, he writes a report and sends it to Rome for members of the Congregation for Bishops to review. It is a process that has sometimes been fraught with church politics.

Last year, Cardinal Wuerl said, Pope Francis came to the Congregation for Bishops and "told us that what the Church needs are bishops who are pastors of souls," he said. "Bishops have to be pastors. They have to be people who are concerned first and foremost for their flock. And that is what you should look for. He told us that if the information comes to you and you look at it and say 'All of these are very fine people, but none of them seem to have much pastoral experience,' then *send it back*."

In the past, Cardinal Wuerl said, "I think there was sometimes a tendency to look for doctrinal formation, theological preparation, or even canonical preparation. The person served in administration and came up through those ranks. Not that there is anything wrong with that, but we are being told that it has to be balanced with pastoral experience. We all know that your response from the ivory tower can be different from your pastoral response in the field hospital."

The pope has often compared the Church to a field hospital in a war zone.

"I think the way the pope has used that image, field hospitals are where the action is. Clearly it's not the perfect medical setting, but it's saving a life. Aren't we supposed to be saving spiritual lives?"

Cardinal Wuerl was an ideal choice for the Congregation for Bishops, Father Rosica said.

"He understands what kind of bishop Pope Francis wants. For a person in Cardinal Wuerl's position, this is a very key position. You are dealing with a lot of Americans and English-speaking appointments. If you have a very seasoned bishop who understands what it is to be a bishop and what the pope expects of bishops, that is very helpful."

The appointment itself was a signal of the kind of bishop Pope Francis wants. Vatican journalist John Allen wrote in the National Catholic Reporter: "Putting in the moderate Wuerl and taking the strongly conservative [Cardinal Raymond] Burke off couldn't help but seem a signal of the kind of bishop Francis intends to elevate in the United States," he wrote. "The kind of man Francis picks for the Congregation for Bishops is, in effect, a proxy for the kind of bishops he wants this panel to identify."[147]

Michael Sean Winters, a commentator on Church matters, wrote in the *Washingtonian* that the appointment marked something far more significant than a personal feud. He cited accounts that Cardinal Wuerl had, in fact, tried to mend the relationship with Cardinal

Burke during the consistory when they were both elevated, and had been rebuffed.

"One can make too much of the politics of Wuerl's new assignment. Popes don't normally use staff decisions to settle personal scores. Nor should Wuerl's promotion be interpreted as a triumph for Catholic progressives. He's no firebrand, and only the most arch of archconservatives would consider him a liberal. Instead he has a track record as a moderate intent on managing staff, reconciling budgets and seeking compromise in a pastoral manner," Winters wrote.[248]

Being a cardinal gave Archbishop Wuerl not only key influence inside the Church, but far greater visibility. Now he has even more opportunities to help the world at large understand Catholic teaching —not the obscure debates of theologians, but the meat and potatoes of doctrine.

With his book The Teaching of Christ, *written with Ronald Lawler and Thomas Comerford Lawler. Courtesy of the Diocesan Archives of the Diocese of Pittsburgh.*

CHAPTER 14:
"MEAT AND POTATOES" DOCTRINE

Father Wuerl's first years as a priest were years of global cultural revolution. New media were beginning to promote a new morality. In the United States and in Europe, there was unrest on college campuses. Old social orders were giving way under pressure from voter initiatives and acts of civil disobedience.

It was perhaps inevitable that the tumult would affect the Church. The decade had begun with a Council, and Pope Saint John XXIII inaugurated the Council with promises to throw open the windows to let fresh air into the Church. Pope John described the event with the Italian word *aggiornamento*—a "todaying" of the Church.

It turned out to be a process fraught with difficulties. Catholic theologians and pundits took up, tested, and applied to the Church one after another of the propositions that were rocking the worlds of culture and politics. Controversy always simmered near the boiling point, as every passionate argument was met with equally passionate counter-arguments.

In his 2015 pastoral letter on Catholic identity, Cardinal Wuerl re-called those days: "When I was a young priest in the 1960s and 1970s, there was much experimentation and confusion in the Church. Teachers and clergy were encouraged by some to communi-cate an experience of God's love, but to do it without reference to the Creed, the sacraments, or Church tradition. It did not work very well. Catholics grew up with the impression that their heritage was little more than warm, vaguely positive feelings about God."[249]

In the heat of the moment, the bishops of the Netherlands commissioned a group of *avant garde* theologians to bring together a catechism reflective of the range of current thought. The result was published in 1966 and soon appeared in English translation as *A New Catechism: Catholic Faith for Adults*. But it was popularly known as "The Dutch Catechism."

Time magazine described the Dutch Catechism as "lively" and "undogmatic," reflective of "the most recent radical insights of theologians and scripture scholars."[250] The Dutch bishops distanced themselves from the text as their colleagues overseas refused to grant the book an *imprimatur*, the sign of Church approval. Pope Blessed Paul VI summoned a commission of six cardinals to evaluate the text. In 1968 the Vatican issued a declaration on the book, judging its presentation of the faith to be defective in many areas—including the doctrines of creation, original sin, the virginal conception of Jesus, the atonement, the sacrifice of the Mass, the hierarchical priesthood, the real presence of Jesus in the Eucharist, and the very foundations of moral theology. In these and other areas, the book presented the Church's official teaching alongside other, contrary views, as if all were equivalent options.

Yet the controversies—and even the condemnations—surrounding the Dutch Catechism only gave the book greater publicity. Sales rocketed in the United States, and it was widely used as a college text by professors advocating for change in the Church's doctrine and practice. By 1973, on the strength of publicity, the book had achieved a quasi-authoritative status in certain circles. Its weak association with the Dutch hierarchy was still the strongest claim of any recent catechism on the market.

• • • • • • •

In Rome, Cardinal John Wright wished to remedy that situation. The Congregation for the Clergy, where both he and Father Wuerl served as officials, had authority over *catechesis*—the teaching of Church doctrine.

In 1973 the cardinal was hosting Pittsburghers at a dinner party in Rome, and the conversation turned toward his concern about the lack of a clear and engaging summary of the Catholic faith. Among the guests were Father Wuerl and Father Ronald Lawler, a Capuchin moral theologian. Another of the dinner guests was Pittsburgh businessman Frank Schneider.[251] As the men discussed the current crisis in the field of catechetics, Cardinal Wright said that what was needed was a new, authoritative catechism. Schneider said that he would gladly fund such a project, and Fathers Lawler and Wuerl volunteered to gather a world-class team of contributing writers. (They were soon joined in the project by Lawler's brother, Thomas, who was a scholar of the early Church Fathers and an executive in the Central Intelligence Agency.)

In recruiting contributors, Wuerl would later recall, "We had clear selection criteria. Our writers had to have competence in their particular area. They had to communicate clearly. And most importantly: *sentire cum ecclesia*—they had to believe with the Church."[252]

Invitations went out to John Finnis, a renowned British lawyer and writer on moral theology; Dominican Father Jordan Aumann, known for his work in spiritual theology; theologians Germain Grisez and Father Lorenzo Albacete; Archbishop John Whealon of Hartford, a scripture scholar; Father John Hugo, a leader in the liturgical renewal; Johannes Quasten, the great scholar of the early Church; and others.

The three editors set to writing their own sections and editing the others' contributions as they came in. They would meet in Washington, D.C., or Pittsburgh for marathon editing sessions. Father Wuerl spent the summer of 1974 hunkered down with the Lawlers in a sweltering monastery basement in Washington, drafting the first edition. They began each day with Mass, then worked till bedtime, breaking for meals and to read the Divine Office. Sometimes Archbishop Whealon would join them and impose his high standards for simplicity and clarity. He named his imaginary ideal reader "Mrs. Magillicuddy," and his constant refrain was: "Mrs. Magillicuddy would not understand that." And, if Mrs. Magillicuddy wouldn't understand, Fathers Wuerl and Lawler had to change the text.[253]

It was a challenge, they said, to make so many brilliant contributions fit well together and speak with one literary voice. Through it
all, they kept in mind their goal of a "meat-and-potatoes catechism,"
Bishop Wuerl said. "We weren't going to do a lot of flourishes. We
were simply going to say what the Church said, with as much as possible in the Church's own words, from Scripture and Tradition."[254]

The finished product was *The Teaching of Christ: A Catholic Catechism for Adults*. It appeared in 1975, published in the United States
by Our Sunday Visitor. Widely respected by theologians and the hierarchy, it became a bestseller and a standard, authoritative text. The
pioneering Dominican theologian Yves Congar called it "a complete
account of Christian teaching and Christian faith."

When the book was published, the three authors presented Pope
Paul VI with a copy.[255] Father Lawler became Father Wuerl's spiritual director, a relationship that lasted until the Capuchin's death in
2003.Forty years later, it is still in print. Revised editions appeared in
1983, 1991, 1995, and 2004.

· · · · · · · ·

The Teaching of Christ had been only a beginning for Father
Wuerl. The mission of teaching sound doctrine became a driving
passion. In addition to his work with the Congregation for the
Clergy, he wrote on doctrinal issues for the Vatican's official newspaper, *L'Osservatore Romano*, as well as for *Our Sunday Visitor*, the
largest-circulation Catholic weekly in the United States.

His program was ambitious. He told one interviewer: "We need to
rebuild our faith from the foundations—the most basic teachings. I
have considered that work essential to my vocation since I was a
young priest."[256]

The doctrinal confusion of the 1960s and '70s had, he observed,
"left so many lay people weak, spiritually and intellectually, and unable to withstand the tsunami of secularism that came in the last
decades of the century. We lost many people because we had failed to
teach them about right and wrong, about the common good, about
the nature of the family and the objective moral order."

The book *The Teaching of Christ* would, in time, become a television series, "The Teaching of Christ," which aired Sunday mornings on Pittsburgh's CBS affiliate for almost two decades. It also appeared for a while on the Eternal Word Television Network and later in cable syndication.

Other spinoffs followed. With the Lawler brothers he prepared a question-and-answer catechism titled *The Gift of Faith* (2001), based on their work in *The Teaching of Christ*. They also produced a study guide and an abridged version of the book. As bishop, Wuerl adapted material from the catechism for use in several video series he hosted, to be used by parishes for sacramental preparation.

As a Vatican official and later as a bishop, he has been a prolific and programmatic author. His early books focused on historical studies: *The Forty Martyrs: New Saints of England and Wales* (1971) and *Fathers of the Church* (1975). Later efforts were largely doctrinal, including a study of holy orders (*The Catholic Priesthood Today,* 1976), and popular books on Catholicism and public life (*Seek First the Kingdom,* 2011), on the creed (*A Faith That Transforms Us,* 2013), on the sacrament of confession (*The Light Is on for You,* 2014), on the Third Person of the Trinity (*Open to the Holy Spirit,* 2014), on marriage (*The Marriage God Wants for You,* 2015), and on prayer (*Ways to Pray,* 2015). He wrote another summary treatment of the faith, *The Catholic Way: Faith for Living Today* (2001), which had been serialized in Columbia magazine, the official publication of the Knights of Columbus.

• • • • • • •

His personal catechesis has been prodigious. The paragraph above lists only a fraction of his book titles. Yet he has always understood that propositions are not the only way—or the primary way—the Church passes on the faith. He made the point as he explained his trilogy of books published between 2011 and 2014. The subjects of those books—*The Mass, The Church,* and *The Feasts*—were, he told interviewers, the three most basic touchstones for an ordinary parishioner.

The arrangement is...intentional. The books focus on three fundamental ways the Church passes on the tradition received from the Apostles.

The primary way is through the liturgy, especially the Mass. At every Sunday Mass we review basic doctrine when we recite the creed; we listen to four readings from Sacred Scripture; we listen to a homily that interprets the Scripture and supplies us with practical spiritual advice; and we offer prayers that Catholics have prayed since the first century. The Mass is not a CCD class, but we can't deny that it's one of the chief ways we're educated in the faith.

In a similar way, our churches are constructed to teach us the saving truths. They do this through representational art, like the Stations of the Cross, but also through the very shape of the building. Our buildings, like our ritual, serve as our tutors in the faith.

Finally, there are the feasts of the Church's calendar. At the beginning of our book we quote a rabbi who said that the calendar is like a catechism. I couldn't agree more. As I said a moment ago, when we celebrate Christmas, we are—effortlessly—reviewing our doctrine of the incarnation of the Son of God. When we celebrate the saints, we are schooling ourselves about our own salvation.

•••••••

Perhaps no area of doctrine has been more misunderstood—and sometimes simply rejected—than Catholic sexual morality. In his years as Bishop of Pittsburgh, Wuerl sought to remedy this through *The Catholic Vision of Love,* a comprehensive curriculum, spanning all ages and every grade, involving not only religion teachers, but families as well. Its materials approached the subject in a positive way —thus its title, which emphasized a vision for family life and society rather than simply the prohibitions of the Commandments. Yet the prohibitions were there, too, presented in the context of the Church's vision.

The program drew opposition from some who dissented from the Church's doctrine on sexual morality, but also from a few who claimed it was a program in "sex education." The charges did not hold up as the curriculum included no detailed discussions of the biology of sex. Bishop Wuerl took criticisms into consideration, ensured parental involvement, and pressed on with the program, which he saw as an urgently needed remedial course in a vital area of Church teaching. "The Church has good news to proclaim about the family, love and human sexuality," Bishop Wuerl wrote in introducing the program in 1994. "This teaching is firmly rooted in sacred scripture and has been constantly taught by the Church through the centuries." In January 1995 the program was reviewed, approved, and praised by the Vatican Congregation for the Clergy, in a letter cosigned by the cardinal prefect and archbishop secretary.

· · · · · · ·

Cardinal Wuerl's episcopal colleagues have recognized his passion for doctrine and elected him chairman of the USCCB's Committee on Doctrine and chairman of the editorial board that oversaw the composition of the *United States Catholic Catechism for Adults.* In his time as chair of the Doctrine Committee, the bishops issued a critique of the work of Elizabeth A. Johnson, a Sister of St. Joseph of Brentwood, N.Y., and a professor at Fordham University. When the bishops' critique drew harsh responses in the media, Cardinal Wuerl produced a guidebook titled "Bishops as Teachers: A Resource for Bishops." In it he once again emphasized the importance of the fundamentals of Catholic faith and identity, even for theologians and even for bishops: "By taking the truth of revelation as a starting point, it should be pointed out that theological inquiry is not diminished but in fact enhanced, since it is only—as in every other discipline—by building on what is confidently known that deeper and fuller investigation can be pursued."

Like his brother bishops in the United States, the popes, too, have often expressed appreciation for Cardinal Wuerl's articulation and defense of authentic Catholic teaching. In 2012, Pope Benedict XVI appointed him a cardinal member of the Congregation for the Doctrine of the Faith. Pope Benedict also appointed him relator general for the 2012 Synod of Bishops on the New Evangelization. In his opening report, Cardinal Wuerl again expressed his concern that "a tsunami of secular influence has swept across the cultural landscape, taking with it such societal markers as marriage, family, the concept of the common good and objective right and wrong." He went on: "Secularization has fashioned two generations of Catholics who do not know the Church's foundational prayers. Many do not sense a value in Mass attendance, fail to receive the sacrament of penance and have often lost a sense of mystery or the transcendent as having any real and verifiable meaning."

His concerns in 2012 match rather exactly those that fueled his first writing efforts in the early 1970s. If the Church has slowed the tide of secularization at all, it is in some measure due to the determined efforts of teachers like Donald Wuerl.

He has often expressed his fidelity in terms of trust. He emphasizes that he is not free to change doctrine to suit his own or anyone else's contrary wishes, whims, or deeply held convictions. "We have received something in the Church that is not ours; it the Lord's. As his faithful stewards, we are accountable to the Lord, not to the contrary demands of the culture. We need to remain connected to Christ and be true to the mission he has entrusted to us."[257]

And sometimes that fidelity means taking a stand that may not be popular. Truth does not change with fashion. Still, Cardinal Wuerl has always tried to put the message of Christ's love first when he tackles the difficult issues.

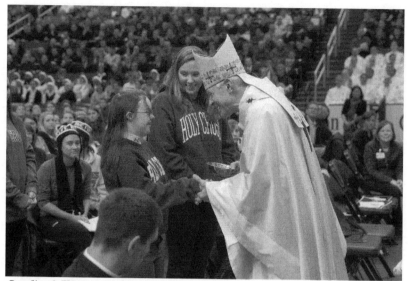

Cardinal Wuerl receives the altar gifts from Academy of the Holy Cross students at the 2015 Youth Rally and Mass for Life in Washington. Catholic Standard *photo by Jaclyn Lippelmann. Used with permission.*

Waving tot the crowd at the Mass for Life. Catholic Standard *photo by Jaclyn Lippelmann. Used with permission.*

Speaking to the media in Rome. Catholic Standard *photos by Paul Fetters.*
Used with permission.

CHAPTER 15:
THE DIFFICULT ISSUES

"A prophet isn't judged by the acceptance of the message but by his fidelity to the message," Cardinal Wuerl once said. "I think that is also true of a bishop. You shouldn't allow yourself to be judged by how popular or how accepted what you had to say was, but by whether or not it is true."

No matter what the issue has been or which diocese he has been in, Cardinal Wuerl has always followed his original charge from Pope John Paul II to maintain unity. He is disturbed by polarization in the Church, whether it is coming from the right or the left, or simply from people upset about a decision involving their parish. He is deeply troubled when people who believe they are defending Church positions do so in ways that reek of hostility and judgmentalism.

The heart of the Church's teaching is summarized in the creeds, but the Church has continually re-examined how those core doctrines are applied pastorally in each era, he said.

"Many times the voices we hear are more reflective of the culture than of the faith, but we shouldn't be too quick to conclude that anything that sounds different from the expression of Church life today must somehow be wrong," he said. "It's very important that we distinguish between what is at the very core and heart of the faith and what are the ways of living it that may be more conditioned by the moment. That is the challenge of balancing. You want to make sure that we are not listening more to a politically correct culture than to the stirrings of the Holy Spirit."

Asked to identify what he considers the most critical issue facing the Church today, he said it's not a specific issue but the underlying premise that there is a right and a wrong for how people are to live. "Whether you are talking about the killing of unborn children or immigration and the question of how to control the flow of people into to the country or the death penalty—morality covers everything," he said.

Within the popular culture "secularists have reduced morality to whatever you can get 51 per cent of the vote for. That becomes right."

Although Cardinal Wuerl is deeply concerned with both public and private morality, "he is not a culture-warrior bishop," said Michael Sean Winters, who writes on Catholic social policy for the liberal *National Catholic Reporter.* "He is a churchman. He is someone who knows Church history, who knows the theology and the canons of the Church. But that is not the same as being a moderate. The moderate is lacking in zeal, and there is nothing fuzzy about him, there is nothing compromised. He is someone who thinks with the mind of the Church."

• • • • • • •

Thinking with the mind of the Church means putting the needs of the poor and helpless first. Although he has never been perceived as a social activist, Cardinal Wuerl has always cared deeply about a broad range of social issues, and has taken action on them, said Father Frank Almade, a Pittsburgh priest who formerly served as his director for social concerns.

When he took that job, Father Almade said, his predecessor told him, "the one thing you will never have to convince Bishop Wuerl of is the value of Catholic social teaching or the social concerns of the Catholic Church. I absolutely found that, especially in matters of health care. I never found him anything other than understanding and supportive."

The first major social issue he addressed in Pittsburgh was not of his own choosing. A few months after his installation, the city council took up a proposed gay-rights ordinance that was drafted in a way that would have required the Catholic Church and other religious bodies to hire teachers and other key employees whose way of life was clearly counter to the teachings of the faith. Rather than denouncing the bill outright, he sought a compromise that would create an exemption for religious bodies.

"Defending civil rights and supporting this specific piece of legislation are two separate issues," he wrote in a letter to his priests. "While I will work with any and all to defend human dignity and civil rights, I must oppose legislation that, under the guise of civil rights, violates the religious rights of all affected by this vague, unclear and undifferentiated view."[258]

That bill was defeated. More than a year later an amended gay-rights bill, drafted after consultation with his office, passed without opposition from the Diocese of Pittsburgh.[259]

But when a similar issue came up in Washington in 2009, there was an explosion of harsh media coverage. The city council decided to force agencies with which it had contracts to provide benefits for same-sex partners. Catholic Charities was receiving close to $20 million a year from the district to provide social services: a Spanish-language medical clinic, tutoring for GEDs, nine homeless shelters, foster care and mental health services.[260] Loss of those contracts could seriously impair those services, archdiocesan officials said, but the Church could not provide same-sex spousal benefits because the Church teaches that marriage can only be between a man and a woman. "That was one of the most difficult periods for the archdiocese," said Jane Belford, who was chancellor at the time. "We were portrayed as bigots and intolerant."

The archdiocese was not trying to stop the city from recognizing same-sex marriage: what it wanted was a religious exemption to allow the Church to uphold its own teaching about the nature of marriage. The Church recognizes that the city council "is firmly committed to opening marriage to homosexual couples," Archbishop Wuerl wrote in an op-ed for the *Washington Post.* "We are asking that new language be developed that more fairly balances different interests— those of the city to redefine marriage and those of faith groups so that they can continue to provide services without compromising their deeply held religious teachings and beliefs."

Catholic Charities serves more than 100,000 people each year in Washington and its Maryland suburbs, without regard to sexual orientation or any other state of life, he wrote. "This legislation won't end Catholic Charities' services, but it would reduce unnecessarily the resources available for outreach."[261]

After lobbying vigorously but unsuccessfully for an exemption for religious institutions, the Cardinal initiated a compromise that kept Catholic Charities open: Although family benefits for current employees would be grandfathered in, future married employees would not receive spousal health insurance. This, however was compensated for by a cash benefit package that helped married employees to pay for such insurance privately.

Cardinal Wuerl said he would have preferred a less confrontational approach, but that was made difficult both by some personalities in District government and by leaders of the U.S. Conference of Catholic Bishops who asked him "not to do anything that would appear to weaken the argument of others who were litigating this issue."

Since then the issue of same-sex civil marriage has been settled by the June 2015 ruling of the U.S. Supreme Court, he said, and the archdiocese is re-examining how to provide spousal benefits in a way that will not confuse people about the difference between a civil marriage and a sacramental union in the Church.

"If the definition in the law says you must give spousal benefits and this person is a spouse, then we would do it," Cardinal Wuerl said. "It's already done with divorce and remarriage" in instances where the second marriage has not been sanctioned by the Church.

Cardinal Wuerl said he has met personally with representatives of gay-advocacy groups since he was Bishop of Pittsburgh. "The conversations are fruitful, I think, because many homosexuals feel wounded by the Church. It's one thing to say that the Church considers what you are doing to be wrong; it's another thing to say that there is something wrong with you. And I think that distinction is becoming increasingly clear."

When Catholics have "difficulty accepting any of the teachings or the discipline of the Church, there is more to be gained by trying to convince them of the truth of the church's position than there is by slamming a door in their face," he said in a 1996 interview that would anticipate the words of Pope Francis nearly two decades later. "You work with people where they are and hope they will move to where you want them to be."[262]

. . . .

He made every effort to reach people, especially young people, with a compelling case for the Church's teaching on sexuality. In Pittsburgh, the diocese developed a K-12 curriculum, "The Catholic Vision of Love," for teaching about marriage and sexuality. He wrote two pastoral letters on the topic specifically for teenagers.

"The deep loneliness of the human heart is to be remedied by a love that is faithful and generous. Sex is not a trivial gift; it is genuine and fully human only when it expresses the kind of love that leads a man and a woman to give themselves entirely to each other and brings them close to God," he wrote in his 1992 pastoral letter *Love and Sexuality*.

"The sexual revolution promised a paradise on earth, but it created instead a wilderness of broken homes, child abuse, epidemics of sexual diseases and an immense increase of pregnancies among the very young. Under its banner many children were born not into secure and loving homes, but into broken families and into circumstances that promised little hope. The cruelty of massive abortion for personal convenience is the deadly fruit of the modern sexual revolution."

. . . .

Abortion is an injustice that he addressed frequently and in multiple contexts.

One of his strongest emphases was on providing and supporting alternatives for women with crisis pregnancies. Early in his tenure the Diocese of Pittsburgh made a commitment to provide social services and pastoral care for women with crisis pregnancies, single mother and women who had had abortions. It accomplished this through a network of diocesan and other services.

Any woman who fears she cannot cope with a pregnancy or with raising a child should "ring the doorbell at the nearest Catholic rectory and say, 'I need help.' The people at the church would take it from there," he said.[263]

He was a frequent visitor and personal supporter of Mom's House —later known as Angel's Place—a pro-life service center providing free day care and parenting support to single parents who are full-time students.[264]

Not only would he visit the Rosalia Center—a home for pregnant women that was founded in the nineteenth century to care for abandoned babies—but he would invite the residents to his own home to watch a movie together. Given their diverse backgrounds and his reserved nature, "that wasn't an easy thing for Cardinal Wuerl to do, but he did it in small doses and he did it intentionally," said Archbishop Hebda, who was his priest-secretary in the early 1990s. "He was always good with kids and wanted them to talk to him. And then they would appear in his homilies."

In 1989 he wrote the first of several pastoral letters on life issues that included abortion.

"These issues include every aspect of human life—prenatal care, birth, nurture, and growth, marriage and family life, housing, employment, care for the disabled and handicapped, ministry to those with AIDS, rehabilitation of those addicted to alcohol and drugs, care of the elderly—indeed any issue related to the dignity of human life," he wrote.

Nevertheless, abortion is "the most important social and moral issue of our age" because it deliberately kills a defenseless unborn child, he wrote. "Sometimes we are told this is a 'rights' issue, the right of a woman to have power over her own body. There is always sentiment in support of personal rights. As Catholics and as Americans we feel an almost instinctive reaction to support 'rights.' Yet in pregnancy we have two lives. We know that it is good and reasonable to limit the 'rights' of one person when they touch the life of another. We seek to limit the 'right' to drink when it comes to drunk driving. We recognize that all civil rights are rooted in the basic human right to life. No 'legal' right to abortion can erase the primordial and God-given right of the child in the womb to life."[265]

That same year, the diocese sponsored a conference on post-abortion counseling, and six years later formally established a Project Rachel ministry to offer healing, support, and reconciliation to women who regretted their abortions. In 2000 post-abortion healing was the sole topic of his Easter pastoral letter during the Great Jubilee.[266]

To illustrate the value of every human life, one of the artists he invited to perform during the diocese's 150th anniversary celebration was Tony Melendez, a singer and guitarist born without arms who played guitar with his toes. In 1994 he dedicated a memorial to unborn children at St. Mary of Mercy, the parish next door to his office in Downtown Pittsburgh.[267]

In 1999 another of his letters on abortion was directed toward people who don't consider themselves pro-life, but who, in fact, support many restrictions on the availability of abortion. The letter put as much emphasis on changing hearts as it did on changing the law.

"The role of the Church is not primarily to deal with legislation but to deal with conscience and the human heart," he wrote in *God's Good Gift of Life*.

It was a good summary of Bishop Wuerl's whole approach to political issues.

· · · · · · ·

Politically, Donald Wuerl was raised in a straight-ticket Democratic neighborhood where union membership was second only to Church membership, and regarded as a gift from God. But as a bishop, he has worked each issue through without concerning himself with its party alignment.

"To this day, I have no idea what Don's political affiliation is," his brother Wayne Wuerl once said.

That's by design. He has consistently urged the bishops to speak as pastors, not as politicians.

"The political preferences of a priest should be personal and private. That goes all the more for a bishop. A bishop should have very strong social-justice positions that grow out of his faith and the teaching of the Church, but he should not be recognized as a partisan politician," Cardinal Wuerl said. "There is no political party that addresses adequately all of the teaching of the Church and all of the positions of the Church. And so why associate yourself with any one party? Associate yourself with the principles and let the people decide how that will be articulated."

Throughout his ministry as a diocesan bishop he has been criticized by some Catholic advocacy groups who expected him to excommunicate or otherwise censure Catholic politicians who voted to support legal abortion. He finds that approach neither pastoral or productive, and has kept his conversations with politicians private.

"When you are dealing with the whole range of human issues, if someone agrees with you on a lot of them and disagrees with you on some of them, don't you still want to keep talking and working? Because on a lot of things that you agree upon, good things for people can be done," he said.[268]

When Bishop Wuerl said he had private conversations with Catholic legislators about the morality of their policies, he meant it, Archbishop Hebda said. "People may think the conversations never took place, but he would have been willing to enter into those hard discussions."

Those hard discussions would have included the subject of abortion. They would also have included another side of the pro-life issue: the death penalty.

· · · · · · ·

Cardinal Wuerl has always taken a firm stand on the death penalty, even in cases where there was strong local sentiment for execution. He listed the death penalty alongside abortion as a life issue in several pastoral letters and in 2005 devoted one solely to that topic.

While the Church must offer support and care to those victimized by deadly crime, he wrote, "How we respond to offenders also says much about what we value. As Christians we must respond to them in ways that are reflective of the teachings of Christ, imitating his steadfast compassion and forgiveness."

Those who follow Jesus "are called to recognize the face of God in everyone—even the criminal."[269]

In 2000, he joined the other bishops of Pennsylvania in pleading for Governor Tom Ridge to grant clemency to Daniel M. Saranchak, who was scheduled to be executed for the murder of his uncle and grandmother seven years earlier. The execution was not carried out.[270]

He opposed the death penalty for two mass murderers who had gone on shooting rampages in Pittsburgh, killing victims at random.

In March 2000, Ronald Taylor was sentenced to death for the racially motivated shooting of three white men in a community just outside of Pittsburgh. One of the victims was a former priest. Bishop Wuerl criticized the use of the death penalty.

"It is regrettable that, once again, a choice has been made to respond to violence with more violence," he said. "We have the means to protect society from even the most violent criminal without having to resort to the death penalty. Life imprisonment without parole serves the need for justice and at the same time reaffirms the essential dignity of all human life."[271]

Less than two months after the Taylor massacre, Richard Baumhammers, a mentally ill attorney, had targeted immigrants and synagogues on a one-day rampage across the region in April 2000, killing five people and paralyzing a sixth. He was given five death sentences.

Bishop Wuerl issued a statement saying that "the use of the death penalty, even in extremely serious circumstances, diminishes our society's commitment to recognize the dignity and worth of all human life, even of a person convicted of the terrible destruction of human life."[272]

In 2003 he joined the leaders of the major Christian traditions in the Pittsburgh region in calling on the governor and state legislature to impose a moratorium on use of the death penalty.[273]

But perhaps Bishop Wuerl's greatest challenge to public opinion in the Pittsburgh region was his high-profile call for gun control.

• • • • • • •

Hunting is a tradition with deep roots in the countryside around Pittsburgh. Many school districts in Southwestern Pennsylvania shut down for the opening of deer season. The bishop himself grew up hunting small game with his older brother.

But his work on the Youth Crime Prevention Council—a regional effort to stem deadly gang violence in the 1990s—had convinced him that measures were necessary. When it was discovered that money embezzled from one of his parishes had been used in part to purchase a gun collection, rather than sell the guns to help recoup the loss, the bishop ordered them melted down.[274] Then, in the spring of 2000, came the Taylor and Baumhammers mass murders.

In both cases, Bishop Wuerl immediately held special Masses to pray for the victims, their families, and the affected communities. But after the second shooting, he went further. At Tree of Life Syn-agogue, he delivered a much-quoted speech on the need for gun con-trol.[275] "Guns must be treated like any other potentially dangerous consumer product," he told the gathering of community leaders. Products from children's pajamas to bottle caps "are all regulated by a society that is more afraid of the lid of an aspirin bottle than it is by an assault weapon.... Guns alone are exempt from such regulation."[276]

"We had some really bad incidents here," he recalled years later. "We talked in those days about what I thought was common-sense gun control. We weren't talking about taking guns away from hunters. We were talking about military-style weapons finding their way into the hands of people. When police officials tell you they have less firepower than some of the people they are tying to corral, you have to say there is an imbalance here."

. . . .

Gun control was a hot issue, but racism was more insidious. Almost everyone agrees in principle that racism is bad, but Bishop Wuerl insisted that Catholics in historically white neighborhoods must grapple with its reality.

In 1996 he wrote a pastoral letter *Confronting Racism Today,* to encourage all people of good will to work together against personal social and institutional racism. It was grounded in the conviction that all human beings are made in the image of God, but it descended to the practical questions of what every Catholic could do to combat racism. "This includes expressly rejecting racial stereotypes, slurs, and jokes. We can also be an influence on co-workers, friends and family members by speaking out on the injustice of racism."

The diocese sponsored gatherings throughout the region for laity, religious and clergy to examine their lives, ministries and parishes for any forms of racism, and eliminate it. In 1999 he revised and updated the pastoral letter in order to continue the push.

His contact with the Urban League of Pittsburgh was critical to sensitizing him both to the level of personal bigotry and to the institutional prejudice manifested in everything from incarceration rates for minor offenses to failure to maintain roads in black neighborhoods. The reality was also driven home by some racist reaction to diocesan programs such as the Extra Mile Foundation, which supported Catholic schools in predominantly black, Protestant neighborhoods in Pittsburgh.

Sister Margaret Hannan, then the chancellor of the diocese, recalled an administrative board meeting at which one of the priests on the staff observed that asking white Catholics to discover their own racism would make a lot of people very uncomfortable. The bishop responded, "That is what we are supposed to do. We have to get them out of their comfort zone."

. . . .

No matter what the issue, Cardinal Wuerl's personal approach has never favored public demonstrations apart from special Masses.

Some pro-life activists wanted him out in the streets with them, "but no one from the chancery has ever been down in front of Planned Parenthood," said Helen Cindrich, president of People Concerned for the Unborn Child, in 2006.[277] That was not a criticism on her part, because she understood his work behind the scenes and his generous donations to pro-life causes and social services. "Bishop Wuerl works on a diplomatic level. He would not be the person you would see [protesting] on the street," she said. Political diplomacy aside, he has a deep, longstanding interest in bioethics and in teaching other Catholic bishops to evaluate new scientific and medical possibilities using the principles of their faith. In 1980, years before he became a bishop, he helped to launch the bi-annual bioethics workshop for bishops sponsored by the National Catholic Bioethics Center.

"The whole idea of the workshops was to help all of us keep up scientifically on what was going on and to hear from the best in moral theology about how you balance what we can do with what we ought to do," he said.

One presentation was by a prominent expert on genetic engineering who began his talk by saying "I don't share your faith and I disagree with many of your conclusions, but you must never stop speaking because, if you do, there will be no one calling us to moral reflection," Cardinal Wuerl recalled.

"I think that is one of the reasons why the Catholic Church is always under so much attack in so much of the media. We are speaking about a morality that so much of Hollywood and so much of modern culture simply doesn't want to hear about."

Just because something is possible doesn't make it right, he said. But the Church also needs to be careful not to reflexively dismiss new possibilities precisely because they are new. It needs time to carefully examine them and consider all the moral implications. "Not everything that you can do you should do," he said. "On the other hand we also need to be looking at all the things that are technologically possible to see if the principles we are using to judge whether they should or shouldn't be done is broad enough," mentioning specifically some practices to help infertile couples conceive. "That brings us back to the natural moral order, which does have a claim on all of us. But it needs a lot of prayerful study before you start applying moral imperatives that flow from it into so many extended and even questionable extensions of our ability to make that moral judgment."

. . . .

Michael Sean Winters observes that Cardinal Wuerl "has an awareness that this is not just a job, it's the Church. It is not just a cause, it's something deeper, and he expects people's best efforts." He is set apart from many other bishops of his era because "I've never heard him do the whole 'we are going to be a smaller, purer Church' thing. It's not okay with him to accept that people are leaving and wash our hands because they are bad and they aren't morally upright like us."

Cardinal Wuerl, said former Pittsburgh auxiliary Bishop Bradley, "defies a label." He is a master at forging consensus, Bishop Bradley said. "He's very analytical. Everything he reads, he retains. After analyzing it he is able to synthesize it and come up with a solution. It's never a solution that's imposed. He has this great gift to say 'Don't you think it would be a good idea if...' and they all come up with a solution that, at least in their heads, everybody thinks is their own."

. . . .

During the 2004 presidential campaign a handful of Catholic bishops made national news when they announced that Senator John Kerry, the Democratic nominee, would not be permitted to receive Communion in their dioceses because of his support for legal abortion. Bishop Wuerl led the charge in developing a wider consensus among the bishops that such politicization of the sacraments is not an appropriate pastoral response.

In May 2004 he spoke at Pittsburgh's Red Mass, an annual event for lawyers, judges and other Catholics in the judicial system. Legislators and others who support access to abortion should voluntarily refrain from receiving Communion, he said, but if they come forward the priest should not make a snap judgment about the state of their soul or withhold the sacrament. The place to address a Catholic's support for a moral evil is in private conversation with that individual.

The focus is to change hearts and minds through helping individuals see that abortion isn't simply a matter of doctrine but a life-and-death decision about an innocent child. "Sanctions won't achieve that goal," he said.[278] A more appropriate and fitting response, he suggested, would be to ban such legislators from speaking in Catholic facilities or receiving awards from the Church. In response, his office was picketed by a dozen anti-abortion demonstrators. They argued that canon law prohibits "those who obstinately persist in manifest grave sin" from being allowed to receive Communion. However, the U.S. Conference of Catholic Bishops was moving toward a set of guidelines that substantially echoed Bishop Wuerl's talk at the Red Mass.[279]

It had been uncharacteristic for Bishop Wuerl to speak out so often and so publicly on a contentious issue in the Church, where he usually preferred to work behind the scenes.

"The reason I spoke up was that all of a sudden we were faced with the fact that politicians were being refused communion, and we were being told that it was something we should all be doing," he said. "But that was never part of the American tradition. The Church in the United States didn't do that. We didn't say that political objectives can be achieved through refusing sacraments. Secondly, there is a fundamental problem with that. St. Paul said that it was on the conscience of each person who presents himself for Communion to determine whether he or she is fit. It has never been the responsibility of the priest or the bishop distributing Communion to judge the conscience of the person coming up in line. I don't know how you can do that."

He called it "an overreach to start using Communion as the way to make your point. And I think the reaction of the bishops was basically ninety-nine percent supportive of that," he said. Such denial of communion "was never done in Rome in all the years I lived there, and we had Catholic politicians in Rome who didn't support all of the Church's teaching. I didn't see it being done anywhere. It struck me as aberrational theology."

The popes themselves have never denied Communion to someone standing in line to receive it, he said.

"I've never seen any of the popes—John XXIII, Paul VI, John Paul, Benedict, Francis—I've never seen any of them invoke sanctions against people, particularly in the political order, when they don't carry out our understanding of the gospel," he said.

"John Paul certainly would have had lots of opportunities had that route been the one he chose, He traveled all over the world, met with everybody."

After the 2004 election he proposed that all of the bishops agree to consult one another before speaking out on public issues—particularly that of Communion for abortion-rights politicians. His proposal appeared in the *Pittsburgh Catholic* newspaper and was picked up nationwide by Catholic News Service.

The actions of about a dozen of the nation's 185 diocesan bishops "caused real difficulties for the other bishops because it made it appear that was the position of all the bishops, when it was not," he wrote. He argued that the Vatican clearly intended for national bishops' conferences to foster "a collegial spirit" among the bishops, and that for individual bishops to take controversial stands without consulting the others violates the unity that the conference is charged with promoting.

He proposed two ways of consolidating that unity. His first choice was a gentlemen's agreement that no bishop would speak out on a divisive national issue without first consulting the others. Failing that, he proposed a mandatory review process, which either the bishops could impose on themselves by a unanimous vote or the Vatican could mandate.[280]

· · · · · · ·

With Archbishop Wuerl's appointment to Washington, D.C., two years later, however, a bright spotlight was turned on his response to Catholics who promoted legal abortion, with calls for him to deny Communion not only to Kerry, but to Representative Nancy Pelosi and others. He held the position he had always held, while also stressing that the vast majority of Catholic politicians were under the jurisdiction of a bishop in their home districts, and it was those bishops who were responsible for their pastoral oversight.

He had worked closely with his predecessor, Cardinal Theodore McCarrick, in recent years to ensure that the sacraments did not become politicized.

"He is so balanced intellectually," Cardinal McCarrick said on the day of the appointment. "He's a man who can hold the middle. And I think we have to hold the middle, because if you hold the middle you can reach out to both ends, and that's important. But if you're on one end, you're going to let the [other] end fall."[281]

In Washington, Archbishop Wuerl experienced a heightened version of something he had encountered for years, what he calls "Good Bishop vs. Bad Bishop Syndrome."

In particular, Church activists focused on his relationship with Cardinal Raymond Burke, a canon lawyer then serving in a high post in the Vatican courts. When he was archbishop of St. Louis, Cardinal Burke had announced that John Kerry was not welcome to receive Communion in his parishes. He was considered a hero by Catholics who believed the Church must draw a hard line and ostracize public dissenters.

The tension reached new heights in 2009 when then-Archbishop Burke appeared in a video made by a prominent anti-abortion activist and seemed to lend support to the activist's contention that Pope Benedict should remove Archbishop Wuerl because he refused to deny Communion to certain legislators. Archbishop Burke later explained that his words had been taken out of context.[282]

The following year both would be made cardinals in the same consistory. In late 2013, in a move widely seen as a major shake-up in how Pope Francis would run the Church, Cardinal Burke was removed from the Congregation for Bishops—which vets bishop appointments worldwide—and Cardinal Wuerl replaced him. Since then Cardinal Burke has been removed from the Vatican court and given a role with a Vatican-related charitable organization.[283]

All of that drew tremendous commentary in the Catholic media, but Cardinal Wuerl is not interested in continuing such quarrels. "What has happened over the past couple of decades is not reasonable or respectful disagreement on issues but rather the emergence of the Good Bishop-Bad Bishop Syndrome," he said. "There are those who say that this bishop is not pro-life enough or that bishop is not social-justice-oriented enough. The result is that you get people clustering around ideological divisions," he said. "The Church," he added, has always recognized "that there are people sitting in the pews who are unhappy with different aspects of the teaching of the Church...It's different parts for different people. But what is happening now is that some say that the people who disagree with them are 'not faithful,' they are not living out the 'true faith.' This ideological approach has succeeded in doing enormous damage to the unity of the Church."

Culture war ideologies, he said, can create narrowly focused division in the Church, which is supposed to be a home of healing and reconciliation. Unfortunately, "just a certain number of issues became somewhat of a litmus test as to whether you are really a good bishop," he said. "The decision of a very few bishops to refuse Communion in a political context was used by some polemicists and writers to criticize the other bishops as 'disobedient' and 'unfaithful.' The vast majority of bishops simply did not refuse Communion, but that does not make them 'bad' bishops. The effort to foster the separation of bishops into these two categories was and continues to be very unfortunate."

It is currently playing out in divisions among some over the response to Pope Francis, he said. "This Pope is trying to say there is much more to the gospel than focusing particularly on civil legislation," he said. "I often find it puzzling. Some people who claim to be

papal, on examination seem to be so only when the pope is in agreement with them."

· · · · · · ·

His convictions about politics, pastoral care and diplomacy did not
prevent him from speaking swiftly and publicly when politicians
made errant attempts to justify their support for abortion by mis-
stating Church history and Catholic theology on national television.
When Rep. Pelosi cited medieval theologians to claim that the
Church has never determined when human life begins, Archbishop
Wuerl was among numerous bishops who cited authoritative teaching going back to the first century. When Vice-President Biden
called the belief that human life begins at conception "a matter of
faith" that he could not impose on others, Archbishop Wuerl explained that it's a matter of easily verifiable science and a human
rights issue.

"Defense of innocent human life is not an imposition of personal
religious conviction, but an act of justice," Archbishop Wuerl said.[284]

Most recently he has taken a leading role in promoting Pope Francis' encyclical on the environment, *Laudato Si*. Not long before its
release in June 15, he was chosen to give a talk at a conference in
Rome, explaining that there is no true conflict between a healthy
planet and a healthy economy. The dignity of the human person
must be the guiding reference for both economic and environmental
concerns, he said.[285]

The cardinal said he was honored to have been asked to make the
presentation. "All you have to do is look around and see the defor-
estation, the lack of water, lack of food, conditions people are living
in to know the planet is being devastated. It doesn't take a lot to say,
'Shouldn't we be caring for this since we only have one?'"

Catholics, he said, "are becoming more aware, thanks to Pope
Francis, that we need to be much more alert to the issues of the
Church universal. We have tended, I think, to concentrate very
much on life issues and they are very important and we need to continue to do that. But around the world there are huge issues of life

and death that have to do with having food and water and housing and education."

Pope Francis' concern for the environment addresses those life-and-death issues. "One of the things I always appreciated about Pope Paul VI was when he said: 'If you want peace, you have to work for social development.' Now the corollary is, if you want social development you have to work for economic development. And Pope Francis is adding: if you want economic development, it has to respect creation."

· · · · · · ·

But he does not believe that bitter partisanship serves any public-policy goal. Christians can take a stand on crucial issues while showing charity and respect for people who disagree with them, he said.

Whether talking about abortion, the environment, the economy or immigration, the current polarized climate in Congress is "disappointing," Cardinal Wuerl said. He believes that both elected officials and their supporters need to back away from personal attack and address the issues with well-reasoned arguments. "Politically in Washington there are a lot of good things going on, and when you sit down at the table with others, it can't just be about pitting one ideology against another or a shouting match," he said. "We used to laugh and say that if you are attacked by both sides, you must be in the right place. But today there is such a tendency go to on talk shows and social media applications and ridicule or attack or demean. Freedom of speech is a constitutionally guaranteed right, but freedom of speech does not abrogate the commandment 'You shall not bear false witness.'"

· · · · · · ·

In a June 2015 letter to his clergy, which also appeared as an installment of his blog "Seek First the Kingdom," Cardinal Wuerl said that faithfulness to Church teaching does not mean turning a cold shoulder to those who do not follow it. "Faithful to her Lord and

Founder, the Church welcomes everyone," he wrote. "This welcome is extended to everyone: married couples with children, unwed mothers and fathers, the single unmarried, couples who struggle with infertility, men and women with same-sex attraction, individuals facing gender issues, those whose marriages have broken down and suffered the trauma of divorce, people with special needs, immigrants, children born and unborn, the young, seniors, and the terminally ill, sinners and saints alive. If the Church were to welcome only those without sin, it would be empty."

Pope Francis, Cardinal Wuerl says, is changing the Church's approach to advocacy so that it is broader and more inclusive of all of the Church's moral concerns. "He comes at issues from the perspective of engagement, not condemnation—which is the opposite of refusing Communion. He comes at issues from the perspective that none of us have it all right, so why don't we work together to at least get some good things done?"

While core Catholic teaching was given by Christ and will not change, he said, the bishops of the United States need to "reflect on the ways we express and apply that teaching. Too often the statements that come out of our conference seem to be more the application of canon law rather than a reflection on how we deal with a living experience. I hear Francis saying, 'Let's take the lived experience and, under the guidance of the Holy Spirit, see what we can do there,'" he said.

That is creating conflict in some Catholic circles because many people are convinced that the fullness of Catholic teaching and pastoral application is already fully described in the catechism and Church canons, he said. But each generation needs to look at what is happening and find new pastoral was to apply that teaching. Right now, he believes, there is too much of a laser focus on sexual sins compared to other kinds of sin.

"Isn't everything disordered by the Fall? Isn't that the heart of our Catholic understanding—that the world after the Fall was not what God intended? So you can't just single out specific issues and say these are the areas that aren't functioning and that everything else is," he said.

Jesus told his followers that they would be judged by how they treated the poor, he said. "I think there is great sympathy today with those who are saying, 'Shouldn't we be as attentive to the poor and to those who are not helping to resolve the issues of the poor, as we are to those who are finding artificial ways to bring about the birth of a child? I suspect there is great empathy among many, many of our people for hearing a more equitable application of the gospel."

While it is and will always be morally wrong and a sin against humanity to kill an unborn child in the womb, there are other reproductive issues that the Church should re-examine, particularly involving solutions for infertility, Cardinal Wuerl said. "That is an area that really needs to be rethought in the Church, both theologically and pastorally," he said. "I believe the natural law is a reality, the rational apprehension of the created order. But then there is the argument over how much detail you can get into with the assurance that this is the only answer. And that is where the Church needs some theological and pastoral investigation."

Along with many other bishops, he has sued the federal government over one stipulation in the federal health insurance program that would require religious institutions to facilitate access to contraceptives, sterilization, and abortifacients in violation of their teaching. In particular he has focused on the new distinction that the government has created between houses of worship—which aren't required to facilitate those services—and the charitable and educational arms of religious faith, as if social outreach in the name of Jesus isn't truly religious.

"Does anyone really think that the work of Mother Teresa wasn't religious?" he asked in an op-ed in the Washington Post. The suit "is not about contraception. Women are able to obtain and use contraception. The assertion that these products are hard to obtain or expensive is not true. Nothing in this lawsuit challenges women's right to obtain these drugs and procedures."[286]

But he has not threatened to close the diocesan social services if the Supreme Court upholds the requirement.

The rule is a bad one, he said. "But how do you balance accepting a law that provides insurance that you don't like for some of your employees against the good you are doing for the poor, the sick, those in need of education, the homeless?"

Cardinal Wuerl speaks with students prior to a Sept. 14, 2014 *Mass for George Washington University Students held at St. Stephen Martyr Church in Washington.* Catholic Standard *photo by Jaclyn Lippelmann. Used with permission.*

With first graders at St. Augustine School. Catholic Standard *photo by Rafael Crisostomo. Used with permission.*

Breaking ground for a new addition at St. Raphael School. Catholic Standard *photo by Rafael Crisostomo. Used with permission.*

CHAPTER 16:
THE EDUCATION BISHOP

Education, like health care, has been for Donald Wuerl a necessary dimension of the Church's work. The Church, as Christ's body, carries on the ministry of Christ. As Jesus healed, so the Church provides health care. As Jesus taught, so the Church provides education.

As a bishop, he has always felt keenly the bishop's call to be a teacher—the principal teacher of faith in the diocese. He looked to Pope John Paul II as his role model. In countless documents, from encyclicals to pastoral reflections, and in all of his Wednesday catechesis for the crowds at his public audience, "he continually and constantly taught the faith. And I think that is the role of the bishop: to stand in the midst of the faithful and make with them the journey of faith while recognizing that it is the bishop's job to teach. The pope, even when he was in an area where he faced hostility from his bishops, like his visit to Holland, he was never a punishing pope. He didn't threaten. He didn't invoke sanctions. He just stood there and said, 'this is what the gospel says.'

"I think today, with some of the tensions in the Church, that is a good lesson to learn: To teach and teach and teach, and hope that you will convince people who will then apply the teaching to whatever field they are engaged in, whether it is medicine or business or law or raising a family."

· · · · · · · ·

The cover story in *Our Sunday Visitor* newspaper, January 3, 1993, described Bishop Wuerl's "magnificent obsession" with Catholic education and proclaimed him "The Education Bishop." The title stuck. The Washington Post used it to describe him in 2006 when he began his tenure as archbishop in D.C.

He is himself a product of Catholic education, having attended Catholic elementary and secondary schools, and then seminaries and graduate schools. He grew up in a period of explosive growth in Catholic schools—an era of "bricks and mortar," launched by the U.S. bishops in the nineteenth century and continued well into the twentieth. Pastors were often encouraged to build a parish school first, and only later raise funds for a permanent church building. In Pittsburgh the schools were sometimes constructed by parishioners —steelworkers who volunteered to work a shift of bricklaying at the school after they finished their shift at the mill. When the Wuerl children were in elementary school, more than 70,000 students were enrolled in Catholic schools in the Diocese of Pittsburgh, and the numbers were on the rise. In 1960, enrollment hit 112,000.

After decades of soaring growth, however, the numbers dropped precipitously in the last quarter of the twentieth century, to 39,000 in 1980 and 30,000 in 1990. Some of the loss was attributable to demographic shifts in Western Pennsylvania. With the decline of the steel industry, younger people—with young children—moved elsewhere for jobs. An aging population had less use for schools and less interest in supporting them. At the same time, the religious orders that had staffed the schools experienced an exodus of members. Always a costly enterprise, Catholic schools began to falter as support weakened.

Yet, in all his years as bishop, Donald Wuerl never wavered in his enthusiasm for the Church's mission of education. In fact, he dug in. In the 1993 story he told *Our Sunday Visitor*'s reporter: "It is high time the Catholic Church stops hiding its light under a bushel when it comes to our schools.... I think our schools at all levels are one of those secrets that we have always kept to ourselves. We have traditionally felt that we were not supposed to toot our own horns when it came to our schools.... I believe we should start letting people know that we have a magnificent system of schools that has educated children well for generations, bringing them up in the faith with a solid system of values and giving them education that has served them extremely well, as evidenced in the success they have had in their lives."

· · · · · · ·

Catholic schools were, of course, the best delivery system for Catholic doctrine—but not only doctrine. Bishop Wuerl held that Catholic schools communicate a worldview, a way of looking at life, a way of living with others. Catholic social teaching, for example, isn't simply taught in Catholic schools. It's "caught" in the interactions among teachers, students, administrators, service personnel, and volunteers.

In 1995 he addressed an audience of four thousand educators and called them to deeper commitment through deep personal conversion: "A Catholic education is essentially a witness to Christ and his Church. A witness has to know what he or she is bearing witness to—to know the faith, and to think with the Church—not to know what some opinions about the faith are, but to know what the Church actually teaches.

"And a witness has to have the courage to bear the witness. Today, in the face of a secularism that is rooted in relativism—'your choice is as good as my choice'—a teacher has to have the courage to say that there is such a thing as right and wrong, truth, chastity, justice....[287]

Catholic education was dependent upon Catholic identity, and a Catholic's deepest identity must be with Jesus Christ.

· · · · · · ·

He was well aware that he was bucking trends as he voiced stronger support for Catholic schools. History itself seemed opposed to him. Many Catholics, especially in leadership positions, had long since beat retreat from the school conversation. Most, it seemed, had made their peace with the "public school plus CCD" model.

The strong sense in many places was that school closings were inevitable; and the attitude only tended to speed the process of closure.

Bishop Wuerl recognized that business-as-usual would not work. He recognized, too, that success would require a high degree of creativity tempered by bracing realism. Over the course of years in Pittsburgh, he launched a variety of innovative programs to shore up the supports for Catholic education.

The Extra Mile Foundation sustains elementary schools in economically disadvantaged inner-city communities. Involving people of many faiths, as well as leaders from the business and philanthropic communities, the program serves hundreds of children, most of them non-Catholic, and many from low-income homes in neighborhoods torn by violence.

The Bishop's Education Fund provides tuition assistance to families of Catholic school students in need. The fund is supported by all parishes in the Pittsburgh diocese and by donations from many regional businesses. It disburses millions of dollars in tuition assistance each year. The goal is that no child should forego a Catholic school education for economic reasons.

The Golden Apple Awards. Sponsored by the Pittsburgh-based Donahue Family Foundation, these annual awards recognize dedicated and exceptional teachers in Catholic schools. Teachers are nominated by their peers and their students, and honorees are chosen by a team of judges. The award includes a monetary stipend, in recognition of the sacrifices made by teachers in Catholic schools, which do not benefit from taxpayer subsidy.

The Total Catholic Education Conference. Designed to provide an intensive experience of spiritual and intellectual formation, this event (held several times during Bishop Wuerl's tenure in Pittsburgh) featured a three-day program of lectures, exhibitions, liturgies, and social events. Its roster of renowned speakers drew attendees from all over the United States and Canada. The goal was to celebrate the mission of Catholic education and motivate teachers and catechists to pursue excellence.

· · · · · · ·

Cardinal Wuerl's commitment to the tradition of Catholic education has grown out of his personal experience. But it is not an exercise in nostalgia. It is forward-looking and open to innovation. He has been alert to emerging trends and open to the possibilities they present the Church.

Homeschooling, or home education, was a small, fringe movement in the 1990s when he first noticed it. In many areas in the United States, religious schools viewed homeschoolers as "competition," and some parishes imposed heavier standards for catechesis that took place in the home.

In 1996 Bishop Wuerl convened a committee to study the issue. It included homeschooling families, parish priests, and chancery officials, as well as Catholic-school teachers and administrators. After a year of consultation, the diocese published *Faith Education in the Home*, the first major document produced by a Catholic diocese on the subject of homeschooling. Prescient in many ways, it provides a nuanced discussion of education, family, and communion with the Church.

His commitment to education—and innovation—has remained strong through his years as Cardinal-archbishop of Washington. When he found a way to keep inner-city Catholic schools open as public charter schools, Eleanor Holmes Norton, the District of Columbia's representative in Congress, applauded the Cardinal's efforts in an op-ed in the *Washington Post:* "this city owes more than it can repay to the Catholic schools that have remained in this largely Protestant town rather than following their parishioners to the suburbs."[288]

Another innovation is St. Francis International School in Silver Spring, Maryland, which opened its doors in September 2010. Its curriculum and services are designed for students whose families are new to the United States. In its first year of operation, the students (or their parents) represented fifty-three countries—in South and Central America, Asia, Africa, Europe, and the Caribbean. The campus is located in a poor area of Montgomery County. Most of the school's students qualify for federal assistance for their meals. Tuition is heavily subsidized by the archdiocese and philanthropic organizations.

In a way, St. Francis International School recalled the role of the ethnic parishes of the early twentieth century—whose elementary schools eased immigrant families into a new environment. The difference is that St. Francis' program serves a wide variety of ethnicities, and all together. School Masses are offered in Spanish, French, and English. Thus, the experience is not simply parochial, but robustly *catholic*—that is, universal.

· · · · · · ·

Another successful new educational venture in the Archdiocese of Washington has been the Don Bosco Cristo Rey High School in Takoma Park, Maryland. Opened in 2007 as a partnership between the archdiocese and the Salesians of Don Bosco, Cristo Rey offers students from very-low-income households a chance to get a college-preparatory education through a corporate work-study program. Students take challenging traditional academic courses; and, one day a week, they work at a steady job in a professional setting, sponsored by local corporations. The corporations cover a large portion of the students' tuition costs. The archdiocese also provides subsidies. The students experience many opportunities that would otherwise be inaccessible to them.

Innovations like these—Saint Francis and Cristo Rey—ensure that Catholic education will be available to many more students in the coming generation.

· · · · · · ·

"The Education Bishop" of 1993 presses on as a cardinal devoted to the same task. In 2008 he issued a pastoral letter that, from its title onward, exuded optimism: *Catholic Education: Looking to the Future with Confidence.* "Looking to the future of Catholic education," he said, "we should do so with hope, confidence and enthusiasm."

His reasons are supernatural.

"This is a time of new Pentecost for the Church in our country and the Church that is our archdiocese. As we begin this new year, we will undertake a review and assessment of our educational efforts as we have said, focusing on our parish education programs and our Catholic schools. Our goal is to participate in that pentecostal outpouring of God's grace and love by providing our young people with an excellent education and understanding of the faith so that they are well equipped to live out their lives as witnesses to Christ and the Gospel."

As with his efforts in catechetics, Cardinal Wuerl's work in education has won the respect of professionals. He has served as chairman of the U.S. bishops' Committee on Education and chairman of the board of directors of the National Catholic Educational Association (NCEA). In 1995 he received the NCEA's prestigious Elizabeth Ann Seton Award for his contributions to Catholic education. He has also received the Lifetime Achievement Award, Catholic Education Foundation (2007) and the NCEA's Emmaus Award for Excellence in Catechesis (2007).

No doubt, the Cardinal's influence in Catholic education is nationwide and Church-wide. But its lasting monument may stand rather close to his birthplace.

In 2014, his home diocese honored him in the most appropriate way, by naming its newly constructed high school in his honor. Cardinal Wuerl North Catholic High School is a private Catholic high school located in Cranberry Township, Butler County, Pennsylvania, a high growth area of the diocese. Its mission is "the formation of Christ-centered young adults who are leaders in their communities, known by their intellectual, practical, ethical and human skills."

His most lasting legacy will be the graduates whose education he inspired and made possible—it will be their accomplishment—and then it will be the education they make possible for the next generation.

End-of-the-year Mass with seminarians at St. John Paul II Seminary.
Catholic Standard *photos by Jaclyn Lippelmann. Used with permission.*

CHAPTER 17:
PRIESTS AND DEACONS FOR THE NEW PENTECOST

In 2011, following a quarter century in which most of the nation's Catholic bishops shut down their nearly empty seminaries, Cardinal Wuerl opened a new college-level seminary for the Archdiocese of Washington D.C. Two years later he built an addition to what is now St. John Paul II seminary because it was overflowing with students.

As of June 2015, the cardinal had seventy-four men preparing for priesthood. The average age at the new, entry-level seminary, was twenty-two.

"They are wholesome, young, energetic. They just want to know how to live as followers of Christ," Cardinal Wuerl said.

That same June he ordained nine new priests—a very large class by current United States standards, but consistent with his earlier ordinations in Washington.

The preparation of these new priests had been very different from what he experienced as a seminarian in the 1950s and 1960s. And that was due in part to his own work on the Vatican seminary study in the 1980s and a subsequent Synod of Bishops on priestly formation in 1990. Archbishop Hebda observed: "It wasn't a bureaucratic task for him. He really wanted the Church to have great priests, and he knew that they had to have really great seminaries if that was to be the case."

When Cardinal Wuerl was a student, seminary education was one-size-fits-all, he recalled. He rarely saw his rector, never spoke with the bishop who initially accepted him as a candidate.

"You were formed by the system. There was a schedule and you were expected to do the things according to that schedule. There were academics. Your spiritual life consisted of Mass or conferences with the spiritual director. The presumption was that you had come out of a good Catholic formation all along," he said. "Today that assumption can't be the starting point."

Today seminary preparation is much more personalized, both in terms of its design and interaction with the faculty, he said. Where his peers were mostly graduates of Catholic schools where they had absorbed both basic theology and good study habits, many of today's students attended public school and may have been raised as nominal Catholics or non-Catholics before a conversion experience led them to seminary. Or they may have been home-schooled by exceptionally devout parents who had them reading St. Thomas Aquinas before they reached their teens.

Each student must be evaluated individually, with programs designed to draw on his strengths and strengthen his weaknesses, he said.

"The result is that we are seeing these young men grow into all of this academically, pastorally, spiritually and humanly with guidance from the faculty," he said. "It's not a system any longer. It's human beings working with other human beings under the direction of the Holy Spirit."

Coupled with his concern for high-quality seminary training has been a concern to provide ongoing education and personal support for priests, so that they are able to develop new skills for changing times and don't become isolated in an era when it is rare to have more than one priest assigned to a parish.

Because of his work on the Vatican study of seminaries in the United States, Father Wuerl was regarded as an expert on the preparation and continuing care of priests before he became a bishop. During his first year as a diocesan bishop, his peers in the U.S. bishops' conference elected him chairman of their Committee on Priestly

Life and Ministry. While in that office he worked on guidelines for helping priests develop and sustain a healthy, mature celibate sexuality. He also promoted high quality retreats for priests, both individually and collectively with their brother diocesan priests.

In August 1990, Pope John Paul II named Bishop Wuerl to the Synod of Bishops on the Formation of Priests in Circumstances of the Present Day. He used his allotted speech to call for the continuing formation and spiritual renewal of priests already ordained.

Such practices were considered innovative when he brought then to the Diocese of Pittsburgh. He instituted twice-yearly convocations for both fellowship and education on topics ranging from preaching to racism to medical ethics. Every third year the fall convocation was a multi-day retreat held in a resort ninety minutes outside Pittsburgh where the priests could enjoy golf, swimming, hiking and other activities between workshops.

There were celebrations for priests observing major anniversaries of their ordinations, Advent socials, and other occasions that might include a softball game between older and younger priests.

"They were important. It was a chance for priests to get away from the parish and get together. Priests need a chance to sit down and talk to each other about they problems they're facing, to say things they can't say from the pulpit," said Father Robert Grecco.

Apart from those fraternal gatherings, he created opportunities to attend short workshops on a wide range of topics in ministry.

"I don't remember any regular programs for post-ordination formation before he came here," said Bishop David Zubik, a priest of Pittsburgh who eventually succeeded him as bishop. "He was big on wanting people to expand their horizons and not get too comfortable or into a slump. There was always a sense of challenge to become better."

• • • • • • •

As we've seen, Bishop Wuerl had earned a well-deserved reputation for swift action against priests who abused the faithful, particular in cases of sexual abuse of minors. But in many situations where a troubled priest's action were immoral but not criminal, he could be supportive and compassionate.

When Father Grecco was his secretary, "I was told that if a priest calls with a problem and needed to see him, that I was to get that priest into the office as soon as possible. I was to clear his schedule," he said.

Because those conversations were so private, many priests tended to see only his tough decisions to remove miscreants, rather than his pastoral care for those struggling with personal issues, said Father Frank Almade. "I've heard stories where guys who were in trouble went to him and he treated them very, very kindly. But it was all behind the scenes. It never got out on the clergy grapevine."

As for the vast majority of priests, "in the main if you—as a pastor —followed the rules and ran your parish as best you could, Wuerl left you alone," Father Almade said. "Only if a priest did something stupid, or against canon law, to publicly embarrass him or the Church, did he get involved."

While there are times that a bishop must intervene, either because a priest is harming the faithful or is publicly dissenting from core tenets of the creeds, a bishop's default should be to trust his pastors, Cardinal Wuerl said.

"We have to place our confidence in our pastors. I have always said the two most important things that a bishop does are to ordain priests and then assigning them as pastors," he said.

"When I hand him the letter of appointment is when I say I am turning over a portion of this flock to you, and the two of us together rare responsible before God for caring for this flock. Then I have to let him go back to that parish and exercise his pastoral judgment."

As a bishop it is his job to proclaim the teachings of the Church so that priests and laity alike understand the life that God has called them to. But priests need to discern how best to work with people who don't yet understand or appreciate that call, he said. "You teach when you are in the pulpit, you teach the full, unvarnished gospel. And then, when you are walking with people, you try to meet them where they are. None of us can say, none of us, 'Well, I am fully living the gospel,'" Cardinal Wuerl said.

"My responsibility is to maintain the unity of the local Church.... At times I have to remind my priests—and I prefer to reflect with them when they are all together—that we are all obliged to follow, not just the teaching but the accepted practice of the church. If something appears very wrong, then I would either invite the pastor in or sometimes have a Mass at that parish."

The late Father Dennis Colamarino was a pastor who welcomed many Catholics who had left other parishes because of irregular marriages or other situations that made them feel unwelcome in their home parishes. His goal was always to bring them into full conformity with the Church, he said in 2006, but Bishop Wuerl understood the way he worked with people who hadn't arrived there.

"Bishop Wuerl affirmed me in that way. He always told me that my style was unique but that it was right for [the city of] Duquesne, where it made for a very viable parish. He understood my sense of humor and my style of ministry," he said when Bishop Wuerl left Pittsburgh for Washington.

He supported the priesthood as a whole during its most difficult days when revelations of child sexual abuse and cover-ups by the bishops in some other dioceses made national news for weeks on end. His longstanding zero-tolerance policy—which some priests feared could make them victims to false allegations—was a reason be was able to express full, public confidence in his priests. And he did so on many public occasions. "He built us up and reminded people to pray for us and support us," Father Grecco recalled.

Ambrose Murray recalled attending a Catholic Charities fundraising dinner in the midst of the scandal when Bishop Wuerl broke from his script to praise the work of the priests of Pittsburgh.

"He pointed out that many priests were present that evening, and that a lot of people didn't like them right now" because of the scandal, Mr. Murray recalled. "He asked them all to stand and said, 'Let's all salute them for their service to God and mankind.' The place went crazy."

· · · · · · ·

As a bishop, Wuerl was especially caring for priests who were ill.

He tried to work with them in each circumstance. In the case of Father Patrick Rager, who battled a very slow-moving form of Lou Gehrig's Disease throughout Bishop Wuerl's years in Pittsburgh, he asked the staff to document the priest's life for a possible later cause for canonization. Father Rager had been able to spend just two years in parish ministry before going to live with his mother in 1987. But because he was still able to speak and write then, Bishop Bevilacqua had made him coordinator of a new office for ministry to people with disabilities. He took calls from, wrote letters to and organized retreats for people with all manner of physical and mental illness.

"When Pat realized how sick he was, he just determined that he was going to make this moment, this ordeal in his life, an occasion of grace for himself and everybody else," Cardinal Wuerl said when Father Rager died in 2010 at the age of 50.

He made every possible effort to offer the funeral Mass for any priest who had died. On the day he buried his own father, he came to the church from his earlier Funeral Mass for a priest.

"Since the bishop is supposed to be the spiritual father of the faithful—and that includes most uniquely his brother priests—he is supposed to be their father in Christ, their spiritual brother, the head of the family—I have always felt that that was by privilege to be able to have the funeral Mass to bury each of the priests," he said.

That extended even to priests who he had very publicly banned from ministry for misdeeds including embezzlement and child sexual abuse. He would celebrate their funeral Mass, sometimes publicly, other times privately, and give them the full dignity of a priest's funeral.[289]

Sometimes he had to boost the morale of all the priests after one of their brothers betrayed them all. Although it was not the worst crime committed by a Pittsburgh priest during his tenure, one of the deepest wounds was caused by Father Walter Benz, who had been a highly respected and trusted pastor before his was discovered to have embezzled more than $1 million from two parishes. He was never officially charged with the crime because, by the time police were ready to act, he was near death from a degenerative brain disease.

Knowledge of the theft "has been devastating," Bishop Wuerl told reporters in a rare public expression of deep emotion. "It is very hard even to talk about it, let alone stand up and have to deal with it. I never had to deal with anything as debilitating as this."[290] A little more than a week after Father Benz's death, Bishop Wuerl held a meeting for all of his priests to talk to them about the case, comfort those who felt as betrayed as he did and to explain that he was appointing a panel of experts to recommend ways that such thefts could be prevented in the future. But his primary mission was to "affirm that we have good, dedicated, honest hard-working priests," he told reporters outside the meeting.

The priests gave him a standing ovation.

"He thanked us for the good work that we do. He spoke to us about our solidarity, about the fact that we are all in this together," said Father Robert Duch, then pastor of St. Scholastica in Aspinwall. "I was very happy that the bishop and his staff took the time to give us the facts. We don't always know if what we see in the media is accurate. I am thankful that it was an uplifting day."[291]

But the biggest morale problem burdening priests was their own dwindling numbers.

• • • • • • •

From the 1930s onward, Pittsburgh had ordained so many priests that its bishops lacked places to assign them all. But ordinations had plummeted in the 1970s, and when he became bishop of Pittsburgh the huge classes from the 1950s were nearing retirement, with those from the 1960s not far behind, and very few new priests stood ready to replace them.

An editorial in the *Pittsburgh Press* in honor of Bishop Wuerl's appointment cited as a problem that there were more than 1,000 Catholics for each of the 866 diocesan and religious priests in his territory—a number that would soon look like a wonderful goal to strive for.[292] The number of active diocesan priests dropped from 520 in 1984 to 314 in 2004. The number was projected to fall to 240 by 2009.

At the time seventy-three percent of parishes nationwide had a resident pastor, but after the Pittsburgh diocesan reorganization of 1992-1994, there was no Pittsburgh parish without a pastor, and half had two priests.[293]

But that could not hold forever. By 2004 he was calling on priests and lay leaders to work together across parish boundaries to plan for how to work together to support ministry in an era of fewer priests.[294]

The most critical work that needed to be done was in vocations— and not just priestly vocations. Bishop Wuerl would restore a long dormant permanent diaconate to Pittsburgh and also call and train lay women and men to follow a call to service in the Church.

Enrollment in the seminary and priestly ordinations grew slowly during his tenure in Pittsburgh, with occasional steps backward. In 1994 he had nine men in the college-level St. Paul Seminary in Pitts-burgh—with more in graduate studies elsewhere. In 1995 he had fifteen students in the entry-level seminary.

However, 1998 became the first year in living memory that no priests were ordained for the Diocese of Pittsburgh. That, in turn, became a catalyst for a surge in vocation awareness that bore fruit. Bishop Wuerl wrote a pastoral letter, *To Walk in the Footsteps of Jesus,* that called for every parish to form a vocations council that would meet weekly to identify and encourage parishioners who were possible candidates for the priesthood and to pray for an increase in vocations.

Although it was far too soon to be a result of those efforts, the following year Bishop Wuerl ordained six new priests. That same week he was scheduled to meet with more than forty men who wanted to explore the possibility of priesthood.[295] And in 2000—when another six men were ordained, seventy men participated in "An Evening with the Bishop" to discuss the possibility of priesthood. In 2001 outreach efforts increased with a seminar for 250 on the various possibilities for ministry—ordained and lay—in the Diocese of Pittsburgh. The diocese, with funding from the estate of the late Mon-signor Francis Rooney, ran television ads during college and profes-sional football games, encouraging men to consider priesthood.[296]

In June 2002, at the height of national publicity over priests who had sexually abused minors, the Diocese had its largest entering class of seminarians in fourteen years. The nine young men who entered included Joseph Freedy, a former quarterback for the University of Buffalo, who as Father Joe Freedy would go on to become an out-standing vocations director for the Diocese of Pittsburgh.[297]

Throughout his ministry, Bishop Wuerl made an effort to get to know his seminarians, Father Grecco said. "He was a regular at the seminary. He would eat dinner with the guys. Guys came to his house for pizza parties. It was a way to get to know them outside of formation so they would know him and he would know them," Father Grecco said.

Meanwhile, as he was working to rebuild his priesthood, he placed a new and renewed interest on other forms of ministry. Vatican II had opened the door to restore the permanent diaconate for married men. For centuries it had been treated only as a transitory ministry for celibate men on the road to priesthood. Bishop Vincent Leonard had ordained a group of permanent deacons in 1974—but neither Bishop Leonard nor his successor ordained any more after that. Twenty-three of them remained in ministry when Bishop Wuerl was appointed to Pittsburgh.

Bishop Wuerl spoke of resuming the permanent diaconate from his first year in Pittsburgh, but there were long delays, in part be-cause the Vatican was re-examining formation standards for them. But in 1995 he accepted class of thirty-six candidates, and ordained thirty-three of them in 1999.[298]

• • • • • • •

With his 2006 transfer to Washington, Archbishop Wuerl fol-lowed in the footsteps of a predecessor who had already overseen a growing number of vocations to the priesthood. Since the archdiocese was largely healthy, Archbishop Wuerl was able to focus his energy on the happy task of improving on that.

The Archdiocese of Washington had never had its own seminary, although it was home to graduate-level seminaries that clustered around the Catholic University of America. "One of the first things he said to me was that it would be really wonderful to have a...college seminary," said Monsignor Robert Panke, who was then the vocations director and is now rector of St. John Paul II Seminary. A college seminary is an entry-level school where students live and receive spiritual direction while taking undergraduate courses in theology and philosophy at a nearby university.

Before the seminary opened in 2011, Washington's new seminarians were scattered among various college seminaries in other dioceses. Archbishop Wuerl "recognized that importance of being formed at home in your own place with your brothers," Msgr. Panke said. "There is something very special about this experience. It will have a lasting impact on priestly fraternity."

"Young men have to have a place in the archdiocese if they are going to serve here. They have to have a place to come to know who they are—and you don't get that by sending them to some other city," Cardinal Wuerl said.

Despite the pressing demands on his time in both Washington and Rome, he has made time with the seminarians a high priority, "He has made an effort to get to know the men here," said Father Carter Griffin, his former priest-secretary who is now vice-rector of St. John Paul II Seminary. "He has made it very clear that this seminary will be a seminary where the men are formed according to the mind of he church and it will not be an idiosyncratic place where personal whims or agendas are advanced. He loves the Church, and he wants that to be conveyed to the men here so they can convey that to others."

When he visits the seminary, "he doesn't sit with the faculty at dinner, he sits with all the guys. Without fail at every dinner you will hear laughter and joy. He loves being with the men who will be his future priests," Msgr. Panke said.

The men are mostly young, and come from a wide variety of back-grounds, including quite a few who were homeschooled, Cardinal Wuerl said. "The ones who were homeschooled come with a profound spiritual formation that is already a part of their life. But we're getting a lot of other young men who realized early in life that the secular world and its values are not really the answer," he said. Many of those come in from Catholic campus ministry programs. In some cases they are converts who first came in touch with the Catholic Church when a Catholic friend invited them to a Mass on campus.

"There are also young people coming out of suffering families" that have been affected by divorce and other difficulties, Cardinal Wuerl said. "They are saying that they think [what the Church teaches] might be the right route. That is what the pope is talking about. The challenge with all of them is to introduce all of the things that are part of being a Catholic."

One young priest who was a convert to Catholicism told him that the first time his seminary class prayed the Stations of the Cross "everyone else started doing it, and he was thinking, 'What is this?'"

In its first year St. John Paul II seminary was filled to capacity with twenty-four seminarians from the archdiocese and another five from elsewhere. The following year ground was broken for a new wing that added room for 20 more students, plus an expanded library, common room workout room and faculty housing, The expansion was funded by Daniel D'Aniello, chairman of the Carlyle Group, a Pittsburgh native who had moved to the Washington area.

The seminary's renovated chapel, which was also supported by Daniel and Gayle D'Aniello, included the altar at which Pope Benedict XVI had celebrated Mass at Nationals Park in 2008 and a first-class relic of St. John Paul—a piece of his blood-stained cassock from the assassination attempt that had nearly killed him in 1981.

The archdiocese is averaging about eight ordinations a year, which is healthy for a diocese of its size. "We have enough priests to go around, but it's not as it once was where you had three priests in a parish," Cardinal Wuerl said.

And that can make things hard on the one priest in the parish.

• • • • • • •

Isolation is as much a risk as burnout in the one-priest parish, and Cardinal Wuerl has focused on building and maintaining fraternal support. "That is something we have to work at all the time, to encourage support groups for the priests. Maybe they can take an evening for prayer together and then go out to dinner so they have priestly camaraderie," he said.

He encourages his priests to take an occasional day off at the seminary, where they can pray, study and perhaps go shopping or sightseeing "but be in a place where there are other priests," he said.

He tries to ensure a built-in support system of priests who are trained to be spiritual directors for other priests, and to offer regular opportunities for mutual support, encouragement, and ongoing education, he said.

He makes every effort to be available to his priests, said Father William Byrne, pastor of Our Lady of Mercy Parish in Potomac, Maryland. "It's well known that any priest who wants to see him is one phone call away. As a shepherd and as a father, he's right there and available to his priests."

"I found that in Washington there was already a strong sense of priestly solidarity, but it's something you have to work at," Cardinal Wuerl said. He tries to build social occasions into liturgical ones, such as a buffet dinner for all the priests before the annual Chrism Mass that celebrates Christ's institution of the priesthood. "We also have ongoing education, lecture series, days of recollection, retreats. They are all intended to provide a sense of all of us being at this together, continuing to grow in our priesthood and grow in our pastoral awareness of needs. It's like a family. You just have to work at bringing everybody together."

• • • • • • • •

Both in order to prevent priest burnout and, more importantly, to follow Jesus' call to serve him, "the real solution is engaging our lay faithful in the ongoing work of the Church, in marriage preparation, religious education, social-service ministry and the ordinary operations of getting everything ready for Mass," Cardinal Wuerl said. "All of that can be done by lay people, volunteers, and it lets the priests concentrate on the Mass, on visitation, care of the sick, confessions, marriages, and funerals."

Permanent deacons have a critical ministry in Washington, especially in serving immigrant groups where a priest who speaks the language may not be available.

"The diaconate has an identity all its own. There are things that deacons do and gifts that deacons bring. They are not second-class priests or a substitute where we don't have enough priests," he said.

"We often associate the deacon with reading the gospel or sometimes with preaching, but the real work of the deacon is in social justice and works of charity. Some of our deacons do an extraordinary job in jails and detention centers. They carry out ministry in our hospitals, visit the sick, as well as in sacramental preparation and helping people prepare for a wedding or for confirmation. It's an almost never-ending list of pastoral things they can do, but it frees up the priest to focus on the things that only a priest can do."

He has a few married priests in his diocese, primarily former Anglicans who converted, so the possibility of a married priesthood is not an alien one. In particular, he said, countries where there a severe priest shortage limits communities to just a few Masses each year may be places where the ordination of married men might be considered.

But celibacy is a tradition that has had great value for the Church, as priests gave their undivided attention to the service of Christ. Ordinations "seem to be cyclic, and we are on an upswing now of priests coming along, so it may not be necessary to [ordain married men]. There is a real value in the celibate priesthood that is wholehearted. Priests are not asked to divide their heart between their family and their parish family."

The ordination of women to the priesthood does not appear possible, he said. When he meets women who feel called to service in the Church, he points out that many executive-level positions in the Church are held by women. He cited the current directors of

Catholic Relief Services and the Catholic Health Association. "Don't get caught up in the idea that if I'm not doing sacramental ministry I'm not being valued," he said. "Rather than get into that argument, look at all the areas where your gifts and talents can bear fruit."

· · · · · · ·

A particular challenge for priests who have been ordained for more than a decade is that they were formed during the papacy of Pope John Paul II, whose emphasis on sound doctrine was very different than the emphasis of Pope Francis on pastoral mercy. Those messages aren't in conflict, Cardinal Wuerl said, and it's important to show priests how to integrate them.

"Saint John Paul's great gift was to remind us of the identity of the faith and the richness of the Church's teaching, but he was also very pastoral. He wasn't driving people away because they didn't live up to the fullness of it," Cardinal Wuerl said. "We were blessed with a twenty-six-year reign in which he said that the Catholic Church does have parameters, it does have teaching, it does expect loyalty. Benedict also said that and Francis is saying it. But at the same time Francis is saying that we have to reach out to those who have difficulty with all of this and let them know that they are still with us. St. John Paul II would have said the same thing in a different way."

It was Pope John Paul II who called for the New Evangelization of the secularized West, Pope Benedict who planned for it, and Pope Francis who is carrying it out. And it is the job of bishops to form priests who can bring the New Evangelization to their neighborhoods and communities.

"We want priests who in their own personal prayer life have a relationship with Christ, who are on fire with that message that Christ is risen and who know Him," Cardinal Wuerl said. "So that formation has to be directed to say that this encounter with Christ is the heart of who we are."

And with that formation, priests can be leaders in the New Evangelization, carrying the message of Christ into a secular world that has forgotten it. It's an exciting time to be a priest. And it's also an exciting time to be a lay Catholic.

Cardinal Wuerl blesses young adults outside St. Matthew the Apostle Cathedral as they prepare to evangelize the streets of downtown Washington during "Light the City." Catholic Standard *photo by Jaclyn Lippelmann. Used with permission.*

With students at the Catholic Student Center at the University of Maryland in College Park. Catholic Standard *photo by Jaclyn Lippelmann. Used with permission.*

CHAPTER 18:
THE NEW EVANGELIZATION

In Rome during the 2014 Synod on the Family, CNN sent a car to bring Cardinal Wuerl to the studio. On the way the producer's aide revealed that he was soon to become a father. The driver chimed in that he had an infant son. They all discussed baby names and the challenges of parenthood.

After the interview on the church's efforts to welcome divorced Catholics, gay people, and others, the producer's aide unexpectedly asked to accompany the cardinal back to the Vatican. In the car he began, "Cardinal, you seem very happy for me about my baby. But you need to know, we are not married."

Then the driver said, "Cardinal, neither are we."

"Well, this is a perfect time for you to reconnect with the Church," Cardinal Wuerl said, ascertaining that both wished to have their children baptized.

The producer's aide turned to face Cardinal Wuerl and asked, "Is there any place for me in the Church?"

"Of course there is," the cardinal began, as the driver also asked if he would be welcome.

He talked with them about how to identify a welcoming parish where their children could be baptized right away and where they could prepare for eventual marriage.

"By this time his eyes had filled up," Cardinal Wuerl remembered later. "It was the most touching moment in the whole two weeks of that synod. He was the very person we were talking about.

"Is there any place for me in the church? That is what Pope Francis is saying: Yes, there is a place. And he is saying to all of us who are already participating in the life of the Church, 'Go out and seek these people and start to walk with them.'"[299]

· · · · · · ·

That is what Cardinal Wuerl has sought to do throughout his ministry: to reach the people who wonder, "Is there any place for me in the Church?"

In recognition of that, Pope Benedict made him the relator for the 2012 Synod on the New Evangelization.

The cardinal drafted his book *New Evangelization: Passing on the Catholic Faith Today* on the plane coming back from that synod.

The New Evangelization, Cardinal Wuerl has said, consists of three elements: renewal of our personal faith, confidence in the truth of scripture and Church teaching, and willingness to share the good news of Jesus with others.

The "new" aspect is the need to re-evangelize large populations that were once Christian but have become secularized. Catholics must engage those who don't agree with the Church, the cardinal said.

The message of Pope Francis is to "tell people that God loves them, tell people that Jesus came so they can experience God's love," he said. "Don't start talking to them immediately about the things they are doing wrong. Invite them to experience God's love and then together we can all try to get close to that love."

Father Thomas Rosica says that Cardinal Wuerl is the foremost interpreter of what Pope Francis is trying to achieve in the New Evangelization.

"The new evangelization isn't a theory, it isn't a book, it isn't a program that you buy from the United States. The new evangelization is a person: Jesus. If you want to see how to do evangelization, look to Pope Francis. If you need someone to explain what Pope Francis is doing, look to Don Wuerl," Father Rosica said.

"He was talking about the New Evangelization way before anyone else was," said Bishop Michael Burbidge of the Diocese of Raleigh. "He understands the importance of how we are to convey this truth of the gospel, this truth of our Catholic faith, in a way that people truly understand, appreciate and are able to articulate."

• • • • • • •

As a young priest in Rome, Father Wuerl spent years quietly building a friendship with a Roman street vendor named Cesare. Cesare hadn't been to church for decades. In fact, he always said that if he ever entered a church it would collapse.

But he asked Father Wuerl to baptize his first grandchild.

"I will, if you will be there," Father Wuerl told him.

The baptism was held in St. Peter's Basilica.

Before the liturgy began, Father Wuerl told the family, "I want everybody to listen very carefully."

They listened in silence.

"I don't hear the dome collapsing," said Father Wuerl.

A big grin lit up Cesare's face. "I'm back," he said.

"Sometimes it just takes a great deal of patience," Cardinal Wuerl remembered years later. "A great deal of patience."

Cardinal Wuerl has quietly continued that kind of personal outreach, often to those whose notoriety or whose extensive theological knowledge from other Christian traditions made them a poor fit for parish-based classes for converts. In 2001 he led Reid Carpenter, a longtime leader in Pittsburgh's evangelical Protestant community, into the Catholic Church. After learning of Carpenter's interest in Catholicism, Bishop Wuerl had invited him to a series of seven dinners at his home.

"He said, 'At the end of the seven dinners, if you decide not to become a Catholic, that will be fine. We will still be great friends. If you decide to do it, I'll be there to welcome you,'" Mr. Carpenter told the Pittsburgh Post-Gazette. "He was a great teacher who...gave me a great deal of love and dignity and respect."

But his outreach wasn't only to community leaders, said Sister Margaret Hannan, his longtime chancellor in Pittsburgh. One night she accompanied him to a dinner with some of the city's wealthiest and most generous Catholics, who had given millions of dollars to the diocese.

"We were walking back into the diocesan building and a gentleman stopped him who was homeless and maybe alcoholic," Sister Margaret said. "He recognized Bishop Wuerl, and the bishop stopped and took his hand and talked with him with as much empathy and as great a respect as he had shown the people at that gathering. He was present to this man in a way that was truly Christlike."

His concern for evangelization is always intertwined with compassion for those who suffer, said Pat Clancy, a parishioner who accompanied him on a 2011 pilgrimage to Lourdes with the Order of Malta. Not only did sixty seriously ill or handicapped people travel in their group of 300, but the streets of Lourdes were filled with thousands of people desperate for healing.

"It was interesting to watch how joyful he was in that situation. He has an ability to have an impact one-on-one with someone who is great need, and provide them with comfort," Mr. Clancy said.

Because he travels often, much of his personal outreach happens in transit. Sometimes his witness is crisis-driven, such as comforting and praying with a flight attendant who burst into tears preparing to board her first flight after the 9/11 terrorist attacks. But more often it is a conversation with someone who spots his clerical collar and assumes he's a parish priest.

One man sitting next to him was reluctantly bound for the first Communion of his nephew. He described himself as "a Catholic who is no longer into the faith," but they discussed Holy Communion, the Mass, and the Eucharist for the duration of the flight. He had had a spotty childhood religious education and did not know some of the most basic Catholic teachings. "He showed real interest in what he thought he already knew, not realizing he was mistaken or simply missing information about the faith of the Church," Cardinal Wuerl said in his address to seminarians in New Orleans. As the plane taxied after landing, "he turned and very seriously said,

'Thanks, Father, for talking to me about this Eucharist thing. It's really cool—I mean really great.'"[300]

That man was part of what the cardinal has long called "the lost generation" of Catholics who grew up amid theological turmoil following Vatican II. Many were introduced to an impoverished lowest-common-denominator version of Catholicism that didn't attract them enough to keep them.

"Teachers and clergy were encouraged to communicate an experience of God's love, but to do it without reference to the Creed, the sacraments, or the tradition. It didn't work very well," Cardinal Wuerl said in an interview with the Knights of Columbus Web site, "Fathers for Good." "Catholics grew up with the impression that their heritage was little more than warm, vaguely positive feelings about God. This left so many lay people weak, spiritually and intellectually, and unable to withstand the tsunami of secularism that came in the last decades of the century. We lost many people because we failed to teach them about right and wrong, about the common good, about the nature of the family and the objective moral order."[301]

This shallow understanding of faith is at the root of bitter divisions in the Church, he said. "It's not that they actively walked away from the Church, but they were never actively invited to understand the wonder of the Eucharist, of God's love, of the Church as our home as we are all struggle in our human condition to embrace God's love. The result has been this reaction where people said, 'This is what it means to be Catholic and you must not be Catholic if you don't do this and this.' So you began to get these divisions.

"The understanding of the Church that I grew up in is that the Church is our wonderful loving mother and we are all doing our best. In the parish I grew up in as a kid, no one ever thought that everyone who was there on Sunday was perfect. It was our spiritual family and we weren't making a judgment about the fitness of anyone else."

Cardinal Wuerl worried that somehow the priorities of the bishops' conference could imply that we were complacent about those who turned away from the Church. In 1995, when a meeting of the bishops' conference committee got bogged down in a debate over which orders of angels to mention in a prayer, he told a reporter that they were majoring in minors. "I might be relieved if people followed the Mass so closely that these changes became a matter of debate," he said. "I'm more concerned about getting people who are not in church back in touch."[302]

Four years later he took the lead in presenting a plan to the bishops for a renewed effort at adult religious education that would also include formation in prayer, scripture study and applying the faith to daily life. "Adults do not grow in faith primarily by learning concepts, but by sharing the life of the Christian community," the document said.[303] One way that he transformed his own catechetical work into evangelization was through the television show "The Teaching of Christ," which aired in Pittsburgh from 1990 to 2006 on the CBS affiliate KDKA, with national exposure through EWTN. He always spoke about an aspect of Catholic teaching, then did an interview segment to explore how it applied to daily living and life in a community.

He believes that liturgy must be inviting to those whose relationship with the Church is distant, broken or nonexistent.

In the early 1990s he supported efforts to translate the church documents and the liturgy using inclusive language for human beings, so that references to both sexes would be translated "men and women," or "sisters and brothers." Throughout his years as a bishop and archbishop he has always spoken that way, even in informal conversation.

Such principles are "sensitive to scripture, they are sensitive to the use of the English language, they are sensitive to public reading, but most of all they are sensitive to the listener who will be hearing those words," he said in 1990.[304]

The Vatican office that oversees liturgy rejected those efforts and mandated that the Mass must be translated literally from the Latin. It explicitly forbade gender inclusiveness in the new Roman Missal of 2011.

Although he loyally promotes the new translation, Cardinal Wuerl believes the stilted language and complex run-on sentences that come straight from Latin have not promoted the reverence that ad-vocates of the new translation intended.

Gender-inclusive language "is such a normal part of life that there has to be a way in which it works into the liturgy. Down the road I think this is going to be revisited again. But I don't expect to be around for that."

• • • • • • •

On the other side of gender concerns, in Pittsburgh he established a group that evangelizes men and brings them into closer relation-ship with the Church. The idea for Catholic Men's Fellowship came from a group of laymen, including Reid Carpenter, the convert who had been a leader among evangelical Protestants. They wanted to share their faith with other men, helping them become better Catholics and better husbands and fathers. Bishop Wuerl gave it his blessing and spoke to 200 of them at the first "Gathering of Catholic Men" in April 2003 at St. Paul's Seminary.

That gathering—which continues today—now draws closer to 2,000. The Cardinal is trying to build something similar in Wash-ington.

"That was one of the areas that was probably least developed—get-ting men to engage in their faith life, getting men to set aside some time on a Saturday to come and pray and go to Confession, to have some spiritual food," he said.

One hope is that spiritually stronger men will have better mar-riages and fewer divorces. But outreach to divorced Catholics, espe-cially those who remarried outside the Church, is one of Cardinal Wuerl's priorities.

"One of the things I have recognized and realized over nearly thirty years as a bishop and forty-eight as a priest is how many people who should be with us aren't because of marriage problems," he said. "When I was bishop of Pittsburgh, the other leaders in our ecumeni-cal group used to say to me jokingly that I should pay dues twice be-cause the Catholic Church was the largest religious entity here and the second-largest was the people who identify themselves as former

Catholics. Almost all of that had to do with marriage problems and the fact that people felt they were no longer welcome. That is where we need to focus our attention."

Pittsburgh had a Catholic ministry to divorced and separated Catholics long before he became bishop. He promoted it, sometimes celebrating the Mass during annual days of enrichment. He also sought to make the annulment process easier and more available, said Sister Margaret Hannan, his chancellor in Pittsburgh. "He would get really annoyed when people were two and three years waiting for documentation. He really tried to speed that up."

When Pope John Paul called for 2000 to be a Great Jubilee of celebrating the 2,000th birthday of Jesus, it was an opportunity for Bishop Wuerl to further promote evangelization and renewal.

One of his favorite initiatives in 2000 was to give to more than 5,000 parishioners at a Eucharistic Congress personal invitations that he had signed, which they could in turn give to fallen-away friends and family inviting them to return to Mass.

"The next time you see them, say, 'The bishop asked me to give you this,'" he told those gathered at the city's convention center.[305]

The effort was so popular that many people called the diocesan Pastoral Center to ask for more invitations. Anecdotal reports indicated that people came back to Mass.

As a result the initiative was expanded to all parishes, with thousands of similar invitations distributed shortly before Christmas. The invitation said, "Often at family gatherings when one member is not present, everyone feels the loss. When we meet as God's family for Sunday Mass, we miss you. You still belong to our family, the Church."[306] As Archbishop of Washington, he launched a similar effort there. Young people were a special concern. Bishop Wuerl found a role model in Pope John Paul II, who inaugurated World Youth Days.

Many bishops were skeptical of the plan to hold World Youth Day in Denver in 1993, saying that young Catholics in the United States had no concept of pilgrimage and that the projected 60,000 young people would never show up.[307] They were happily shocked when final registration was about 225,000, with an estimated 500,000 at the papal Mass.[308]

Bishop Wuerl was one of the featured speakers, telling 90,000 teens and young adults in Mile High Stadium, "The Catholic faith does not make us less human but more human. It urges us to be faithful to the deepest longings of the human spirit, to be bearers of peace and to be a blessing to others."[309]

In Denver he met with the young people from Pittsburgh and answered their questions. One young man asked, "You know, like, you're the big cheese in our diocese. So, what's it like meeting the bigger cheese?"

The bishop replied, "Every time I get on my knees, I realize there is a much bigger cheese."[310] That World Youth Day sparked many local initiatives in Pittsburgh. He interviewed four young people who had been in Denver on his TV show, "The Teaching of Christ." In July 1994 he held a listening session with young people from across the diocese to hear their views on the Church. This became an annual event: "Youth Speak Out." In 1995 he held a session focused on their role in evangelization. The 1996 session drew 260 teens. In 2001 more than 2,000 young people went on a World Youth Day cruise at the confluence of Pittsburgh's three rivers.[311]

Another tradition began in 2000 with the first Hosanna gathering for 2,500 teens on Palm Sunday. Held on a college campus, it was a pep rally fused with a retreat to the tune of uptempo music.[312] That event continues in Pittsburgh. With help from Youthtowne, a local Catholic foundation, Pittsburgh regularly sent one of the largest delegations to World Youth Day in cities across the globe.

Just a month after World Youth Day in Denver, the Diocese of Pittsburgh celebrated its 150th anniversary with a Mass in the Civic Arena. The hockey scoreboard was draped in green, gold, purple, scarlet, and magenta streamers to transform it into a baldacchino above the raised altar.

As the *Pittsburgh Post-Gazette* described it, "When 10,000 faithful made the sign of the cross...the movement rippled through the arena like a demure rendition of 'The Wave.'"

Bishop Wuerl called on the laity to be evangelizers.

"You are our primary witness in the world. Through you the world is to be transformed," he said. "In all the things you do in your home or in your school, in your neighborhood and where you work, you have been called to bring the spirit of Christ into your life and the lives of others."[313] One of his favorite liturgical events is the Rite of Election, which welcomes new Catholics into the Church. Bishop Wuerl encouraged every parish to have a formal program of instructing and mentoring prospective Catholics—known as the Rite of Christian Initiation of Adults, or RCIA.

Each year in Pittsburgh typically saw an increase, from about 600 when he came to well over 1,000 such converts. Some would cite Bishop Wuerl's direct influence on their decision to convert through his TV show "The Teaching of Christ."[314]

In Washington, the numbers of adults participating in the Rite of Election grew following Cardinal Wuerl's arrival, and is now so large that it has to be held over the course of two weekends at the Basilica of the National Shrine of the Immaculate Conception. In 2015, over 1,300 adults participated in the ritual.

Popular religious holidays were an occasion for outreach. At Christmastime he worked across denominational lines to keep Jesus uppermost in minds and hearts. There were ecumenical Christmas concerts at the city's major theaters. But since 1999 the centerpiece has been the Pittsburgh Creche, the only replica of the larger-than-life-size nativity scene that Pope John Paul II commissioned for St. Peter's Square.

It was the idea of Louis Astorino, a Pittsburgh architect. A few years earlier, Bishop Wuerl had helped advise him when he was commissioned to design a chapel for the guest house the Vatican was building to house important visitors, as well as cardinals who would vote in any future conclave. Though it remained obscure for many years, it is now famous as the one where Pope Francis celebrates daily Mass each morning, as he has elected to live in that guest house.[315] Bishop Wuerl pulled together a non-profit ecumenical organization to support the crèche project. Many volunteers also help, from nuns who make clothes for the figures to a theater company that assembles, maintains and stores the figures.

The crèche is erected in the USX Plaza, in a busy stretch of Downtown. It has become a place where marriage proposals take place, where homeless people seek God, where people bring their joys and sorrows to the manger, said Father Ronald Lengwin, the unofficial chaplain who spends most nights during Advent talking with people at the crèche.[316]

• • • • • • •

Archbishop Wuerl arrived in Washington with evangelization at the top of his agenda.

"Our task is to continually remind people of their relationship with God," he said in an online chat on WashingtonPost.com, in response to a question about urgent priorities. "One of the priorities of the Church today is to reach out to those who have fallen away from the practice of the faith and those who have never really heard the story of Jesus and his gospel."[317]

He became a popular speaker at Theology on Tap, which brings young adult Catholics to a pub to hear a speaker and ask questions. He speaks often at college campus ministry groups.

"The cardinal recently celebrated a liturgy for young adults down at the cathedral, and it was jammed," said Father Mark Knestout. "He enjoys the fact that the cathedral has a thriving young adult population. The evening Mass on Sundays is very popular with them. The cardinal is aware of that and has gone a number of times to that Mass."

Young people are a key reason why the cardinal—never known as a first adopter of new technology—prioritized social media outreach.

"Young people today aren't watching television," Cardinal Wuerl said. "But the need to communicate remains. You can never communicate enough."

• • • • • • •

One of Cardinal Wuerl's signature initiatives, "The Light Is On for You," begun in Pittsburgh in 1999, reached new heights in Washington and has been endorsed by the U.S. Conference of Catholic Bishops for use nationwide.

A well-documented collapse in the number of Catholics going to Confession, coupled with his belief that return to that sacrament will be the precursor of a great renewal of faith, inspired The Light is On for You.

The earliest version began as preparation for the Great Jubilee. The Diocese advertised that parishes would be open for Confession on Wednesdays during Advent 1999. The Diocese created a simple brochure for those unfamiliar with the sacrament. Bishop Wuerl urged priests to preach about Confession, write letters inviting estranged Catholics to "come home" through the sacrament of Reconciliation, to make Confession more available, and to go to Confession themselves.[318] That December he personally heard confessions at parishes in three different counties.[319]

In Washington he expanded the program. All churches are open on Wednesdays during Lent, which is heavily advertised through all media from bus signs to Twitter.

In his 2008 pastoral letter, *Reflections on God's Mercy and Our Forgiveness: The Light is Always On!* he wrote about the overwhelming response.

Hundreds, perhaps thousands, of people who had not been to Confession for decades came back.

"In many parishes each successive Wednesday brought more people to church for reconciliation, and in some cases during Wednesday of Holy Week priests heard confessions for three, four, five hours," he wrote. Some pastors increased the hours for Confession year-round.

In 2014 Cardinal Wuerl published a book about the sacrament of Reconciliation, also called *The Light is On for You.* "Some readers might be afraid of the Confessional. I hope this book can help them get over their fear and into the sacrament," he told Pete Socks of "The Catholic Book Blogger." His message, he said, is "Don't be afraid. Everyone is rooting for you. None of your sins will shock the priest who hears your Confession. He's heard everything in his years in the confessional. He knows that everybody sins. He wants you to succeed and he'll help you."[320] The cardinal called on lay Catholics to be the front line evangelizers.

"He is trying to activate the latent apostolic zeal of the lay faithful," said Father Carter Griffin, his former priest-secretary who is now vocations director and vice-rector of St. John Paul II Seminary in Washington.

"The first evangelization took place from one Christian to another. If that doesn't happen, then the New Evangelization won't be what the Holy Father is hoping for. So his preaching and teaching is to the ordinary lay faithful, so that they will understand that they are not simply recipients of the good news, but that they have to become messengers of the good news."

His multimedia staff produced TV ads. One for Christmastime has no words but shows people moving to the tune of "Joy to the World," from school children tapping their desks to nuns dancing with a woman in her wheelchair.

"The idea was to go for the lowest common denominator and reach people not with a heavily theological message, but with one that reaches the heart," said Father William Byrne, who as the secretary for pastoral ministry and social concerns oversaw evangelization initiatives in the Archdiocese of Washington. "His evangelization style is more open arms than a pointing finger."[321] The next year at Lent, the Archdiocese of Washington launched a multimedia outreach: "Longing for Something? Maybe it's God." It used subway ads, YouTube videos, radio and newspaper ads and lawn signs to invite people back. Parishes distributed 50,000 invitation cards in English and Spanish, which parishioners could use to invite loved ones back to Mass.[322]

The effort was meant to be a gentle wake-up call to people who think they are doing just fine without God, the Cardinal said. "This just plants the seed. Are you really all that happy? Is there something missing? It's just to say that God is. He is here, and he is inviting you into a relationship."

• • • • • • •

Pope Francis has been a role model for how to do the new evangelization, with his message of love and welcome for all.

Cardinal Wuerl soon became an important advisor to Pope Francis, as well as a leading defender of the pope when he is criticized by
more conservative Catholics.

In February 2015 he wrote a blog post about watching on television as Pope Francis addressed an adoring crowd of tens of thousands
in St. Peter's Square, as his inbox filled with emails "including an interview and an article by brother bishops who are less than enthusiastic about Pope Francis," he wrote.

It caused him to reflect on when, as a twenty-year-old seminarian,
he was scandalized by self-proclaimed faithful Catholics who denounced the encyclical of Pope John XXIII, *Mater et Magistra*. One
of the priests at the seminary, he wrote, reminded him that there
have always been currents of dissent in the Church, including among
the cardinals. Cardinal Wuerl cited attacks on Pope Paul VI from
both the left and the right, on Pope John Paul I for allegedly abusing
the dignity of his office by smiling too much, and on Pope John Paul
II again from right and left for his social encyclicals and teachings on
evangelization respectively.

The common thread in all of that, he said, is that "they disagree
with the Pope because he does not agree with them and therefore follow their position. Disagreement is perhaps something we will always
have, lamentable as it is, but we will also have Peter and his successor
as the rock and touchstone of both our faith and out unity."[323]

Pope Francis, Cardinal Wuerl said, is reaching people who have
turned away from the Church because they sense his genuine love for
them. "Pope Francis is such a wonderful example in inviting people
to draw close to Christ. If you meet them where they are and start to
talk with them and walk with them, you can begin to talk about how
maybe they aren't as close to Christ as they might want to be. But
you can't have that conversation if you have not met and engaged
them."

Less than six months after Pope Francis' election, Cardinal Wuerl
was among the speakers as a standing-room-only crowd overflowed a
750-seat hall at Georgetown University for a forum on "The Francis

Factor." It had been moved to that hall from a 200-seater after advance registration soared far above normal levels and drew a much younger crowd than similar events. It was also a very mixed crowd, ideologically and theologically.[324]

"This is not a political program or ideological agenda, but faith in action, the Gospel at work," the cardinal told them. "Pope Francis is teaching us not only that we should know the Gospel, but how to 'do' the Gospel....Pope Francis is a model of civility and service that a polarized and paralyzed Washington could learn from and follow."[325]

• • • • • • •

Not long after Pope Francis' first anniversary, the Archdiocese of Washington welcomed its largest group of Catholic converts ever: 1,306. Nearly a third were under age 36.[326]

Those numbers reflect conversations the cardinal has had with many people since March 13, 2013. At a baggage carousel in Washington he was approached by a woman who identified herself as a lapsed Catholic.

"She said, 'This pope has made me feel so welcomed that I've started to go back to Mass.' I asked her what made her feel welcomed, what had Pope Francis said that made her feel that way. She said, 'He makes me feel that it's not all my fault.' All I could say is, 'That's the theology of original sin and the human condition. It's not all our fault.' St. Paul talked about that struggle between what we want to do and what we end up doing. I said to her, 'The next time you identify yourself, why don't you say you're an ex-lapsed Catholic?'"

Priests worldwide are overjoyed with the interest that Pope Francis has inspired in people who have been estranged from the Church, he said. "My priests tell me they feel so empowered by what is going on. They have been trying to reach out to people all along. Now they know that, from the pope on down, the Church is saying that people don't have to be perfect to be welcomed in. That makes all the difference."

• • • • • • •

The New Evangelization isn't just a *program* in the Archdiocese of Washington, said Msgr. Robert Panke, rector of St. John Paul II Seminary. It's a way of life. In 2013 the seminarians developed an on-going initiative to do street evangelization. "They've become active in wanting to bring faith to the people. The seminarians went on their own initiative. They've done some work with parishes going door to door. They are looking for ways to talk about their faith and to witness in class to other students at the Catholic University of America. It's become a very significant thing, this need to reach out to those who are on the fringe."

"We have so many young adults coming along who are telling us, 'I'd like to know about the Catholic Church. Can you tell me what it's all about?'" Cardinal Wuerl said. "They don't know much more than the generation before them. The difference is that they want to know."

Cardinal Wuerl greets parishioners at Our Lady of Mercy Church in Potomac, Maryland. Catholic Standard *photo by Jaclyn Lippelmann. Used with permission.*

Cardinal Wuerl greets catechumens, candidates, their godparents and spon-
sors during the Rite of Election and Call to Continuing Conversion Liturgy.
Catholic Standard *photo by Jaclyn Lippelmann. Used with permission.*

CHAPTER 19:
FUTURE DIRECTIONS

Poems, they say, are never finished, only abandoned. And the same must be said of any "real-time" attempt to chronicle the work of Donald Wuerl. As long as he is alive and able, he will be a fast-moving target.

In the time between our manuscript's completion and its production as a book (just a few short weeks), he has hosted a papal visit to the United States...represented the country's bishops in the rite for the canonization of Junipero Serra...appeared on several network news programs...and flown off to attend the 2015 meetings of the Vatican Synod on the family. From Rome he is registering regular reports by video; and his contributions to the Synod are the regular fodder of news on television and in the electronic and print media. Pope Francis has appointed Cardinal Wuerl as one of six prelates who will draft the final report on the Synod.

Two major publishers have announced books forthcoming from the Cardinal, one on martyrdom and another on prayer. Both are substantial studies. Both are due out in the weeks to come.

Our book will hardly be the last word about Cardinal Donald Wuerl. We believe he will continue to make history, and history will continue to reflect on the contributions he has already made. This is a beginning, now to be abandoned to the reading public, but soon, no doubt, to be superseded.

"Pastoral" is the word his colleagues use most often to describe him. Yet, after thirty years a bishop and almost fifty a priest, he is still eager to improve—to do something still "more pastoral."

With Pope Francis in Washington, 2015. Catholic Standard *photo by Paul Fetters. Used with permission.*

AFTERWORD

By Mark Zimmermann

As the late great Yankees catcher and accidental philosopher Yogi Berra said, it was "like deja vu all over again."

On a sunny fall day in September 2015 in Washington, D.C., I stood on the press riser overlooking the 25,000 people gathered outside the Basilica of the National Shrine of the Immaculate Conception for the canonization Mass for Blessed Junípero Serra, and I had a front-row view of Pope Francis passing by in his popemobile, smiling and waving to the cheering crowd. And there riding in the back seat was our Archbishop of Washington, Cardinal Donald Wuerl, whom I as editor of the *Catholic Standard* newspaper of the Archdiocese of Washington, along with our reporters and photographers, have been covering since his appointment to the nation's capital. What an amazing ride that must have been for him! Cardinal Wuerl later joked that if he had to come up with a title for the papal visit, it might be "Scenes from the Popemobile."

And even more amazing, seven and a half years earlier in April 2008, I had watched from a nearby vantage point, on the basilica's steps, as the popemobile carrying a smiling, waving Pope Benedict XVI passed by, with that same passenger, then-Archbishop Wuerl, who was named a cardinal two years later.

When Archbishop Wuerl welcomed Pope Benedict at the outdoor Papal Mass at the newly opened Nationals Park, he said the diverse crowd of nearly 50,000 people represented the face of the Catholic Church in America—people from many different ethnic and cultural backgrounds, "a faith family that includes women and men, young and old."

A few days after Pope Francis left Washington, Cardinal Wuerl reflected on what he told the Holy Father as they rode in the popemobile through the campus of The Catholic University of America that adjoins the basilica, that as the pope looked out over the thousands of students and young adults in the crowd he was seeing the "future of the Church in this country." No wonder Pope Francis surprised the event organizers by having the popemobile turn around and swing by again for another look. Then moments later, the pope had another view of the Church's future, as he stepped inside the basilica and was greeted by loud cheers of thousands of seminarians and novices from across the country. After the Mass, Pope Francis visited the Archdiocese of Washington's Saint John Paul II Seminary, which Cardinal Wuerl established in 2011 to train the next generation of priests who will serve local Catholics. The pope encouraged the 49 seminarians studying there to be men of prayer and to adore Jesus in their lives and work.

Cardinal Wuerl has said the faith and vitality of young adults inspires him and gives him great hope for the future of the Catholic Church, and he has spoken to that age group at Theology on Tap gatherings at Washington pubs, and at Masses and dinners for college students at the University of Maryland and George Washington University. Six months before Pope Francis's arrival, Cardinal Wuerl had celebrated a special Mass for young adults at the Cathedral of Saint Matthew The Apostle, and then they participated in a "Light the City" evangelization event, carrying candles as a sign of Christ's light and walking together on the darkened city streets, to invite people to come to the cathedral and pray with them.

Fittingly, cheering young adults were among the most vocal people in the crowd to welcome Pope Francis to Washington after his arrival at Joint Base Andrews, where the Holy Father was greeted by President Barack Obama and the First Lady. The cardinal also made sure that rotating groups of students from nearly all 139 parishes and 95 Catholic schools in the archdiocese would be present for all eight comings and goings that Pope Francis had from the Apostolic Nunciature, where he stayed during his two-day visit to Washington. That way, nearly 2,100 youth had the chance to see the pope up close, and quite a few were able to shake his hand or pose for a selfie with him.

At the homily for his 2006 installation Mass in Washington, Archbishop Wuerl addressed his new family of faith and spoke of what lay ahead—"our faith journey together." The two papal visits which he hosted in Washington reflected that spirit, as Cardinal Wuerl sought to engage his archdiocese and the community as a whole to welcome first Pope Benedict XVI, and later Pope Francis, by bringing help and hope to others.

One day before Pope Francis arrived, Catholic Charities of the Archdiocese of Washington announced that more than 100,000 people had taken the "Walk with Francis Pledge" to pray, serve, or act on behalf of those in need. Those making the pledge included a boy who donated his birthday money to the poor, and a parish young adults group that bagged and delivered 80,000 pounds of potatoes to soup kitchens around the city.

To honor Pope Benedict XVI on his visit to Washington, Catholics at local parishes and schools collected 227,837 pounds of food for the Archdiocesan Hunger to Hope Food Drive coordinated by Catholic Charities.

Throughout his leadership of the Archdiocese of Washington, Cardinal Wuerl has encouraged local Catholics to take up the call to the New Evangelization, to deepen their faith, grow confident in its truth, and share it with others.

When he marked his 25th anniversary as a bishop in 2011, Cardinal Wuerl celebrated a Mass and presented Manifesting the Kingdom Awards to 201 unsung heroes from local Catholic parishes, schools and Catholic agencies, thanking them for helping to build God's kingdom in their community.

Then to mark the 75th anniversary of the Archdiocese of Washington three years later, the cardinal convoked the first Archdiocesan Synod, with the stated goal of "building the best Church we can be." The 200 Synod participants included lay men and women from across the archdiocese representing different backgrounds, and

priests, women religious, deacons and bishops. The Synod participants analyzed more than 15,000 suggestions offered through parish
and regional listening sessions and online surveys. Cardinal Wuerl
accepted 79 recommendations and related statutes from the dele-
gates, which charted a blueprint for the local Church's future outreach in the key areas of worship, education, community, service and
stewardship/administration.

In 2007, then-Archbishop Wuerl called a Convocation for
Catholic Education that brought together 500 educational leaders
from throughout the Archdiocese of Washington, who looked at
current challenges facing Catholic schools and discussed the need for
working together on future strategic planning in order to sustain
Catholic schools. In a related pastoral letter the next year, titled,
"Catholic Education: Looking to the Future with Confidence," Cardinal Wuerl wrote, "The future of our Catholic schools depends on
the ability of all of us working together to meet their increasing costs
and to assist families who are making sacrifices to give their children
a Catholic school education."

Following the convocation, task forces were formed, research was
done into best practices, surveys were sent to 12,000 people, focus
groups met, archdiocesan consultative groups reviewed proposals,
and regional consultations were held. That extensive consultation
and collaboration resulted in new Catholic School Policies being
adopted for the archdiocese in 2009, which were aimed at strength-
ening the Catholic identity, academic excellence, governance and af-
fordability and accessibility of Catholic schools.

A progress report in 2013, five years after the cardinal's education
pastoral, noted that through a revised offertory program, people at
every parish throughout the archdiocese were investing in Catholic
education, including at 112 out of 139 parishes that had entered into
regional school sponsorship agreements. Archdiocesan tuition assistance has risen from $800,000 in 2007 to nearly $6 million annu-
ally by 2015, which helped make the dream of a Catholic education
possible for 5,500 families that school year.

Known nationally as the "education bishop" for his teaching ministry that has included books, pastoral letters, TV programs and ra-

dio spots, Cardinal Wuerl now also writes blogs and e-letters, and the Archdiocese of Washington's papal visit coverage included reporting by its English and Spanish language newspapers, and also live tweets and Facebook postings by its digital media team, and videos by its multimedia crew posted on the archdiocese's own YouTube channel.

As this book shows, the cardinal is both a teacher and a pastor, which he has demonstrated in good and challenging times. He has crisscrossed the archdiocese to celebrate parish and school anniversary Masses, and he also joined religious leaders in a Unity Walk to mark the fifth anniversary of the 9/11 terrorist attacks, and he celebrated a Mass for healing on the day after shootings at the Washington Navy Yard in 2013 left 12 people dead.

That same year, Cardinal Wuerl joined volunteers at a Catholic Charities food line, serving a warm meal to some of Washington's homeless. He personally greeted each man and woman in line, smiling at them and shaking their hands.

"It's very important to ask their name," the cardinal said. "It's important to ask people who they are." They are not just numbers coming through the line, he said. "Every one has a story."

The cardinal said Catholic Charities provides more than just food and shelter. "It (this outreach) says God loves you... God is with you, and this here is a sign of that. It's not just giving people food, it's letting them know they are loved. Catholic Charities is a visible sign of God's love, because of the support of everyone who makes it possible."

The next morning after their popemobile ride near the National Shrine, Pope Francis became the first pontiff to address a joint meeting of Congress, then the Holy Father paid a visit to that same Catholic Charities food line where Cardinal Wuerl sometimes volunteers.

The popemobile ride may be over, but Cardinal Wuerl has said that the "Walk with Francis" should continue, as people emulate the pope's example of sharing the Gospel with others and bringing Christ's love to those in need, two hallmarks of the cardinal's ministry in the nation's capital and his earlier service in his hometown of

Pittsburgh, where then and now, he has felt called to "do something more pastoral."

Zimmermann is editor of the Catholic Standard *newspaper of the Archdiocese of Washington.*

With Pope Francis and seminarians at St. John Paul Seminary during the papal visit, 2015. L'Osservatore Romano photo. Used with permission.

With Pope Francis at Mass for the canonization of Junípero Serra, Basilica Shrine of the Immaculate Conception, 2015. Catholic Standard photo by Paul Fetters. Used with permission.

Notes

1 "Francis J. Wuerl, Whose 4 Children Included a Bishop," *Pittsburgh Post-Gazette*, May 14, 1994.

2 "The Bishop Moves Ahead," *Pittsburgh Post-Gazette*, March 24, 1996.

3 Dan Donovan, "Pope Names Wuerl Bishop Here," *Pittsburgh Press*, February 12, 1988.

4 *Pittsburgh Press Sunday Magazine*, March 12, 1989, 22.

5 Reminiscence of Christopher Wolfe, as recounted to the authors.

6 Desmond O'Grady, "An American with a Roman Connection," *National Catholic Reporter*, August 4, 1972, 6.

7 McDowell, 52.

8 Unsigned editorial, "Wright the Enigma," *National Catholic Reporter*, August 4, 1972.

9 Robert McClory, "Looking Ahead: Bishop Wuerl of Pittsburgh," *National Catholic Reporter*, March 4, 1988, 1.

10 M. J. Wilson, "When in Rome, Pittsburgh Priest Donald Wuerl Lived Differently: He Saw the Pope Get Elected," *People Magazine*, March 12, 1979.

11 "The Bishop Moves Ahead," *Pittsburgh Post-Gazette*, March 24, 1996.

12 Patricia Rhule, "Pope Paul Eulogized at Mass Here," *Pittsburgh Press*, August 15, 1978.

13 "Wuerl Gives Thanks to Leadership of Pope John Paul II," *Pittsburgh Post-Gazette*, October 16, 1998.

14 *Pittsburgh Press Sunday Magazine*, March 12, 1989, 24.

15 Jerry Filteau, "Wuerl in 1978 Conclave That Elected John Paul II," *National Catholic Reporter*, November 20, 2010.

16 McDowell, 84.

17 "The Bishop Moves Ahead," *Pittsburgh Post-Gazette*, March 24, 1996.

18 Ann Rodgers-Melnick, "Bishop Leonard is Remembered as a Priest's Priest," *Pittsburgh Post-Gazette*, September 2, 1994.

19 Donald W. Wuerl and Michael Wilson and Piero Cipolat, *A Visit to the Vatican for Young People* (Boston, MA: St. Paul Editions, 1980).

20 "The Bishop Moves Ahead," *Pittsburgh Post-Gazette*, March 24, 1996.

21 Karen J. Terry et al., *The Causes and Context of Sexual Abuse of Minors by Catholic Priests in the United States*, 1950-2010 (Washington, DC: USCCB, 2011), 40-47.

22 "Crackdown May Come on 'Conscience' Cases," *National Catholic Reporter*, August 4, 1972, 1; see also "Remarried Receive Communion," 16, and "St. Louis Official Criticizes Communion for Remarried Persons," 16.

23 *National Catholic Reporter*, November 7, 1986, 23-25.

24 "The Bishop Moves Ahead," *Pittsburgh Post-Gazette*, March 24, 1996.

25 Cited in Patricia Bartos, "Bishop Wuerl Explains, Denies Myths in Seattle," *Pittsburgh Catholic*, June 10, 1987.

26 Patricia Bartos, "Bishop Wuerl Explains, Denies Myths in Seattle," *Pittsburgh Catholic*, June 10, 1987; see also the chronology of events involving the Archdiocese of Seattle, printed in *National Catholic Reporter*, November 7, 1986, 23-25.

27 Patricia Bartos, "Bishop Wuerl Explains, Denies Myths in Seattle," *Pittsburgh Catholic*, June 10, 1987.

28 "Seattle Saga: From Wuerl to Murphy in Four Years," June 5, 1987, 19; see also Patricia Bartos, "Bishop Wuerl Explains, Denies Myths in Seattle," *Pittsburgh Catholic*, June 10, 1987.

29 Chronology of events printed in *National Catholic Reporter*, November 7, 1986, 23-27.

30 Interview for *Pittsburgh Post-Gazette*, December, 1995.

31 Knight-News-Tribune news service, *Pittsburgh Press*, September 13, 1986.

32 Patricia Bartos, "Bishop Wuerl Explains, Denies Myths in Seattle," *Pittsburgh Catholic*, June 10, 1987.

33 Tim McCarthy, "Rome Opposition among Seattle Catholics 'Deep,'" *National Catholic Reporter*, October 3, 1986; see also Tim McCarthy, "Seattle Prelates Still Ride Stormbound Sea," *National Catholic Reporter*, October 10, 1986.

34 Tim McCarthy, "Seattle Prelates Still Ride Stormbound Sea," *National Catholic Reporter*, October 10, 1986.

35 Tim McCarthy, "Rome Opposition among Seattle Catholics 'Deep,'" *National Catholic Reporter*, October 3, 1986; see also Tim McCarthy, "Seattle Prelates Still Ride Stormbound Sea," *National Catholic Reporter*, October 10, 1986.

36 Eleanor Bergholz, "Priests Ask Wuerl to Leave Seattle," *Pittsburgh Post-Gazette*, December 3, 1986.

37 Dan Morris, "Ovation Greets Hunthausen at Mentor's Funeral," November 7, 1986, 23.

38 "Ratzinger '85 Letter Outlines Road to Orthodoxy," *National Catholic Reporter*, June 5, 1987, 24.

39 "Hunthausen: My Understanding Differs," *National Catholic Reporter*, November 7, 1986, 25.

40 Eleanor Bergholz, "Wuerl Says Seattle Glad to See Him Go," *Pittsburgh Post-Gazette*, June 3, 1987.

41 "The Bishop Moves Ahead," *Pittsburgh Post-Gazette*, March 24, 1996.

42 Patricia Bartos, "Bishop Wuerl Explains, Denies Myths in Seattle," *Pittsburgh Catholic*, June 10, 1987.

43 UPI, *Pittsburgh Press*, November 14, 1986, A12.

44 AP, "U.S. Bishops Support Vatican in Disciplining of Seattle Prelate," *Pittsburgh Press*, November 12, 1986.

45 Brad Reynolds, "Seattle Focus Back on Hunthausen," *National Catholic Reporter*, May 1, 1987, 1.

46 "Pope Reinstates Archbishop Hunthausen," *Pittsburgh Press*, May 27, 1987 (*Los Angeles Times* wire story); see also Eleanor Bergholz, "Wuerl Says Seattle Glad to See Him Go," *Pittsburgh Post-Gazette*,

June 23, 1987.

47 Patricia Bartos, "Bishop Wuerl Explains, Denies Myths in Seattle," *Pittsburgh Catholic*, June 10, 1987.

48 Unsigned editorial, *Seattle Post-Intelligencer*, as cited in Patricia Bartos, "Bishop Wuerl Explains, Denies Myths in Seattle," *Pittsburgh Catholic*, June 10, 1987.

49 Jerry Filteau, "Bishop Wuerl: Glad It's Over," *Florida Catholic*, June 5, 1987, 11.

50 *Shepherd Touched All Areas of Local Church*, commemorative supplement to the *Pittsburgh Catholic*, June 9, 2006, 4.

51 Tim Vercellotti, "Long Walk Ahead, Wuerl Says at Ceremony," *Pittsburgh Press*, March 26, 1988.

52 "Bishop as Administrator," speech to new bishops in Rome September 20, 2005.

53 Ann Rodgers-Melnick, "Bishop Wuerl Washes Feet of 12 County Jail Inmates," *Pittsburgh Press*, March 24, 1989.

54 Archbishop Donald Wuerl, "The Bishop as Administrator," address, Rome, September 20, 2005.

55 Bishop Donald Wuerl, *Future Directions*, pastoral letter, September 19, 1993.

56 Ann Rodgers-Melnick, "Catholic Charities to Open Clinic," *Pittsburgh Post-Gazette*, May 8, 2003.

57 Pamela Gaynor, "Hospital Merger Plan Collapses," *Pittsburgh Post-Gazette*, January 31, 2002; see also Teresa Lindemann, "St. Francis to Close; Children's Moving in," *Pittsburgh Post-Gazette*, August 20, 2002.

58 Marylynn Uricchio, "Seen," *Pittsburgh Post-Gazette*, December 2, 2003.

59 Mary Niederberger, "Diocesan Task Force to Study Cuts in Debt," *Pittsburgh Press*, April 16, 1988.

60 Mary Niederberger, "Wuerl Vows to Recover from $2.8 Million Deficit," *Pittsburgh Press*, March 20, 1989; see also "Bishop Reaches 5th Anniversary as Head of Pittsburgh Diocese," *Pittsburgh Catholic*, February 12, 1993.

61 Ann Rodgers-Melnick, "Parishioners Increase Giving," *Pittsburgh Press,* January 10, 1991.

62 Bill Zlatos, "Schools Draining Diocese Finances, Wuerl Says," *Pittsburgh Press,* October 29, 1988.

63 "Policies for Financing Elementary Schools, Diocese of Pittsburgh," May, 1995, 8.

64 Bill Zlatos, "Schools Draining Diocese Finances, Wuerl Says," *Pittsburgh Press,* October 29, 1988.

65 Ann Rodgers-Melnick, "Help Promised for Catholic Parishes in Debt," *Pittsburgh Press,* June 22, 1988.

66

67 "Policies for Financing Elementary Schools," Diocese of Pittsburgh, 1995

68 Bill Zlatos, "Schools Draining Diocese Finances, Wuerl Says," *Pittsburgh Press,* October 29, 1988.

69 Ann Rodgers-Melnick, "Parishioners Increase Giving," *Pittsburgh Press,* January 10, 1991.

70 Bill Zlatos, "Schools Draining Diocese Finances, Wuerl Says," *Pittsburgh Press,* October 29, 1988.

71 Interview with Ambrose Murray, Pittsburgh.

72 Bill Steigerwald, "Hope and a Prayer," *Pittsburgh Post-Gazette,* April 10, 1994.

73 Bill Steigerwald, "Hope and a Prayer," *Pittsburgh Post-Gazette,* April 10, 1994.

74 Bill Zlatos, "Firm to Help Poor Attend Diocese Schools," *Pittsburgh Press,* May 5, 1991.

75 Ann Rodgers, "Peace, Farewell," *Pittsburgh Post-Gazette,* June 11, 2006.

76 Tony Eichelberger et al., "Evaluation of Four Extra Mile Catholic Elementary Schools of the Pittsburgh Diocese," University of Pittsburgh, 2007.

77 Carmen J. Lee, "Former President Bush Goes the Extra Mile Here," *Pittsburgh Post-Gazette,* October 8, 1999.

78"Catholic Schools Get Tuition Fund," *Pittsburgh Post-Gazette*, September 13, 1994, B6.

79"Grants for Catholic Pupils Rise," *Pittsburgh Post-Gazette*, June 23, 1999, B3.

80C. T. Maier, *Shepherd Touched All Areas of Local Church*, special supplement to the *Pittsburgh Catholic*, June 9, 2006.

81Johnna A. Pro, "Fire Guts Former Church," *Pittsburgh Post-Gazette*, January 31, 2001.

82Johnna A. Pro et al., "Counting Up the Costs," *Pittsburgh Post-Gazette*, September 21, 2004.

83Ann Rodgers-Melnick, "Somber Wuerl Addresses 2 Parishes," *Pittsburgh Post-Gazette*, August 17, 1998.

84Ann Rodgers-Melnick, "Bingo Hall Voices Saddened by Word of Parish Closings," *Pittsburgh Press*, January 26, 1992.

85Ann Rodgers-Melnick, "Although Painful, Mergers Succeed," *Pittsburgh Post-Gazette*, October 8, 1995; see also Mackenzie Carpenter, "New Parish in North Hills," *Pittsburgh Post-Gazette*, December 5, 1993.

86"Bishop Presides as Work Starts on Parish Hall," *Pittsburgh Post-Gazette*, June 1, 1995; see also Kathleen Ganster, "FBI Chaplain Takes Over at Franklin Park Church," *Pittsburgh Post-Gazette*, August 11, 2002.

87Interview with Ann Rodgers, September 28, 2014, Pittsburgh.

88Ann Rodgers-Melnick, "Although Painful, Mergers Succeed," *Pittsburgh Post-Gazette*, October 8, 1995.

89Ann Rodgers-Melnick, "Although Painful, Mergers Succeed," *Pittsburgh Post-Gazette*, October 8, 1995.

90Ann Rodgers-Melnick, "64 Parishes in Diocese on Fast Track for Change," *Pittsburgh Press*, October 11, 1991.

91Ann Rodgers-Melnick, "Reorganized Parishes Face Spiritual Goal," *Pittsburgh Post-Gazette*, March 15, 1994.

92"45 More Catholic Parishes in Reorganization Study," *Allegheny Bulletin*, September 11, 1992.

93 Ann Rodgers-Melnick, "Diocese Takes Steps to Preserve Cultures," *Pittsburgh Post-Gazette*, Feb 4, 1994.

94 Ann Rodgers-Melnick, "6 More Parishes Are Closing, 59 Catholic Sites Are Affected in 4th Part of Consolidations; Church Closures Now Total 36," *Pittsburgh Post-Gazette*, December 6, 1993.

95 Ann Rodgers-Melnick, "Group Spreads the Word: You Can Sue Bishop," *Pittsburgh Post-Gazette*, October 23, 1993; see also "Experts on Catholic Canon Law Say Parish Lawsuits Doomed to Fail," *Pittsburgh Post-Gazette*, September 26, 1993; "Lawyer Questions Vatican Letter on Closing," *Pittsburgh Post-Gazette*, August 26, 1993; "Parish Closings Prompt Lawyer's Quixotic Crusade," *Pittsburgh Post-Gazette*, September 26, 1993; "Diocese Has Right to Shut Its Parishes, Court Rules," *Pittsburgh Post-Gazette*, December 20, 1995; Jon Schmitz, "Although Painful, Mergers Succeed," *Pittsburgh Post-Gazette*, October 8, 1995.

96 Ann Rodgers-Melnick, "Cause for Rejoicing, Reorganization Ends with One Church Closing, Many Reprieves," *Pittsburgh Post-Gazette*, March 14, 1994.

97 Ann Rodgers-Melnick, "Although Painful, Mergers Succeed," *Pittsburgh Post-Gazette*, October 8, 1995.

98 Ann Rodgers-Melnick, "Vatican OKs Closings in Diocese," *Pittsburgh Post-Gazette*, October 5, 1994; see also "Vatican Appeal Fails," *Pittsburgh Post-Gazette*, June 23, 1997.

99 Ann Rodgers-Melnick, "Cause for Rejoicing, Reorganization Ends with One Church Closing, Many Reprieves," *Pittsburgh Post-Gazette*, March 14, 1994.

100 Ann Rodgers-Melnick, "Reorganized Parishes Face Spiritual Goal," *Pittsburgh Post-Gazette*, March 15, 1994; see also "Parish Priests Hit Hardest by Merger Fallout," *Pittsburgh Post-Gazette*, October 9, 1995.

101 Ann Rodgers-Melnick, "Although Painful, Mergers Succeed," *Pittsburgh Post-Gazette*, October 8, 1995; see also "Merged Parishes Offer Bigger Menu of Ministries to All," *Pittsburgh Post-Gazette*, October 11, 1995.

102 Editorial, "Religious Revival: The Catholic Diocese Gets Reorganized for the Future," *Pittsburgh Post-Gazette*, March 17, 1994.

103Ann Rodgers-Melnick, "Although Painful, Mergers Succeed," *Pittsburgh Post-Gazette*, October 8, 1995; see also Ann Rodgers, "Bishop to Name Collaborators to Manage Priestless Parishes," *Pittsburgh Post-Gazette*, April 26, 2006.

104Ann Rodgers-Melnick, "The Bishop Moves Ahead," *Pittsburgh Post-Gazette*, March 24, 1996.

105Karen J. Terry et al., *The Causes and Context of Sexual Abuse of Minors by Catholic Priests in the United States*, 1950-2010 (Washington, DC: USCCB, 2011), 47.

106Ann Rodgers-Melnick, "Wuerl's Tough Record on Sex Abuse," *Pittsburgh Post-Gazette*, June 15, 2003.

107Interview with Ann Rodgers, July 8, 2014, Pittsburgh.

108Ann Rodgers-Melnick, "Wuerl's Tough Record on Sex Abuse," *Pittsburgh Post-Gazette*, June 15, 2003.

109Ann Rodgers-Melnick, "Wuerl Openly to Address Sex Charge Against Priest," *Pittsburgh Press*, October 19, 1988.

110Ann Rodgers-Melnick, "Wuerl's Tough Record on Sex Abuse," *Pittsburgh Post-Gazette*, June 15, 2003.

111Ann Rodgers-Melnick, "Diocese Revises Policy for Priest Misconduct Cases," *Pittsburgh Post-Gazette*, March 11, 1993.

112Ann Rodgers, "Duquesne U. Dean's Book Tells How Church Dealt with Pedophile Priests," *Pittsburgh Post-Gazette*, April 7, 2008.

113Ann Rodgers-Melnick, "Addressing the Agony of Child Sexual Abuse," *Pittsburgh Post-Gazette*, June 18, 1993; see also "Bishops Call for Openness," *Pittsburgh Post-Gazette*, November 16, 1994.

114Ann Rodgers-Melnick and Dan Donovan, "Wuerl Says Money Request Preceded Sex Abuse Claims," *Pittsburgh Press*, November 23, 1988.

115Ann Rodgers-Melnick, "Vatican Alters Rules for Disciplining Priests," *Pittsburgh Post-Gazette*, October 13, 1995.

116Ann Rodgers-Melnick, "Wuerl's Tough Record on Sex Abuse," *Pittsburgh Post-Gazette*, June 15, 2003.

117"Vatican Clears Priest, Wuerl Rejects Verdict," *Pittsburgh Post-Gazette*, March 21, 1993.

118Ann Rodgers-Melnick, "Duquesne U Dean's Book Tells How Church Dealt with Pedophile Priests," *Pittsburgh Post-Gazette*, April 7, 2008.

119Ann Rodgers-Melnick, "Diocese Acts after New Grasp of Canon Law," *Pittsburgh Post-Gazette*, March 25, 1993.

120Ann Rodgers-Melnick, "Molestation Suit Settled with Church," *Pittsburgh Post-Gazette*, October 1, 1993.

121Ann Rodgers-Melnick, "Banned Priest Says Mass on TV," *Pittsburgh Post-Gazette*, Feb 18, 1994; see also "Rare Sanction Imposed on Priest," *Pittsburgh Post-Gazette*, November 16, 2002.

122Ann Rodgers-Melnick, "Vatican Alters Rules for Disciplining Priests," *Pittsburgh Post-Gazette*, October 13, 1995.

123Ann Rodgers-Melnick, "Rare Sanction Imposed on Priest," *Pittsburgh Post-Gazette*, November 16, 2002.

124Ann Rodgers-Melnick, "The Bishop Moves Ahead," *Pittsburgh Post-Gazette*, March 24, 1996.

125Ann Rodgers-Melnick, "Wuerl's Tough Record on Sex Abuse," *Pittsburgh Post-Gazette*, June 15, 2003.

126Ann Rodgers-Melnick, "Wuerl Won't Identify Priests He Removed," *Pittsburgh Post-Gazette*, March 8, 2002.

127Ann Rodgers-Melnick, "Wuerl Removes 'Several' Priests," *Pittsburgh Post-Gazette*, March 7, 2002; see also "Judging Credibility in Abuse Cases is a Tough Call," *Pittsburgh Post-Gazette*, March 17, 2002; "Wuerl Won't Identify Priests He Removed," *Pittsburgh Post-Gazette*, March 8, 2002.

128Ann Rodgers-Melnick, "Bishop Sings Praises of Battered Priesthood," *Pittsburgh Post-Gazette*, March 29, 2001.

129Ann Rodgers-Melnick, "Zappala, Wuerl Define Policies, Roles in Abuse Cases," *Pittsburgh Post-Gazette*, April 17, 2002; see also Steve Levin, "Diocese Expands Meetings with District Attorneys," *Pittsburgh Post-Gazette*, April 26, 2002.

130Ann Rodgers-Melnick, "Diocese to Alert Police to All Abuse Reports," *Pittsburgh Post-Gazette*, May 8, 2002.

131 Ann Rodgers-Melnick, "Local Policies Exceed Proposals," *Pittsburgh Post-Gazette*, June 5, 2002; see also "Wuerl Argues That One Credible Allegation of Molestation Should Cause Removal from Ministry," *Pittsburgh Post-Gazette*, June 9, 2002.

132 Ann Rodgers-Melnick, "Wuerl Argues That One Credible Allegation of Molestation Should Cause Removal from Ministry," *Pittsburgh Post-Gazette*, June 9, 2002; see also Steve Levin and Ernie Hoffman, "Wuerl Takes Aim at Pedophiles," *Pittsburgh Post-Gazette*, June 11, 2002.

133 Ann Rodgers-Melnick, "Bishops Are Told They're to Blame," *Pittsburgh Post-Gazette*, June 14, 2002.

134 Ann Rodgers-Melnick, "U.S. Bishops Get Tough on Sex Abusers," *Pittsburgh Post-Gazette*, June 15, 2002; see also "The Nature and Scope of Sexual Abuse of Minors by Catholic Priests and Deacons in the United States 1950-2002," John Jay College, February 2004.

135 Ann Rodgers-Melnick, "U.S. Bishops Get Tough on Sex Abusers," *Pittsburgh Post-Gazette*, June 15, 2002.

136 Ann Rodgers-Melnick, "Duquesne Dean on Catholic Panel," *Pittsburgh Post-Gazette*, July 21, 2002.

137 Bishop Donald W. Wuerl, *To Heal, Restore and Renew*, June 17, 2002.

138 Ann Rodgers-Melnick, "Bishops' Policy on Abuse Satisfies Wuerl," *Pittsburgh Post-Gazette*, June 16, 2002.

139 Ann Rodgers-Melnick, "New Catholic Rules on Priest Sex Abuse Violate the Clergy's Rights, Lawyer Says," *Pittsburgh Post-Gazette*, September 27, 2002.

140 Ann Rodgers-Melnick, "Report Finds Most Dioceses Doing Better on Abuse," *Pittsburgh Post-Gazette*, January 4, 2004; see also "Diocese's Response on Abuse Praised," *Pittsburgh Post-Gazette*, October 11, 2003.

141 Ann Rodgers-Melnick, "Wuerl Named to New Panel to Oversee Sex Abuse Charter," *Pittsburgh Post-Gazette*, October 3, 2002.

142 Ann Rodgers-Melnick, "Catholic Bishops Approve Revised Sex Abuse Policy," *Pittsburgh Post-Gazette*, November 14, 2002.

143Ann Rodgers-Melnick, "Vatican Permits Swift Justice Against Offending Priests," *Pittsburgh Post-Gazette*, February 27, 2003.

144Ann Rodgers, "Sex Abuse Lawsuit Pursues Dioceses, Not Priests," *Pittsburgh Post-Gazette*, July 5, 2004.

145Ann Rodgers, "Diocese Accused of Abuse Cover-Up," *Pittsburgh Post-Gazette*, January 15, 2004.

146Ann Rodgers, "Diocese Accused of Abuse Cover-Up," *Pittsburgh Post-Gazette*, January 15, 2004; see also Ann Rodgers, "Suits Claim Diocese Cover-Up of Ex-Priests," *Pittsburgh Post-Gazette*, March 17, 2004; Jim McKinnon, "Lawsuits Target Catholic Diocese," *Pittsburgh Post-Gazette*, April 29, 2004; Ann Rodgers, "Diocesan Cover-Up Alleged in Abuse," *Pittsburgh Post-Gazette*, July 1, 2004.

147Ann Rodgers, "Sex Abuse Lawsuit Pursues Dioceses, Not Priests," *Pittsburgh Post-Gazette*, July 5, 2004; see also "Accused Priest Had Prior Offense," *Pittsburgh Post-Gazette*, July 9, 2004.

148John E. Murray et al., "Stale Claims, Justice and the Catholic Diocese of Pittsburgh," *Pittsburgh Post-Gazette*, August 9, 2004.

149Ann Rodgers, "Time Has Run Out for Abuse Cases, Diocesan Lawyers Say," *Pittsburgh Post-Gazette*, July 7, 2004; see also "City Diocese Settles Abuse Cases," *Pittsburgh Post-Gazette*, September 18, 2007.

150Ann Rodgers, "U.S. Bishops Disagree over Liturgy," *Pittsburgh Post-Gazette*, November 12, 2005.

151Victor L. Simpson, "Abuse Victims Pray with Pope," *Pittsburgh Post-Gazette*, April 18, 2008.

152William Wan, "Vatican Issues Rules on Clergy Abuse; Activists Call Them Weak," *Washington Post*, July 16, 2010.

153Ann Rodgers-Melnick, "Mourning the Victims of Flight 427," *Pittsburgh Post-Gazette*, September 13, 1994.

154Ann Rodgers-Melnick and Rebekah Scott, "Finding Solace in the Church Community," *Pittsburgh Post-Gazette*, September 12, 1994.

155Grace Rishell, "Airport Priest Pilots a Diverse Congregation," *Pittsburgh Post-Gazette*, April 15, 1998.

156Press kit for February 12, 1988, press conference.

157Ann Rodgers, "Award Recognizes 50 Years of Jewish-Catholic Relations," *Pittsburgh Post-Gazette*, June 21, 2010.

158"Briefs," *Pittsburgh Post-Gazette*, June 18, 2005.

159Tim Grant, "Rabbis Teach Catholics About Church's Persecution," *Pittsburgh Post-Gazette*, October 17, 2005.

160Steve Levin, "Tree of Life Rabbi, Wuerl in Vatican for Holocaust Memorial Dedication," *Pittsburgh Post-Gazette*, April 13, 1999.

161"Briefs," *Pittsburgh Post-Gazette*, May 21, 2003.

162Dennis Roddy, "Pope in Peace Concert," *Pittsburgh Post-Gazette*, January 18, 2004.

163Ann Rodgers, "Peace, Farewell," *Pittsburgh Post-Gazette*, June 11, 2006.

164Carmen J. Lee, Steve Levin, and Barbara White Stack, "Religious Leaders Ask for Prayers and Peace," *Pittsburgh Post-Gazette*, September 12, 2001.

165Sally Kalson, "Local Religious Leaders Gather to Pray and to Denounce Hatred," *Pittsburgh Post-Gazette*, September 21, 2001.

166Ann Rodgers, "The Long Walk Ends," *Pittsburgh Post-Gazette*, June 12, 2006.

167Paul Meyer, "3-Run 9th Gives Mets 4-1 Victory," *Pittsburgh Post-Gazette*, September 18, 2001.

168Johnna Pro, "Wuerl Consoles Homewood Pupils," *Pittsburgh Post-Gazette*, February 2, 2002.

169Robert Dvorchak, "Killing Spree Rattles an Image of Safety," *Pittsburgh Post-Gazette*, May 2, 2000.

170Jan Ackerman, "Clerics Create a Marine Chapel in Boat Blessing," *Pittsburgh Post-Gazette*, May 27, 1996.

171Ann Rodgers-Melnick, "Christian Unity...and Dissension," *Pittsburgh Post-Gazette*, February 12, 1993.

172Ann Rodgers-Melnick, "Bishops of 3 Churches Sign Cooperation Pledge," *Pittsburgh Post-Gazette*, February 14, 1996.

173Ann Rodgers-Melnick, "Wuerl in 1st Meeting with Lutheran Leaders Here," *The Pittsburgh Press*, June 9, 1989.

174Jan Ackerman, "Catholics, Lutherans End Dispute," *Pittsburgh Post-Gazette*, November 1, 1999.

175Ann Rodgers-Melnick, "Catholics and Graham Have Come a Long Way," *Pittsburgh Post-Gazette*, May 30, 1993.

176"AIDS Center Celebrates," *Pittsburgh Post-Gazette*, October 10, 1994.

177Ann Rodgers, "Region's Religious Groups to Help Burned Churches," *Pittsburgh Post-Gazette*, June 19, 1996.

178Ann Rodgers-Melnick, "District Raises Black Church Arson Funds," *Pittsburgh Post-Gazette*, October 2, 1996.

179Ann Rodgers-Melnick, "Wuerl: Others Can be Saved," *Pittsburgh Post-Gazette*, September 7, 2000.

180Dennis Roddy, "Wuerl: Pray, Fast to Halt Violence," *Pittsburgh Post-Gazette*, March 17, 1994.

181Ann Rodgers, "Peace, Farewell," *Pittsburgh Post-Gazette*, June 11, 2006.

182Michael A. Fuoco, "Prosecution and Prevention Cut Gang Crime Here," *Pittsburgh Post-Gazette*, October 3, 1997.

183Johnna Pro, "Speakers Seek Unity, Justice," *Pittsburgh Post-Gazette*, July 4, 1996.

184Jan Ackerman, "Civic Leaders to Public: Ignore Klan," *Pittsburgh Post-Gazette*, April 3, 1997.

185Dennis B. Roddy, "Klansman Says He's a New Man," *Pittsburgh Post-Gazette*, August 30, 1997.

186Mike Clark, "Pittsburgh was Blessed by Bishop's Leadership," *Pittsburgh Catholic*, June 9, 2006.

187Bishop Michael Pfeifer, interview with Ann Rodgers, 2014, Baltimore.

188Ann Rodgers-Melnick, "Wuerl at Center of 2 Debates by U.S. Catholic Bishops," *Pittsburgh Press*, November 15, 1988.

189Ann Rodgers-Melnick, "Wuerl to Defend Vatican Teaching Position in National Conference of 300 Bishops," November 13, 1988, *Pittsburgh Press*.

190 Ann Rodgers-Melnick, "Bishops Withdraw Paper on Authority," *Pittsburgh Press*, November 14, 1988.

191 "Wuerl Defends Cardinal's Request," *The Pittsburgh Press*, October 30, 1990.

192 "Wuerl Gets Rome Letter on Meeting Wed Priests," *Pittsburgh Press*, October 24, 1990.

193 Ann Rodgers-Melnick, "Wuerl Defends Meeting with Dissidents," *Pittsburgh Press*, October 25, 1990.

194 Ann Rodgers-Melnick, "Wuerl a Whirlwind at National Conference," *Pittsburgh Post-Gazette*, November 21, 1993.

195 Ann Rodgers-Melnick, "Bishops Are Urged to Support Priests," *Pittsburgh Post-Gazette*, November 12, 1996; see also "Bishops Mourn a Respected and Beloved Brother," *Pittsburgh Post-Gazette*, November 15, 1996.

196 Ann Rodgers-Melnick, "Conservative Catholic Critics Less Visible, More Active," *Pittsburgh Post-Gazette*, November 20, 1994.

197 Ann Rodgers-Melnick, "Bishops Ponder Translations, Elect Black to Lead Conference," *Pittsburgh Post-Gazette*, November 14, 2001; see also Ann Rodgers, "U.S. Bishops Disagree over Changes in Liturgy," *Pittsburgh Post-Gazette*, November 15, 2005.

198 Michelle Boorstein, "Archdiocese Chancellor Retires after a Busy Era," *Washington Post*, January 11, 2014, B2.

199 "Happy Five Star Friday," *The Open Door*, June 13, 2014.

200 Rosilind S. Heldeman and Derek Kravitz, "Man Beaten outside Md. Church on Christmas Eve," *Washington Post*, December 26, 2008; see also David Hill, "Church Beating Suspect Pleads Guilty to Attempted Murder," *Gazette.net*, July 28, 2009.

201 Daniel LeDuc and Mary Beth Sheridan, "Nats New Cathedral to Baseball Prepares for Pontiff," *Washington Post*, April 15, 2008.

202 Christy Goodman, "Rebuilt Chapel Opens Doors onto Maryland's Colonial Past," *Washington Post*, September 24, 2009.

203 Rebecca J. Barnabi, "St. Joseph's Marks Congregation's 250th Anniversary," *Washington Post*, October 3, 2013.

204Michelle Boorstein, "Leading and Following," *Washington Post*, April 29, 2014.

205Archbishop Donald Wuerl, *The Church, Our Spiritual Home,* pastoral letter, September 14, 2012.

206"Religion briefs," *Washington Post*, December 21, 2006.

207Ann Rodgers, "Washington Welcomes Wuerl," *Pittsburgh Post-Gazette*, June 23, 2006.

208Steve Hendrix, "Biden, 5 Justices Maintain Tradition of the Red Mass," *Washington Post*, October 10, 2010.

209"Ask the Archbishop," *WashingtonPost.com*, December 20, 2006.

210Joe Heim, "Just Asking: Cardinal Donald Wuerl," *Washington Post*, August 8, 2014.

211Mary Beth Sheridan, "Faith Leaders Urge Cuba to Free Man," *Washington Post*, January 11, 2011.

212Archbishop Donald Wuerl, *Catholic Education: Looking to the Future with Confidence,* pastoral letter, September 14, 2008, 13.

213"Archbishop Talks about DC Catholic Schools," live chat on *WashingtonPost.com*, September 14, 2007.

214Archbishop Donald Wuerl, *Catholic Education: Looking to the Future with Confidence,* September 14, 2008, 13.

215Theola Labb, "7 Catholic schools to be Converted to Charters," *Washington Post*, November 6, 2007.

216Erin Donaghue, "From One Mother's Idea, Many Are Helped," *Washington Post*, October 22, 2009.

217Ann Rodgers-Melnick, "Archaic Procedures Govern Synod Activity," *Pittsburgh Post-Gazette*, November 16, 1997.

218Ann Rodgers-Melnick, "Papal Selection May Prophesy Higher Calling," *Pittsburgh Press*, August 31, 1990.

219Ann Rodgers-Melnick, "American Bishops Meeting at Vatican," *Pittsburgh Post-Gazette*, November 16, 1997.

220Ann Rodgers-Melnick, "Wuerl Pledges Local Help for Priesthood in East Europe," *Pittsburgh Press*, October 10, 1990.

221Bishop's logbook.

222Eric Slagle, "Cardinal Visits to Mark Church's 50 Years," *Pittsburgh Post-Gazette,* May 11, 2006.

223Ann Rodgers, "Wuerl Urges Bishops to be Accountable," *Pittsburgh Post-Gazette,* September 23, 2005.

224Nicole Winfield, "Pope Opens Major Meeting with Bishops," *Pittsburgh Post-Gazette,* October 3, 2005.

225Ann Rodgers, "Is Wuerl Leaving for Post in Rome?" *Pittsburgh Post-Gazette,* November 2, 2005.

226Michelle Boorstein, "Friends Join Archbishop Wuerl in Rome," *Washington Post,* November 16, 2010.

227Ann Rodgers, "Crowds Roar Their Approval of Cardinal Wuerl," *Pittsburgh Post-Gazette,* November 21, 2010.

228Ann Rodgers, "Pope Presents Rings to Wuerl, 23 Other New Cardinals," *Pittsburgh Post-Gazette,* November 22, 2010.

229Michelle Boorstein, "DC Archbishop Off to Rome, Along with 400 Faithful Friends," *Washington Post,* November 16, 2010; see also Ann Rodgers, "Wuerl Celebrates Mass for Pilgrims," *Pittsburgh Post-Gazette,* November 19, 2010.

230Ann Rodgers, "New Title Means Some New Vestments for Wuerl," *Pittsburgh Post-Gazette,* November 20, 2010; see also "Liturgical Welcome Home Party for Cardinal Wuerl," *Pittsburgh Post-Gazette,* December 13, 2010.

231Ann Rodgers, "Wuerl Celebrates Mass for Pilgrims," *Pittsburgh Post-Gazette,* November 19, 2010.

232Ann Rodgers, "Cardinal Wuerl: Next Pope Must Make Faith Compelling," *Pittsburgh Post-Gazette,* March 3, 2013.

233Ann Rodgers, "Cardinal Wuerl Appointed to 2 Vatican Offices," *Pittsburgh Post-Gazette,* December 30, 2010.

234Ann Rodgers, "Americans in Papal Chase," *Pittsburgh Post-Gazette,* March 12, 2013.

235Michelle Boorstein, "Next Pope Must Reach Those Who've Left Church, Wuerl Says," *Washington Post,* February 23, 2013.

236Ann Rodgers, "Cardinal Wuerl: Next Pope Must Make Faith Compelling," *Pittsburgh Post-Gazette*, March 3, 2013.

237Interview, May 30, 2013, Pittsburgh.

238Ann Rodgers, "Francis: Argentine Cardinal Jorge Bergoglio is Elected Pope," *Pittsburgh Post-Gazette*, March 14, 2013.

239Ann Rodgers, "New Pope 'a Universal Pastor'," *Pittsburgh Post-Gazette*, March 15, 2013.

240David Gibson, "Two Years in, Pope Francis Faces Headwinds in Reforming the Vatican," *Religion News Service*, March 11, 2015.

241Peter Smith, "Bishops Say Issues in US Align with Pope's Mission," *Pittsburgh Post-Gazette*, November 12, 2013.

242Phone interview, December 31, 2014.

243"We Are Not Bystanders," *Plough Quarterly*, Summer 2014.

244Cardinal Donald W. Wuerl, "Pope Francis, the New Evangelization: A Pastoral Message the Church Needs Today," *America Magazine*, September 24, 2013.

245"Seek First the Kingdom," March 11, 2015.

246"Pope's Appointment of Cardinal Wuerl Extends Ties Between the City and the Vatican," *Pittsburgh Post-Gazette*, December 17, 2013; see also "Two US Bishops Lose Vatican Posts," *New York Times*, December 17, 2013.

247John L. Allen, Jr., "Preparing a Generation of 'Francis Bishops'," *National Catholic Reporter*, December 17, 2013.

248Michael Sean Winters, *Washingtonian Magazine*, March, 2014.

249Cardinal Donald Wuerl, *Being Catholic Today: Catholic Identity in an Age of Challenge* (Washington, DC: Archdiocese of Washington, 2015).

250"Roman Catholics: Catechism in Dutch," *Time*, December 1, 1967.

251"Catechism Co-Authored by Wuerl Remains Popular after 25 Years," *Pittsburgh Post-Gazette*, January 22, 2001.

252Mike Aquilina, "Still 'Teaching' after All These Years," *Pittsburgh Catholic*, July 14, 1995.

253Ann Rodgers-Melnick, "Catechism Co-Authored by Wuerl Remains Popular after 25 Years," *Pittsburgh Post-Gazette*, January 22, 2001, A3.

254Mike Aquilina, "Still 'Teaching' after All These Years," *Pittsburgh Catholic*, July 14, 1995.

255McDowell, 49.

256Brian Caulfield, "Inside the Church," *FathersForGood.org*, March 2013.

257Cardinal Donald Wuerl, *Being Catholic Today: Catholic Identity in an Age of Challenge* (Washington, DC: Archdiocese of Washington, 2015).

258"Text of Bishop's Message to Priests," *Pittsburgh Press*, September 14, 1988.

259Ann Rodgers, "Quiet Bishop Plans to be Heard," *Pittsburgh Post-Gazette*, May 21, 2006.

260Michelle Boorstein and Carol Morello, "DC Council Digs in on Same-Sex Nuptials," *Washington Post*, November 13, 2009.

261Archbishop Donald W. Wuerl, "D.C.'s Same-Sex Marriage Bill: Finding the Right Balance," *Washington Post*, November 22, 2009.

262Ann Rodgers-Melnick, "The Bishop Moves Ahead," *Pittsburgh Post-Gazette*, March 24, 1996.

263Ann Rodgers-Melnick, "Catholic Bishops Focusing on Abortion, Aid to Africa," *Pittsburgh Post-Gazette*, November 15, 2001.

264Ann Rodgers-Melnick, "Spirituality is His Specialty," *Pittsburgh Press Magazine*, March 12, 1989.

265Bishop Donald W. Wuerl, "Respect for Life," September 27, 1989.

266Bishop Donald W. Wuerl, "Post-Abortion Reconciliation and Healing," April 23, 2000.

267Jean Bryant, "Wuerl Decries Violence While Honoring Unborn," *Pittsburgh Post-Gazette*, August 1, 1994.

268Ann Rodgers, "Quiet Bishop Plans to be Heard," *Pittsburgh Post-Gazette*, May 21, 2006.

269 Bishop Donald W. Wuerl, *A Fresh Look at the Death Penalty*, Holy Week, 2005.

270 Ann Belser, "Execution Set Tonight; Protests Planned," *Pittsburgh Post-Gazette*, November 8, 2000.

271 Tom Barnes, "Taylor Gets Death Sentence," *Pittsburgh Post-Gazette*, November 12, 2001.

272 Jim McKinnon, "Baumhammers Gets 5 Death Sentences, Plus Hundreds of Years in Jail," *Pittsburgh Post-Gazette*, September 7, 2001.

273 Ann Rodgers-Melnick, "Churches Seek Halt in Death Penalty," *Pittsburgh Post-Gazette*, July 4, 2003.

274 Ann Rodgers-Melnick, "Wuerl, Others, to Address Gun Violence," *Pittsburgh Post-Gazette*, May 10, 2000.

275 Robert Dvorchak, "Killing Spree Rattles an Image of Safety," *Pittsburgh Post-Gazette*, May 2, 2000.

276 Ann Rodgers-Melnick, "Wuerl Calls for Safety Locks, Limits on Sales of Weapons," *Pittsburgh Post-Gazette*, May 13, 2000.

277 Ann Rodgers, "Quiet Bishop Plans to be Heard," *Pittsburgh Post-Gazette*, May 21, 2006.

278 Ervin Dyer and Mackenzie Carpenter, "Wuerl Favors Communion Choice," *Pittsburgh Post-Gazette*, May 26, 2004.

279 Ann Rodgers, "Protesters Urge Bishop to Deny Communion to Pro-Abortion Legislators," *Pittsburgh Post-Gazette*, June 17, 2004.

280 Ann Rodgers-Melnick, "Wuerl Urges US Bishops to Consult on Hot Issues," *Pittsburgh Post-Gazette*, August 31, 2005.

281 Ann Rodgers-Melnick, "Wuerl Urges US Bishops to Consult on Hot Issues," *Pittsburgh Post-Gazette*, August 31, 2005.

282 Jacqueline L. Salmon, "Vatican Archbishop Issues Apology," *Washington Post*, March 27, 2009.

283 Inés San Martín, "Cardinal Burke Denies Rift with Pope, Warns of 'Gay Agenda' for Synod," *www.cruxnow.com*, April 1, 2015.

284 Jacqueline Salmon, "Archbishop Disputes Pelosi's Statements," *Washington Post*, August 27, 2008; see also "Bishops Criticize Biden,

Pelosi on Abortion Remarks," *Washington Post*, September 13, 2008.

285Brian Roewe, "D.C. Cardinal: Free Enterprise, Environmental Protection Are Compatible Goals," *National Catholic Reporter*, May 20, 2015.

286Cardinal Donald W. Wuerl, "Protecting our Catholic Conscience," *Washington Post*, May 25, 2012.

287Mike Aquilina, "'Water' Renews Catholic Education: Conference Draws 4,200 to Prayer, Formation," *Pittsburgh Catholic*, November 10, 1995, 1-3.

288Eleanor Holmes Norton, "Real Choices for D.C. Students," *Washington Post*, June 17, 2008, A17.

289Ann Rodgers-Melnick, "Murdered Man Regains Full Measure of Priesthood," *Pittsburgh Post-Gazette*, June 12, 2001.

290Ann Rodgers-Melnick, "Somber Wuerl Addresses 2 Parishes," *Pittsburgh Post-Gazette*, August 17, 1998.

291Lawrence Walsh and Ann Rodgers-Melnick, "Bishop Wuerl Gives Message to Boost Morale for Priests," *Pittsburgh Post-Gazette*, September 17, 1998.

292"A Homegrown Bishop," *Pittsburgh Press*, February 13, 1988.

293Ann Rodgers-Melnick, "Bishops Look at Ways to Ease Priest Shortage," *Pittsburgh Post-Gazette*, June 16, 2000.

294Ann Rodgers, "Bishop Tells Parishioners to Prepare for Fewer Priests," *Pittsburgh Post-Gazette*, September 17, 2004.

295Ann Rodgers-Melnick, "Bishops Look at Ways to Ease Priest Shortage," *Pittsburgh Post-Gazette*, June 16, 2000.

296Scott Deacle, "Career with a Calling: Diocese Recruits Priests, Nuns at Daylong Event," *Pittsburgh Post-Gazette*, December 5, 2001.

297Ann Rodgers-Melnick, "More Men Choosing Priesthood in Diocese," *Pittsburgh Post-Gazette*, September 14, 2002.

298Anita Srikameswaran, "Bishop Wuerl Ordains 33 Men as Deacons," *Pittsburgh Post-Gazette*, June 27, 1999.

299Interview with Ann Rodgers, Pittsburgh, November 26, 2014.

300 Speech at Notre Dame Seminary, New Orleans, February 17, 2014.

301 Brian Caulfield, "Inside the Church," FathersForGood.org.

302 Ann Rodgers-Melnick, "Angels Fall from Liturgy after Debate by Bishops," *Pittsburgh Post-Gazette*, November 20, 1995.

303 Ann Rodgers-Melnick, "Catholic Bishops Seek to Educate 'Lost Generation' of Adults," *Pittsburgh Post-Gazette*, November 16, 1999.

304 Ann Rodgers-Melnick, "Women Top Overloaded Agenda for Nation's Catholic Bishops," *Pittsburgh Press*, November 11, 1990.

305 Ann Rodgers-Melnick, "Catholics Flock to Eucharistic Congress," *Pittsburgh Post-Gazette*, October 29, 2000.

306 Kim Paskorz, "Catholic Officials Try to Boost Attendance at Mass," *Pittsburgh Post-Gazette*, December 24, 2000.

307 Ann Rodgers-Melnick, "Bishops Call for Universal Health Care," *Pittsburgh Post-Gazette*, June 19, 1993; see also "Colorado Teens' Fervor a Joy to Bishops," *Pittsburgh Post-Gazette*, August 22, 1993.

308 Wayne Laugesen, "Looking at the Good Fruit of World Youth Day Denver 1993," *National Catholic Register*, August 23, 201.

309 Andrea Jacobs, "Pittsburgh Diocese Youth Gather to Rejoice, Pray with Their Bishop," *Pittsburgh Post-Gazette*, August 14, 1993.

310 Ann Rodgers-Melnick, "The Bishop Moves Ahead," *Pittsburgh Post-Gazette*, March 24, 1996.

311 Bishop's logbook, October 2001, Pittsburgh.

312 Tom Barnes, "In the Spirit, Singing, Dancing and Shouting Were Part of a Catholic Youth Event Celebrating the Jubilee Year," *Pittsburgh Post-Gazette*, April 17, 2000.

313 Ann Rodgers-Melnick, "10,000 Mark First 150 Years of Diocese," *Pittsburgh Post-Gazette*, Sept 20, 1993.

314 Ann Rodgers-Melnick, "Catholics, Presbyterians Struggle for Converts," *Pittsburgh Post-Gazette*, February 25, 2002; see also "Faith the Tie That Binds 750 New Catholics," *Pittsburgh Post-Gazette*, April 19, 1992.

315 Donald Miller, "The Divine Design of Chapel at Vatican," *Pittsburgh Post-Gazette*, June 27, 1999.

316 Jonathan Silver, "Replica of Vatican Creche to Grace USX Plaza," *Pittsburgh Post-Gazette*, November 11, 1999; see also Ann Rodgers interview with Father Lengwin, July 8, 2014, Pittsburgh.

317 Online chat transcript, *WashingtonPost.com*, December 20, 2006.

318 Ann Rodgers-Melnick, "Wuerl Calls Catholics to Confession," *Pittsburgh Post-Gazette*, January 16, 1999.

319 Bishop's logbook, Pittsburgh, January, May, December 1999.

320 Pete Socks, "CBB Interview with Cardinal Donald Wuerl," Patheos.com, April 13, 2014.

321 Father William Byrne, interview with Ann Rodgers, Washington, D.C., September 4, 2014.

322 Emily Langer, "Lapsed Catholic Targeted in Area Marketing Blitz," *Washington Post*, February 21, 2009.

323 "Seek First the Kingdom," February 12, 2015.

324 Melinda Henneberger, "At Georgetown, Considering 'The Francis Factor'," *Washingtonpost.com*, October 3, 2013.

325 Cardinal Donald Wuerl, "Address to Initiative on Catholic Social Thought and Public Life," Georgetown University, October 1, 2013.

326 Tara Bahrampour, "A Growing Flock," *Washington Post*, April 20, 2014.